W9-ADZ-854
ST. MARY'S CITY, MARYLAND 20686

Sociology after
Bosnia and Kosovo

Postmodern Social Futures
Stjepan Mestrovic, Series Editor

Ways of Escape (1994), by Chris Rojek
Reluctant Modernity (1998), by Aleš Debeljak
Feeling and Form in Social Life (1998), by Lloyd E. Sandelands
Provocateur (1999), by Anthony J. Cortese
Civilization and the Human Subject (1999), by John Mandalios
Sociology after Bosnia and Kosovo (2000), by Keith Doubt

Forthcoming:

Agency and Power, by Blasco José Sobrinho
Science as Metaphor, Knowledge as Democracy, by Donald R. LaMagdeleine
Compassionate Temperament, by Natan Sznaider

Sociology after Bosnia and Kosovo

Recovering Justice

Keith Doubt

ROWMAN & LITTLEFIELD PUBLISHERS, INC.
Lanham • Boulder • New York • Oxford

ROWMAN & LITTLEFIELD PUBLISHERS, INC.

Published in the United States of America
by Rowman & Littlefield Publishers, Inc.
4720 Boston Way, Lanham, Maryland 20706
http://www.rowmanlittlefield.com

12 Hid's Copse Road
Cumnor Hill, Oxford OX2 9JJ, England

Copyright © 2000 by Rowman & Littlefield Publishers, Inc.

Chapters 2 and 14 are reprinted from *The Conceit of Innocence:Losing the Conscience of the West in the War against Bosnia,* edited by Stjepan Mestrovic, by permission of the Texas A&M University Press. Copyright 1997. They also previously appeared in *Dijalog* (2) 1999 under the title "Moral i Politka."

Chapter 12 was previously published in *Novi Izraz* 1999 under the title "O nepravdi postmodernizma: Peter Handke o Srbiji I lekcija iz Bosne."

All rights reserved. No part of this publication may be reproduced, stored in a retrieval system, or transmitted in any form or by any means, electronic, mechanical, photocopying, recording, or otherwise, without the prior permission of the publisher.

British Library Cataloguing in Publication Information Available

Library of Congress Cataloging-in-Publication Data
Doubt, Keith.
    Sociology after Bosnia and Kosovo : recovering justice / Keith Doubt.
        p. cm.
    Includes bibliographical references and index.
    ISBN 0-8476-9376-7 (alk. paper) – ISBN 0-8476-9377-5 (pbk. : alk. paper)
        1. Yugoslav War, 1991-1995—Social aspects. 2. Yugoslav War, 1991-1995—
Bosnia and Hercegovina. 3. Kosovo (Serbia)—History—Civil War, 1998---Social
aspects. 4. War and society. 5. Bosnia and Hercegovina—Ethnic relations. 6. Kosovo
(Serbia)—Ethnic relations. I. Title.

DR1313.7.S64 D68 2000
949.703—dc21

                                                                        99-049771
Printed in the United States of America

⊖™ The paper used in this publication meets the minimum requirements of American National Standard for Information Sciences—Permanence of Paper for Printed Library Materials, ANSI Z39.48-1992.

In Memory

Margaret Elizabeth Brown

Contents

Editor's Foreword

THIS IS A SIGNIFICANT book for many reasons. First, Keith Doubt is one of only a handful of sociologists in the entire world who has expressed professional concern with the wars in the former Yugoslavia that began in 1991. Additionally, Doubt's book is the first and only bona fide sociological treatment of the wars in Bosnia and Kosovo. It is a book about sociology and about Bosnia and Kosovo simultaneously. To be sure, there exist implicitly sociological works that approach these wars from the vantage points of journalism, history, postmodernism, or some other aspect of cultural studies. But Doubt is using "real" sociologists—Max Weber, Harold Garfinkel, Robert Merton, Erving Goffman, Talcott Parsons, Thomas Scheff, among many others—to make genuinely sociological points about these wars. Doubt deserves enormous credit for being a sociological pioneer in this regard. And the fact that few other sociologists applied their professional expertise to Bosnia and Kosovo should force others in the profession to question this neglect. For example, why have sociology's experts on race and ethnic relations not shared their wealth of knowledge with those seeking to promote a multiethnic and multicultural society in the former Yugoslavia, and why have they refused to let their thinking be challenged and deepened by the particular nature of the serious ethnic problems in the Balkans?

Second, Doubt recasts existing material by journalists, historians, and witnesses, among others, vis-à-vis sociological theory. I can easily foresee sociologists using this book to illustrate Max Weber's concept of charisma, for example, in relation to Serbian General Ratko Mladić, or Robert K. Merton's deceptively enigmatic concept of latent functions in relation to the functions of so-called "ethnic cleansing." In other words, one of the important things Doubt does is to unify the plethora of scattered writings on Bosnia and Kosovo into a sociological template of sorts. Without such a conceptual template, the reader who is confronted by literally hundreds of articles and books on the wars in the former Yugoslavia is more likely to experience stress than understanding.

Third, Doubt is a forerunner among thinkers who recognize that the term "ethnic cleansing" is a profoundly ambiguous and ultimately unsuitable concept for social analysis. It is a term invented by the Serbs and co-opted by Western diplomats, journalists, and even laypersons that serves as a kind of euphemism for genocide, as a kind of excuse for inaction (because of the assumption that "everybody" engages in "ethnic cleansing"), and ultimately, as a catch-all term that means everything and ultimately, nothing. For example, the Serbs are accused of "ethnic cleansing," but so are the Croats for liberating the Krajina, and so are the Kosovar Albanians when Serbs flee Kosovo following the return of about a million persons who had been expelled by the Serbs. Akbar Ahmed[1] is right to claim that ultimately, "ethnic cleansing" has become a metaphor for our times, such that one can, and persons often do, refer to "ethnic cleansing" in Los Angeles, Karachi, London, *and* Srebrenica. The term, "ethnic cleansing" may have come into vogue as a way to avoid the conceptual difficulties associated with the term genocide, which carries with it conceptual baggage from World War II that may or may not be relevant to the Balkans (namely, rational, top-down, ends-means, bureaucratic thinking associated with the Holocaust). One may and perhaps should speculate as to other reasons why both terms, "ethnic cleansing" and genocide, are problematic. But the more important point is that Doubt seeks to supercede both terms conceptually with the invention of his own term, "sociocide," to capture the destruction of society by external as well as internal forces in wartime situations. I believe that this is a remarkable break-through in conceptualization that holds analytic potential for revamping thinking about genocide, civil wars, war crimes, and international law.

One of the ironies that emerges from between the lines of Doubt's analysis is that the Holocaust is an instance of historical genocide that was given a name and is regarded as unique by many analysts, but the genocide in Bosnia has no name. Whatever happened in Bosnia—whether one calls it genocide or "ethnic cleansing"—has ultimately become genocide with a small, not a capital, "g," and it is described as if it were one genocide among so many others. Ironically, the invention of the term genocide, meant to sensitize humankind to one of its most evil crimes, ends up desensitizing and alienating persons from its horrors. One senses that Doubt uses both terms (genocide and ethnic cleansing) because he is forced to do so by convention, but ultimately, he is struggling to find a vocabulary that will, at long last, be an emotional and morally appropriate response to the suffering that occurred in the former Yugoslavia.

Another irony is that Doubt's analysis is simultaneously "mainstream" and "marginal" in relation to sociology's core concerns. What I mean by this is that Doubt uses the standard, "classical," "big name" sociologists for his conceptual

---

[1] Akbar Ahmed, "Ethnic Cleansing: A Metaphor for Our Time," ed. S.G. Meštrović, *The Conceit of Innocence: Losing the Conscience of the West in the War Against Bosnia* (College Station: Texas A & M University Press, 1997), 35–64.

arsenal, from Weber to Parsons. Doubt's work is not some esoteric exercise in small-time sociology: this is real, hard-core sociology at its best. Yet "mainstream" sociology has largely ignored the wars in the former Yugoslavia and has thereby made itself "marginal" to world events and to issues and concerns of colleagues in other fields, such as lawyers at the International Criminal Tribunal for the former Yugoslavia (ICTY). How many sociologists are available to the ICTY to serve as expert witnesses in trying to explain to the world what happened in the former Yugoslavia in the 1990s, and why? Not many. By taking up issues that are "marginal" to sociology—namely, Bosnia and Kosovo—Doubt has forced sociological theory into the "mainstream" of the world's concerns. For as Doubt points out in his book, Bosnia and Kosovo have mesmerized the world's collective consciousness: "Bosnia became a global media screen, a theater, upon which we witnessed a gripping and horrifying moral tale" (p. 162). But unlike the postmodernists, who also regard the world as a screen or text, Doubt does not leave the reader with the discontented feeling that follows reading Jean Baudrillard's writings on Bosnia or any other war. For Baudrillard and most postmodernists, the wars in the former Yugoslavia are hyperreal, simulations of reality. Postmodernism is still marginal in intellectual circles because most persons are disturbed by the idea of dismissing the real deaths of innocents as "hyperreal." Let us admit honestly that most professionals who work outside academia have no use for postmodernism's disdain for reality. Lawyers, judges, medical doctors, social workers, and other professionals have to make informed decisions on life and death matters on a daily basis. They need understanding, not jargon. In contrast to the postmodernists, Doubt's passion, morality, and empathetic concern come through in this analysis. In contrast to the mainstream sociologists, Doubt shows that core sociological concepts developed in Eurocentric, Western, "biased" milieus can be applied successfully to a setting (the Balkans) that involves Muslim and other cultures that are regarded by many as only partly Western.

The reader who feels conceptual vertigo when confronted by the complexity of issues regarding Bosnia and Kosovo will be grateful to the author for supplying a glossary of both names and concepts. In general, this is a book that will help the layperson and professional alike finally understand what happened in the former Yugoslavia. Doubt's approach is multifaceted and complex, so that his book will stimulate discussion and thought. I hope that it will stimulate other sociologists to apply their rich storehouse of concepts to other neglected sites of cruelty in the world, from Rwanda to New York City to East Timor.

Stjepan G. Meštrović

Acknowledgments

I WOULD LIKE TO acknowledge the people who helped with this study from its birth to its completion. I have benefited from Stjepan Meštrović's confidence. His generous counsel and timely support have been crucial to the development of this work. At Truman State University, five students, Ann Lacey, Heather Burgess, Daniel Capotosto, Erin Donovan, and Hristina Toshkova, contributed their considerable talents and energies to this endeavor, despite their heavy class loads. I especially thank Heather Burgess for her invaluable work to help me complete the project. I am also indebted to Jennifer Top for her professional and diligent work with the manuscript preparation. I am grateful to Truman State University for its generous support of this research, and I would also like to thank Sharon Hackney, director of our Media Library, for helping me attain several video documentaries, which have become indispensable to my teaching and research.

In 1998 I attended two seminars in Bosnia: "Strengthening Democracy and Human Rights in Multi-Ethic Societies" sponsored by the Institute for Strengthening Democracy and Human Rights and organized by Džemal Sokolović, and "Bosnian Paradigm International" organized by the International Forum Bosnia. At both seminars I learned as a sociologist and gained as a person. I was able to converse with several people whose books I had only been able to read. During my visits to Sarajevo, I was moved by the goodwill of many people, for instance, Beverly Allen, Margarat Vandiver, Tom Cushman, Norman Cigar, and Rašid Durić. I would like to acknowledge two people in particular: Professor Rusmir Mahmutćehajić and Dr. Ešref Karaiković. I ask readers of this book to recognize, as I myself did during my visits to Bosnia, that the commitment to human rights and the belief in the good of humanity are cherished and poignantly articulated in a tragically afflicted but deeply compelling nation.

Chapter 1

Sociology after Bosnia

As images of "human nature" become more problematic, an increasing need is felt to pay closer yet more imaginative attention to the social routines and catastrophes which reveal (and which shape) man's nature in this time of civil unrest and ideological conflict.

—C. W. Mills
The Sociological Imagination

The Holocaust has more to say about the state of sociology than sociology in its present shape is able to add to our knowledge of the Holocaust.

—Zymunt Bauman
"Sociology after the Holocaust"

AT THE ANNUAL meeting of the American Sociological Association in 1998, approximately 2,300 papers were presented. Only two were on Bosnia. The same year, at the triannual World Congress of Sociology, approximately 3,500 studies were presented. Only one, "From Armenia to Bosnia: Genocide and Integral Nationalism" by Alma Begicević, was on Bosnia. Why is there this dearth of sociological work on the recent history and current situation in Bosnia? Sociologists not only in the United States but throughout the world seem to mirror the incredulous gaze of the world toward Bosnia. Can sociology sustain itself as a viable study of society when it ignores perhaps the most pressing and difficult subject in its time?

This book redresses this torpidity within the discipline of sociology. Drawing upon the tradition of sociology, it provides a series of distinctive studies on Bosnia and Kosovo. Each chapter constructs, not necessarily a causally adequate account, but a meaningfully adequate account of the experiences of people in Bosnia as well as the world's response to these experiences.[1]

In 1992, a fairly healthy and relatively functional society was viciously attacked and sadistically abused. Bosnia seemed to digress into what Thomas Hobbes calls a natural state of war. The only cardinal virtues were force and fraud. Might was right. The world watched, and, the world abetted this process. Can sociologists ignore such an event?

Thomas Hobbes says that, in fact, the presocial state of nature has never existed and never will. For Hobbes, the presocial state of nature is an ideal type. Hobbes reasons that the natural state is too painful to last for any period of time. He uses the notion of the Hobbesian jungle—for heuristic purposes—to explain the origins of society. Did it, then, really exist in Bosnia? Here is the question that sociologists must face and answer, and it is a question that challenges the root of the discipline.

What was the situation in Bosnia? Every day children, women, and unarmed men were murdered. Every week mass murders occurred. Sadistic rape camps were constructed. The motivation behind this conduct was to destroy a community and demolish the social order upon which the community had thrived for centuries. The social fabric of a community was shredded. In 1999 this entire pattern repeated itself in Kosovo.

At this time, sociologists need to bring the best works in their tradition and within their field to bear on the contemporary social history of Bosnia. One reward will be the construction of meaningfully adequate accounts of events in Bosnia. A second reward will be that this knowledge will influence political thinking and positive social action within and outside of Bosnia. A third reward will be the awakening of sociologists' dormant interest in their own discipline. The final reward will be sociologists' clearer recognition of the compelling issues within their own communities. To date, few sociologists have recognized or contributed to this project.[2]

Why is this? Bosnia confronts sociology. The weight of Bosnia, the long-term suffering and unconscionable pain that its people suffered, may be too heavy for conventional sociology to comprehend. In other words, sociology no

---

[1]Max Weber, *The Theory of Social and Economic Organization,* Talcott Parsons, ed., trans. A. M. Henderson and Talcott Parsons (New York: Free Press, 1964), 94–96.

[2]For some strong exceptions, see Stjepan Meštrović, *The Balkanization of the West: The Confluence of Postmodernism and Postcommunism* (London: Routledge, 1994); Tom Cushman and Stjepan Meštrović, eds., *This Time We Knew: Western Responses to Genocide in Bosnia* (New York: New York University Press, 1996); and Rusmir Mahmutćehajić, *Twisted Politics: Readings of History and Community Relationships in Bosnia,* trans. Francis R. Jones and Marina Bowder (Sarajevo: Did, 1998).

longer holds a privileged position vis-à-vis Bosnia. Bosnia humbles sociology. Thus, Bosnia has become a subject with which sociology must risk itself. If, as it is currently practiced, sociology is unable to explain events in Bosnia, then the scope of sociological knowledge needs to be assessed and extended. If sociology falls short, weaknesses within sociology are exposed and opportunities for developing sociology appear. Sociology needs to risk this experience of deconstruction and address its consequences.

Many courageous journalists reported the atrocities that occurred in Bosnia. I will name a few: Roy Gutman, Peter Maass, Roger Cohen, David Rieff, and David Rhode.[3] In the spring of 1999, few journalists were able or willing to cover comparable events in Kosovo; for one thing, the Belgrade regime learned to suppress, not only its media, but also the global media and to restrict their influence on world opinion.

Journalism, however, is still a distinct discipline from sociology. The events that journalists objectively report raise issues that sociologists objectively examine; given the low level of attention that sociologists have given to Bosnia, journalists have done the work of not only journalism, but also ethnography. In their reports, journalists ask the following: How was social life experienced before, during, and after the ethnic cleansing that occurred in Bosnia? What was the character of social order, not only before, but also during the genocidal activities of paramilitary soldiers? How was social order challenged under the most trying of times and how was social order sustained under the most trying of times? Journalists keenly raise these questions, but they are often left unexamined from the vantage point of the sociological tradition.

Along the same line, several outstanding historians provided comprehensive explanations of the complex past and different traditions that give character to Bosnia as a social entity. See, for example, the work of Noel Malcolm, Ivo Banac, Robert J. Donia and John V. A. Fine, or Rusmir Mahmutćehajić.[4] History, however, no matter how insightful and objective it is vis-à-vis the disfigured sto-

---

[3]See Roy Gutman, *A Witness to Genocide: The 1993 Pulitzer Prize-Winning Dispatches on the "Ethnic Cleansing" of Bosnia* (New York: Macmillian, 1993); Peter Maass, *Love Thy Neighbor: A Story of War* (New York: Vintage Books, 1997); Roger Cohen, *Hearts Grown Brutal: Sagas of Sarajevo* (New York: Random House, 1998); David Rieff, *Slaughterhouse: Bosnia and the Failure of the West* (New York: Simon and Schuster, 1996); David Rohde, *Endgame: The Betrayal and Fall of Srebrenica, Europe's Worst Massacre since World War II* (New York: Farrar, Straus, and Giroux, 1997).

[4]See Noel Malcolm, *Bosnia: A Short History* (Washington Square: New York University Press, 1994); Ivo Banac, *The National Question in Yugoslavia: Origins, History, Politics* (Ithaca: Cornell University Press, 1984); Robert J. Donia and John V. A. Fine, *Bosnia and Hercegovina: A Tradition Betrayed* (New York: Columbia University Press, 1994); and Rusmir Mahmutćehajić, *Twisted Politics: Readings of History and Community Relationships in Bosnia* (Sarajevo: Did, 1998).

ries of nationalistic ideologies, provides only a partial account of what happened to Bosnia's society. Historical accounts are indispensable to understanding contemporary events in Bosnia, but alone they are insufficient for understanding these events from a sociological perspective.

Likewise, political scientists have written telling commentaries on nationalism, the persuasiveness of propaganda, and the self-serving practices of the power elite. Political scientists focus on the dominant variables influencing events in Bosnia; they explain the conduct of the power elite to the exclusion of the conduct of everyday people. Sociologists, though, explain not only the activities of the power elite, but also the activities of everyday people; from the viewpoint of sociology, the activities of everyday people are as revealing and telltale as those of the power elite.

During the war, several writers from Bosnia published compelling memoirs that bear witness. If one were to read only one, I would recommend Rezak Hukanović's *The Tenth Circle of Hell: A Memoir of Life in the Death Camps of Bosnia*. These memoirs hold a special place in the literature and culture of Bosnia. The character with which they are written moves and enlightens readers. Memoirs, however, no matter how gripping and telltale, do not displace the need for sociological accounts of events in Bosnia.

It would be a mistake, I believe, to say that only those who suffered an event can speak authentically to the event. This position, while widely accepted in everyday life and the academy, allows the recounting of the event by the one who experienced it to be the sole authority for comprehending the event.[5]

Within postmodernism, there is tension as to what, if anything, constitutes an authentic speaking position. One way in which postmodernism resolves this issue is to claim that there is no privileged speaking position, and this assertion, which displaces all privileged speaking positions, comes to stand as the most privileged of privileged speaking positions. Conversation dies. Another way that postmodernism resolves this issue is to claim that only speakers who are directly acquainted with an event can authentically speak to the event. Thus, postmodernism advocates the exclusive legitimacy of the original speaker against the hegemony of science and the authority of reason.

However incomparable and unique events in Bosnia are, it is a mistake, I believe, to assume that they are unrelated to events outside of and external to Bosnia. It is a mistake to assume that events in Bosnia cannot be shared with outsiders. Such a position is unhealthy for both Bosnia and the world. It is the pariah's position, which postmodernism defends and this book resists. If unimaginable, never-ending crimes are events that defy discourse, then all we can do is gaze at the event as if it occurred in the realm of nature rather than the social

---

[5]See Alan Blum, "Victim, Patient, Client, Pariah: Steps in the Self-Understanding of Suffering and Affliction," *Canadian Journal of Visual Impairment* 1 (1992): 56–65.

world. More and more, this attitude governs today's intellectualizing. Only by demonstrating a refutation to this perspective can sociology reclaim its vocation and rescue itself from the implications of its failure to address the most complex and pressing subject in this time.

Not only do Bosnians need constructive accounts of their experiences during the war and the world's response to these experiences, but sociology needs to examine the current situation in Bosnia. When we try to understand the recent history of Bosnia, it is impossible not to turn to the field of sociology. In turn, when we engage in sociology, it is self-defeating and hypocritical not to turn our attention to Bosnia. The relation between Bosnia and sociology is dialectical. Each subject rewards the other. In fact, sociology now needs Bosnia as much as Bosnia needs sociology.

Genocide is perhaps an inadequate term to describe the activity of "ethnic cleansing" in Bosnia and Kosovo. Some argue, drawing upon quantitative and semantic reasons, that the activity of ethnic cleansing in Bosnia and Kosovo falls short of the meaning of the term genocide. Terms like "population transfer" are preferred.

In contrast, I argue that the term genocide does not match the conduct of ethnic cleansing. "Sociocide"—to kill a society—is not a word found in the dictionary. The word, however, is a more accurate term than genocide to describe what happened in Bosnia and Kosovo. Sociocide more accurately describes the character and more fully encompasses the consequences of ethnic cleansing.

The work of this study is to demonstrate this argument. The task is to recognize and address what sociocide is. The question now is how the society resurrects itself. While human nature may attempt sociocide, there is something immortal about society.

Where, then, are the sociologists within the discipline to investigate this societal destruction? Sociologists need to recognize and address the crime. The evidence needs to be gathered and the clues collected. Not only the perpetrators, but also the accomplices, need to be identified; their conduct needs to be understood and judged. In the here and now justice needs to be achieved because justice is the foundation upon which societies are reborn. Justice is the notion through which societies realize their immortality.

Chapter 2

On the Pathetic Hegemony of Face-Work

> The more the individual is concerned with the reality that is not available to perception, the more must he concentrate his attention on appearances.
>
> —Erving Goffman
> *The Presentation of Self in Everyday Life*

TO START, THIS chapter employs Erving Goffman's early accounts of face-work to examine the moral issues that arise from the war in Bosnia and the responses of Western leaders to this war. Concepts like "face" ("the positive social value that a person effectively claims for himself by the line others assume he has taken during a particular interaction"), "face-saving" ("the process by which the person sustains an impression for others that he has not lost face"), and "face-giving" ("to arrange for another to take a better line than he might otherwise have been able to take") are applied to the media descriptions of selected performances on this stage.[1]

Bosnia became a theater. It became a stage on which the tensions between and within various ideologies like nationalism, modernity, democracy, liberalism, postmodernism, and morality were sharply dramatized.[2] Bosnia, however, is also more than a stage. It is a social entity. It is a reality that the theater analogy alone cannot grasp. For this reason Bosnia refuses to be either defined by or counter-

---

[1]Erving Goffman, *Interaction Ritual: Essays on Face-to-Face Behavior* (New York: Pantheon Books, 1967), 5–15.

[2]For an incisive discussion of these matters, see Stjepan G. Meštrović, *The Balkanization of the West: The Confluence of Postmodernism and Postcommunism* (London: Routledge, 1994).

acted with the "face-work" of Western leaders or its participants.

On November 16, 1995, in the *New York Times*, Roger Cohen reported the following banal comment by a Western official observing the peace talks at Dayton, Ohio: "But there comes a time, when you have to choose between some absolute justice and moving forward in peace."[3] The comment echoes a refrain frequently heard and widely discussed in the media. The statement creates a dichotomy; the dichotomy asserts a truism. On the one hand, to seek justice means to abandon the possibility of establishing peace. On the other hand, to work toward peace means to ignore justice as a necessary standard for social relations. Peace, the Western official asserts, is established when people stop insisting that justice be the appropriate measure of social and political structure. Justice hinders the establishment of peace. Goffman explains the social attitude that informs the official's comment: "Perhaps the main principle of the ritual order is not justice but face, and what any offender receives is not what he deserves but what will sustain for the moment the line to which he has committed himself, and through this the line to which he has committed the interaction."[4]

The official's comment distributes status, and it distributes status unequally. Those who seek peace are more aware, more worldly; those who demand justice are living in an unreal world, shall we say, a metaphysical or idealistic realm. The comment creates a hierarchy and disabuses those whose commitment is to justice.

To add some details to the setting within which this comment is made, the Bosnian delegation (at this point in the peace talks at Dayton) is insisting that the towns of Srebrenica and Žepa be returned to the Republic of Bosnia and Herzegovina. Their end is justice. As Cohen writes, "By every standard of morality or justice, Bosnian control of the towns makes complete sense because they were the scenes of Serbian atrocities against Muslim communities in eastern Bosnian towns."[5] Srebrenica and Žepa (like Bihać, Gorazde, and Tuzla) were designated safe areas by the United Nations Security Council. The UN promised to protect these people from violence.[6] As part of this promise, UN forces removed the heavy weapons that the Bosnian government army held in the town of Srebrenica. Removing these weapons made the inhabitants more vulnerable to attacks and more dependent upon the UN for protection. When the UN removed the heavy weapons of the Bosnian government soldiers (but not the heavy weapons of the nationalist Serb army in the surrounding area), the Bosnian government focused on the promises of the UN Security Council to protect the civilians in Srebrenica if attacked by the Bosnian Serb army. Disarmed, the safe havens

[3]Roger Cohen, "Two Towns, Symbols of Serbian Killings, Snag Balkan Talks," *New York Times* (November 16, 1995): A6.

[4]Goffman, *Interaction Ritual,* 44.

[5]Cohen, "Two Towns," A6.

[6]UN Resolution no. 819 passed on April 16, 1993.

fell in July 1995 to the attacks of the Serbian army, and killings, rapes, and sadistic actions (a grandfather was forced to eat his grandson's liver; a mother was forced to drink her dead son's blood) were inflicted on the people living in these towns.[7] "By every standard of morality and justice," these towns should have been returned to the Bosnian government.

The Serb delegation, however, insisted that they be allowed to keep the towns. Their end was peace, more specifically the peace that they see achieved in the creation of a Greater Serbia, that is, an apartheid state where non-Serbs have neither political nor civil rights, no right to worship, own property, vote, or live. Cohen writes, "The Serbs will not relinquish the towns because they are determined that their territory adjoining Serbia be as cohesive as possible." "Put bluntly," Cohen continues, "Bosnian control of Srebrenica and Žepa now makes no sense politically or diplomatically, because the towns would be vulnerable islands surrounded by Serbs and the likely seeds of renewed violence."[8]

What, then, is being said with the statement, "But there comes a time, when you have to choose between some absolute justice and moving forward in peace"? The comment exemplifies several important features of face-work, the modern practice of sophistry, as formulated by Goffman. For one thing, the official asserts "the positive social value" that controls the interactions at Dayton and the behavior of its participants (whether successfully or not). The official draws the "line," which the parties are expected to respect. This line, Goffman adds, "tends to be of a legitimate institutionalized kind."[9]

The dramaturgical point is not whether this line is true or correct. The point is not even whether the parties agree with this line or whether any party agrees. The point is that this line identifies "the basic structural features of interaction, especially the interaction of face-to-face talk." "It is typically a 'working' acceptance, not a 'real' one, since it tends," Goffman writes, "to be based not on agreement of candidly expressed heart-felt evaluations, but upon a willingness to give temporary lip service to judgments with which the participants do not really agree."[10]

With the comment, "But there comes a time, when you have to choose between some absolute justice and moving forward in peace," the official is "giving face." This is the power in the official's comment, and this power has consequences. The official is giving face to the Serb delegation. Given the unconscionable injustices that the nationalist Serb army and its paramilitary groups inflicted against non-Serbs, and given the nationalist Serbs' policy of genocide, euphemistically called "ethnic cleansing," it would seem difficult for

---

[7]"The Fall of Srebrenica and the Failure of UN Peacekeeping," *Human Rights Watch/ Helsinki Report* 7, no. 13 (October 1995).

[8]Cohen, "Two Towns," A6.

[9]Goffman, *Interaction Ritual*, 7.

[10]Goffman, *Interaction Ritual,* 11.

the Serb delegation to maintain face with leaders from democratically governed, human rights-based countries. The Serb delegation is therefore dependent upon Western leaders to provide a line through which they can participate in these interactions. "One can say," Goffman writes, "that *to give face* is to arrange for another to take a better line than he might otherwise have been able to take, the other thereby gets face given him, this being one way in which he can gain face."[11]

This is the strategy of U.S. diplomats leading the Dayton talks: "Give-face" to the Serbian delegation and, in particular, the Serbian leader, Slobodan Milošević, who controls the Serb delegation. It is widely known that Milošević is the person most responsible for the war for a Greater Serbia and its brutalities throughout former Yugoslavia, starting perhaps with the attack on Vukovar in 1991.[12] In this setting, Milošević, however, is cast as a peacemaker. He is pictured as someone who is different, genuinely different. U.S. diplomats gainsay Milošević's well-documented infamy and in this way arrange for him to take a better line than he might otherwise have been able to take.

The "carrot" used to compel Milošević to assume this face is the promise of lifting economic sanctions against Serbia. Serbia has been deeply involved and highly supportive of the war for a Greater Serbia. Milošević gave birth to and nurtured the war. Economic sanctions have caused many people in Serbia to live an impoverished and limited life. Lifting economic sanctions helps Milošević maintain his power.

The "stick" used to compel Milošević to put on this face is the threat of releasing U.S. intelligence reports to the International Tribunal for War Crimes at The Hague, which has been investigating war crimes in former Yugoslavia and which has brought indictments against the Bosnian Serb leaders, General Ratko Mladić and Dr. Radovan Karadžić, as well as others. These intelligence reports implicate Milošević as a war criminal in the same vein as the others. Richard Goldstone, the Tribunal's prosecutor and a judge from South Africa, who was "a dogged opponent of apartheid," had asked the United States to turn over any such documents in its possession.[13] International law, Francis A. Boyle points out, requires that the U.S. government does so. If Milošević is indicted, the United States will be required to apprehend Milošević and place him in the custody of the War Crimes Tribunal.

Despite his criminal record, Milošević is the recipient of the face-giving treatment of U.S. diplomats, and given his own dramaturgical skills, Milošević

---

[11]Goffman, *Interaction Ritual*, 42.

[12]See Laura Silber and Allan Little, *Yugoslavia: The Death of a Nation* (New York: TV Books, Inc., 1996), as well as the video documentary by the same name produced by Brian Lapping Associates. See also Jean Hatzfeld, "The Fall of Vukovar," *Granta* 47 (1994): 197–222.

[13]See Robin Knight in *U.S. News and World Report* (December 4, 1995): 30.

carries the line given him perhaps farther than his benefactors intended, which is how Milošević achieves a certain autonomy in these interactions. Goffman calls such behavior "tact regarding tact," that is, Milošević ensures that U.S. diplomats continue their face-giving treatment toward him by reciprocating their tactfulness with his own.[14] The more tactful Western leaders are with Milošević the more tactful Milošević is toward the Western leaders. Milošević, despite igniting the flames of Serbian nationalism that brought hell to so many people in the former Yugoslavia, is trusted dramaturgically. He is trusted to play the face-giving game and play it well. "Trouble," Goffman writes, "is caused by a person who cannot be relied upon to play the face-saving game."[15]

What else is being said with the comment, "But there comes a time, when you have to choose between some absolute justice and moving forward in peace"? The comment puts the Bosnian delegation in "wrong-face." Insofar as the Bosnian delegation does not defer to "the institutional line" that structures these negotiations, the Bosnian delegation can be said to be "out of face." They are perceived as causing trouble. "A person may *be out of face* when he partici-pates in a contact with others without having ready a line of the kind participants in such situations are expected to take."[16] The Bosnian delegation, from the point of view of U.S. diplomats, cannot be relied upon to play the face-saving game.[17] The Bosnian delegation seeks justice; the Republic of Bosnia and Herzegovina, a sovereign nation, was invaded by a foreign force; an arms embargo prevented its soldiers from protecting its land and people; the arms embargo was requested by the invading force, which holds an overwhelming superiority. Many Western leaders insisted that it was right to respect this request.

At Dayton, the more the Bosnian delegation insists on justice, the less the Bosnian delegation is viewed as being interested in peace. The interest in justice is viewed as "out of line." The interest in justice is reduced to a desire for revenge, a desire that is antithetical to the attainment of peace. By insisting upon "some absolute justice," the Bosnian government is "not playing fair." It is viewed by U.S. diplomats as exemplifying an injustice toward the "line" that organizes this setting. "A person may be said to 'be in wrong face' when infor-mation is brought forth in some way about his social worth that cannot," Goff-man writes, "be integrated, even with effort, into the line that is being sustained for him."[18] Paradoxically, while the Bosnian delegation is committed to the prin-

---

[14]Goffman, *The Presentation of Self*, 234–37.

[15]Goffman, *Interaction Ritual,* 31.

[16]Goffman, *Interaction Ritual,* 8.

[17]Think here of the untimely apprehension of the Bosnian Serb General Djordje Djukić, a suspected war criminal, by the Bosnian government shortly after the signing of the Dayton Peace Accord and the embarrassment that it caused IFOR and IFOR's face-work with respect to implementing the Dayton Accord.

[18]Goffman, *Interaction Ritual*, 8.

ciple of justice, this comitment reflects an unfair relation to the interactional line guiding the peace talks at Dayton.

What else, in terms of face-work, is the official saying? "But there comes a time, when you have to choose between some absolute justice and moving forward in peace" saves face. The statement saves face for Western leaders, most of whom have lost face given the numerous ways they have responded to, tolerated, appeased, and acerbated the conflict in Bosnia.

There are various methods that Western leaders employ to "save face." For instance, as the towns of Srebrenica and Žepa were falling to the nationalist Serb army, Western leaders of the Contact Group (France, Germany, Great Britain, the United States, and Russia) held an emergency meeting in London organized by the British government. Western leaders concluded their gathering by replicating a promise that had already been made to the people living in Srebrenica and Žepa. This time, however, they promised to protect the people living in Goražde, a third enclave to the south of Srebrenica and Žepa, which remained under control of the Bosnian government, although it, too, had suffered fierce attacks against civilians and even its hospital by General Mladić's forces. Western leaders concluded their emergency meeting by promising to protect Goražde if, after completing their work in Srebrenica and Žepa, the Serb army proceeded to this third enclave.

In terms of face-work, Western leaders are maintaining poise. "Through poise," Goffman writes, "the person controls his embarrassment and hence the embarrassment that he and others might have over his embarrassment."[19] Western leaders give the appearance of keeping their promise to Srebrenica and Žepa even as they do not. They keep their promise by repeating the same promise to another town. (Žepa was still defending itself as this announcement was being made, and the military commander of the Bosnian government forces defending Žepa, Col. Avdo Palić, was thereafter murdered by Serb soldiers while trying to negotiate a surrender.) Western leaders, by transferring to Goražde the promise they made to Srebrenica and Žepa, maintain face. They are committed to the promise but not the ones to whom the promise is made. Hyperreality, the hypothetical situation that Goražde would be overrun, displaces reality, which is that Srebrenica and Žepa have been overrun. In the discourse of Western leaders, what is happening in Srebrenica and Žepa becomes unreal and so unnecessary to deal with.

After overrunning Srebrenica, Serbian soldiers ordered UN Dutch soldiers stationed at Potocari just north of Srebrenica to surrender their uniforms and vehicles. (Potocari was an area around which thousands of unarmed civilians herded themselves for protection from the Serbian army, only to be lied to, abused, and murdered by Serb soldiers within earshot of UN soldiers.) Wearing UN uniforms and driving UN vehicles, the Serb soldiers then drove to the hills

---

[19]Goffman, *Interaction Ritual*, 13.

and called out to civilians hiding in the forests. After enticing civilians to come out, Serb soldiers killed these people, many of whom were women and children.

Dramaturgically, Serb soldiers were playing the "discrepant role" of shill or claque. Goffman writes, "The designations 'shill' and 'claque' employed in the entertainment business, have come into common use."[20] A shill is a member of the audience who works directly against the interests of the audience in league with the performer, unbeknownst to the audience. The shill exploits the audience's trust that he or she is one of them. This trust makes the audience vulnerable, vulnerable to the interests of the performer. In this context, Serb soldiers (who were "on the opposing side") deceived the civilians under the guise of being UN soldiers (who were "on their side"). The fraud helped Serb soldiers achieve their interest in murdering more people and doing so more efficiently—people who were Bosniaks.[21]

Within the microcosm of this interaction, Serb soldiers parody the macrocosm of the Western leaders' response to their long-planned attack on a safe area and the idea of ethnic cleansing. Serb soldiers parody the Western leaders' betrayal and mock the possibility that there are UN soldiers in the area willing to protect the people who have been attacked and under siege for years. Serb soldiers exploit their victims' trust, a trust that Western leaders insisted was warranted and that grounded their relationship to Europe.

The evil in the Serbs' performance is that it erases the possibility of sincerity in human discourse. Evil reduces life to sheer play. Drawing evil's conclusion, Goffman writes, "There is, then, a statistical relation between appearance and reality, not an intrinsic or necessary one."[22] Wearing UN uniforms and driving UN vehicles, Serb soldiers simulate the possibility that the UN is collaborating with their murders of non-Serbs, which nationalist Serb leaders call "ethnic cleansing." The question, which still paralyzes the world media and enrages academic discourse, is whether this simulation is a statistical possibility or an intrinsic and necessary one. In Srebrenica, UNPROFO (United Nations Protection Force) complied with whatever demands General Mladić made of them, for instance, the demand to turn over the Bosnian translators working for UNPROFO, who were thereafter murdered by Serb soldiers. See as well David Rieff's painful description of the assassination of Dr. Hakija Turaljić, vice president of the Republic of Bosnia and Herzegovina, while riding in a UN armored personnel carrier under the protection of French and British soldiers.[23]

The actors and circumstances in Bosnia and subsequently Kosovo seem to

---

[20]Goffman, *Presentation of Self,* 146.

[21]The term "Bosniak" encompasses without prejudice the cultural and historical legacy of Bosnians who embrace and are influenced by the Muslim faith.

[22]Goffman, *Presentation of Self,* 71.

[23]David Rieff, *Slaughterhouse: Bosnia and the Failure of the West* (New York: Simon and Schuster, 1996), 150–51.

change constantly. New sets are displayed, and different actors play the same role. Face-work, however, remains a ubiquitous feature of the performances on this stage. What is needed, then, to transcend these descriptively interesting but ultimately unsatisfying accounts? The discussion here could continue endlessly. Are the insights gained from what Roland Barthes would call the attitude of sarcasm sufficient for understanding this subject?[24] "What I claim," Barthes writes, "is to live to the full the contradiction of my time, which may well make sarcasm the condition of truth."[25] Is sarcasm, however, the best relation that a social theorist can have to truth?[26] At what point does sarcasm change to irony? At what point does irony shun sarcasm? The advantage of sarcasm is its detachment from its subject; this detachment can lead to astute insights. The advantage of irony is its objectivity, an objectivity that is not detached from but involved with its subject.

> Objectivity is by no means nonparticipation (which is altogether outside both subjective and objective interaction), but a positive and specific kind of participation—just as the objectivity of a theoretical observation does not refer to the mind as a passive *tabula rasa* on which things inscribe their qualities, but on the contrary, to its full activity that operates according to its own laws.[27]

[24]See Žlatko Dizdarević, *Sarajevo: A War Journal,* Ammiel Alcalay, ed., Midhat Ridjanović, trans. (New York: Fromm International, 1993). Although the use of sarcasm throughout this telling memoir is an effective and pointed device, the most poignant accounts are not the ones narrated with sarcasm.

[25]Roland Barthes, *Mythologies*, Annette Lavers, trans. (New York: Noonday Press, 1972), 12.

[26]"The mythologist is condemned to live in a theoretical sociality; for him, to be in society is, at best, to be truthful: his utmost sociality dwells in his utmost morality. His connection with the world is of the order of sarcasm" (Barthes, *Mythologies*, 157).

[27]Georg Simmel, "The Stranger," in *The Sociology of Georg Simmel,* trans. and ed. with an introduction by Kurt H. Wolff (Glencoe, Ill.: Free Press, 1950), 404.

Chapter 3

On the Latent Function of Ethnic Cleansing in Bosnia

No State Shall, during War, Permit Such Acts of Hostility Which Would Make Mutual Confidence in the Subsequent Peace Impossible.

—Immanuel Kant
Perpetual Peace

Anything that obscures the fundamentally moral nature of the social problem is harmful, no matter whether it proceeds from the side of physical or psychological theory. Any doctrine that eliminates or even obscures the function of choice of values and enlistment of desires and emotions on behalf of those chosen weakens personal responsibility for judgment and for action. It thus helps create the attitudes that welcome and support the totalitarian state.

—John Dewey
Freedom and Culture

"ETHNIC CLEANSING" IS a widely used euphemism for the arrests, rapes, murders and expulsions of Bosnian citizens from their homes. The phrase is euphemistic because the word "cleansing" implies an activity that is harmless, ordinary, and even good. The analogy that the phrase establishes, however, is perverse. Were the arrests, rapes, murders, and expulsions of Bosnian citizens a matter of cleansing? Were the arrests, rapes, murders, and expulsions of Bosnian citizens a matter of cleaning an area? In what sense was this activity beneficial? For what reason was it necessary? Was there anything ordinary about the murders, arrests, rapes and expulsions of Bosnian citizens? The use of this phrase by victimizers and victims alike obstructs an adequate understanding of the activity that the term describes.

The use of this phrase also promotes the prejudice that motivates the conduct. The term "ethnic cleansing" patronizes and indulges the rationalization of the actors' victimizing people under the guise of ethnic cleansing because the word "cleansing," by itself, is filled with positive images. Whenever the phrase is used, it leaves unchallenged the assumptions and opinions of those engaged in and committed to ethnic cleansing.

Perhaps because the conduct being identified is so painful to witness and accept, it is necessary to employ a normalizing language. Nevertheless, ethnic cleansing refers to a planned and methodical act of genocide in Europe in the 1990s. The task now is to understand and critique the significance of the conduct that the phrase identifies.

In *Bosnia: A Short History*, Noel Malcolm concludes his account of Bosnia's history from the middle ages to the present time with a keen observation of contemporary events. First, Malcolm describes the conscious motivation for ethnic cleansing.

> The pattern was set by young urban gangsters in expensive sunglasses from Serbia, members of the paramilitary forces raised by Arkan and others...what they were doing was to carry out a rational strategy dictated by their political leaders—a method carefully calculated to drive out two ethnic populations and radicalize a third.[1]

One implication is that the conscious motivation is rational. It represents the actors' decision regarding the most efficient means for attaining a selected end. This motivation on the part of the Belgrade regime has been documented carefully; Norman Cigar, Roy Gutman, Peter Maass, and many others have provided abundant evidence to support this description of the manifest function of ethnic cleansing in Bosnia as well as Croatia and Kosovo.

Malcolm implicitly draws upon a well-known but infrequently used concept in the sociology of Robert K. Merton. In his essay "Manifest and Latent Functions," Merton says that functional analysis is an interpretive scheme, a certain style of hermeneutics.[2] With the distinction between manifest and latent function,

---

[1]Noel Malcolm, *Bosnia: A Short History* (Washington Square: New York University Press, 1994), 252.

[2]Robert K. Merton, "Manifest and Latent Functions" in *Social Theory and Social Structure* (New York: Free Press, 1968), 73–138. See also Robert K. Merton, "The

Merton establishes one dominant and particular way of doing interpretation in sociological inquiry. Drawing upon the model of the biological sciences, functional analysis examines social conduct in terms of how it contributes to the maintenance of an organic whole. It addresses what role social conduct plays in the vitality of this whole. From a functionalist point of view, how did ethnic cleansing operate so as to maintain the vitality of a whole to which it was subject? What social organization did ethnic cleansing serve or disserve? The manifest function of ethnic cleansing was to drive apart two ethnic populations and radicalize a third. Bosnian Muslims and Bosnian Croats were driven apart and Bosnian Serbs were radicalized. Does this conscious motivation, however, adequately explain why the conduct occurred?

After describing the conscious motivation for ethnic cleansing, Malcolm then identifies a more telltale understanding of why ethnic cleansing occurred in Bosnia. This insight stands as the conclusion to Malcolm's book. Malcolm cites the historian Richard Pipes, and the strength of Pipes's concluding words is that they identify what Merton would call the latent function of ethnic cleansing.

> But perhaps the best comment on the tactic of Milošević and Mladić and on what they have achieved in Bosnia...is a judgment by another historian on another country's descent into blood.... "The Bolsheviks had to spill blood in order to bind their waving adherents with a band of collective guilt. The more innocent victims the Bolshevik Party had on its conscience, the more the Bolshevik rank and file had to realize there was no retreating, no faltering, no compromising, that they were inextricably bound to their leaders, and could only march with them to 'total victory' regardless of the cost."[3]

Merton argues that, as long as functional analysis restricts its focus to the manifest function of social conduct, it remains deficient and undeveloped. The business of functional analysis, Merton asserts, is to explain the real or causal function of social conduct. In sociology, function, Merton says, is determined, not by the subjective dispositions of social conduct or the rational motivations of the activity, for instance, motives, but by the objective consequences of the conduct. Aims and purposes, Merton argues, more often than not have little to do with the objective consequences of conduct. According to Merton, in social life subjective dispositions and objective consequences operate independently of each other. Thus to understand what governs conduct "causally," it is necessary

---

Unanticipated Consequences of Purposive Social Action," *American Sociological Review* 1 (1936): 894–904 and Kenneth E. Boulding, *The Image* (Ann Arbor: University of Michigan Press, 1969).

[3]Malcolm, *Bosnia*, 252.

to address the objective consequences of the conduct. Often, the objective consequences are unintended and unrecognized, which is why Merton insists upon the concept of latent function for sociological inquiry.[4]

What was the objective consequence of ethnic cleansing? What function then did ethnic cleansing perform? Why did it occur with the sadism and unconscionable violence that it did? While the manifest function describes, from the viewpoint of the actors engaged in the conduct, a rationalization for ethnic cleansing, the latent function explains the unrecognized or unintended logic that governs the activity. As Malcolm points out, the latent function of ethnic cleansing was to bind together with a band of collective guilt the wavering adherents within the Serbian population.[5] The more ambivalent Bosnian Serbs are about the aim of ethnic cleansing, the more gruesome the practice has to be. The more uncertain Bosnian Serbs are about the purpose of ethnic cleansing, the more perverse the conduct becomes. The more skeptical Bosnian Serbs are about the purpose of ethnic cleansing, the more sadistic the activity is.

The reason why ethnic cleansing took on its most abusive form in Bosnia is not because there was a long-standing history of tribal hatreds in Bosnia. On the contrary, ethnic cleansing took its most abusive form in Bosnia because there is a long-standing history of tolerance and openness in Bosnia. Moreover, there has been among Bosnians a long-standing history of goodwill toward each other and different sacred traditions. From the viewpoint of Bosnian Serbs who saw themselves not just as Serbian but also as Bosnian, there was no need for ethnic cleansing. From the viewpoint of Bosnian Serbs who saw themselves as Yugoslavs rather than Serbs, there was no purpose for ethnic cleansing. From the perspective of Bosnian Serbs whose spouses were non-Serbs, there was no desire for ethnic cleansing.[6]

Given the normative orientations that had historically held the Bosnian community together, ethnic cleansing had to be done in ways that were categorical. Given the shared values that integrated the Bosnian society, ethnic cleansing had

[4]For a critique of this position, see Colin Campbell, "A Dubious Distinction? An Inquiry into the Value and Use of Merton's Concepts of Manifest and Latent Function," *American Sociological Review* 47 (February 1982): 29–44.

[5]The same dynamic holds for any group engaged in ethnic cleansing. When Croats, for example, ethnically cleanse parts of Bosnia of non-Croats, the latent function is to bind together with a band of guilt the wavering adherents within the Croation population.

[6]There are several excellent books to support these points: Rusmir Mahmutćehajić, *Twisted Politics: Readings of History and Community Relationships in Bosnia*, trans. Francis R. Jones and Marina Bowder (Sarajevo: Did, 1998); Robert J. Donia and John V. A. Fine, Jr., *Bosnia and Hercegovina: A Tradition Betrayed* (New York: Columbia University Press, 1994); Kemal Kurspahić, *As Long as Sarajevo Exists*, trans. Collen London, (Stony Creek, Conn.: Pamphleteer's Press, 1997); and Noel Malcolm, *Bosnia: A Short History,* cited in this chapter.

to be done in ways that were absolute and ruthless. Otherwise, the uncertainty and ambivalence of Bosnian Serbs could not be overcome. The objective consequence of ethnic cleansing, as Malcolm points out, was to force Bosnian Serbs "to realize there was no retreating, no faltering, no compromising, that they were inextricably bound to their leaders, and could only march with them to 'total victory' regardless of the cost."[7]

Examples of this objective consequence of ethnic cleansing are easy to find. Consider the following telling passages from Michael A. Sells's *The Bridge Betrayed: Religion and Genocide in Bosnia*, Peter Maass' *Love Thy Neighbor: A Story of War*, and David Rohde's *Endgame: The Betrayal and Fall of Srebrenica: Europe's Worst Massacre since World War II*.

First, Sells makes the following report:

> Serbs who refused to participate in the persecution of Muslims were killed. In a Serb-army occupied area of Sarajevo, Serb militants killed a Serb officer who objected to atrocities against civilians; they left his body on the street for over a week as an object lesson. During one of the "selections" carried out by Serb militants in Sarajevo, an old Serb named Ljubo objected to being separated out from his Muslim friends and neighbors; they beat him to death on the spot. In Zvornik, Serb militiamen slit the throat of a seventeen-year-old Serb girl who protested the shooting of Muslim civilians. In the Prijedor region, Serb militants put Serbs accused of helping non-Serb neighbors into the camps with those they tried to help.[8]

Sells also brings our attention to the following practice:

> Commanders of the killing camps made a practice of opening them to local Serb radicals, gangsters, and grudge-holders, who would come each night to beat, torture, and kill the detainees. This practice had the effect of spreading complicity throughout the neighboring area. Distribution of stolen and abandoned goods also spread complicity. Every town "cleansed" meant the availability of automobiles, appliances, stereo and television equipment. Once a family had in their home something that had belonged to a neighbor, they were less likely to object to the "ethnic cleansing."[9]

Remember here the concluding words of Malcolm's book:

> The Bolsheviks had to spill blood in order to bind their waving adherents with a band of collective guilt. The more innocent victims the Bolshevik Party had on its conscience, the more the Bolshevik rank and file had to realize there was no

---

[7]Malcolm, *Bosnia*, 252.

[8]Michael Sells, *The Bridge Betrayed: Religion and Genocide in Bosnia* (Berkeley: University of California Press, 1996), 73.

[9]Sells, *Bridge Betrayed*, 74.

retreating, no faltering, no compromising, that they were inextricably bound to their leaders, and could only march with them to "total victory" regardless of the cost.[10]

In *Love Thy Neighbor,* Maass likewise identifies the objective consequence of ethnic cleansing in Bosnia.

> Gaining the support of ordinary people...is a crucial element of any successful reign of terror. The wavering masses, the silent majority, the good men, they must feel stained by the same blood as the Visigoths who fired the first shots. They must be made into accomplices to the crime. Once this is done, once their moral backs are broken, they will do virtually anything. Like Želja [a Serb sniper on the front line in the hills of Sarajevo] they will even fire shots that might kill their own parents [Želja's parents lived in Sarajevo during its siege].[11]

Rohde's *Endgame* chronicles the fall of Srebrenica from the viewpoint of those who experienced or participated in the atrocity. Reporting an anecdote from Dražen Erdemović, an executioner during the Srebrenica massacre found guilty in June 1996 of crimes against humanity before the International War Crimes Tribunal, Rohde notes the following from Erdemović's recount:

> Before the last group were executed, Gojković [the squad's commander] entered the bus and handed a Kalashnikov to the driver. "You must each kill one, " he said to the horrified driver. He didn't want anyone talking. Everyone would be guilty.[12]

During the fall of Srebrenica, not only were individuals co-opted into the conduct of ethnic cleansing, but entire villages and towns were implicated by the process. Consider the collective ritual by which Muslim men, who were retained in Bratunac, a Serb-held town northeast of Srebrenica, were executed.

> [Six hundred] Muslim prisoners who had sweltered through Mladić's speech on the Nova Kasaba soccer field were packed shoulder to shoulder in two sixty-foot-long, sixteen-wheel trucks.... For three hours, the men stood in the stifling trucks. At 11 P.M., guards finally lifted the top off the back entrance of the truck. Local Serb men and women from Bratunac were waiting. They asked if any Muslims from Bratunac or any old friends they knew were on board. "We brought you dinner," they said, or "We brought you cigarettes." About twenty Muslims got off the truck. They were asked questions briefly and then the Serbs

[10]Malcolm, *Bosnia*, 252.

[11]Peter Maass, *Love Thy Neighbor: A Story of War* (New York: Vintage Books, 1997), 112.

[12]David Rohde, *Endgame: The Betrayal and Fall of Srebrenica, Europe's Worst Massacre since World War II* (New York: Farrar, Straus, and Giroux, 1997), 309.

began to beat them. The men in the truck listened to their cries, and then heard pistol fire. None of the twenty returned.

At 12:30 A.M., more people appeared at the back of Hodžić's truck, wanting to know if there were any Muslims from the villages of Kravica and Lolići on the truck. About twenty Muslim men, either deciding that they wanted to die or believing somehow that their friends would spare them, got off. They were immediately beaten. "Fuck your Gypsy mother!" one Serb shouted. Again, shots were heard. Again, none of the twenty returned.[13]

What was the latent function of ethnic cleansing in Bosnia? The function was to disfigure the normative orientation to which Bosnian Serbs were both dependent and subject as members of the Bosnian community. The objective consequence was to maim the collective sentiments that integrated Bosnian Serbs in their society and guided them in their interactions with others. The result was to detach Bosnian Serbs from the value elements that they use to make judgments not only about others but also about themselves.[14]

In Bosnia the moral sentiments of nationalist Serbs were transformed into the mind-set of a crowd. Gustave Le Bon says that, while a crowd is a social phenomenon with a distinct structure, a crowd, nevertheless, lacks the form of a society. While a social entity, a crowd is a deficient and dysfunctional society. Le Bon, however, notes that sometimes, "An entire nation may become a crowd under the action of certain influences."[15]

Given the influence of ethnic cleansing, the normative orientation upon which the Bosnian Serb community depended became the delusional mind-set of a crowd. Drawing upon a passage from *Catch-22,* Maass provides a caricature of this crowd mentality that overtook not only nationalist Bosnian Serbs, but also Bosnian Croats and (to a lesser degree) Bosnian Muslims.

> Everyone knew that sin was evil and that no good could come from evil. But…it was almost no trick at all…to turn vice into virtue, and slander into truth, impotence into abstinence, arrogance into humility, plunder into philanthropy, thievery into honor, blasphemy into wisdom, brutality into patriotism, and sadism into justice. Anybody could do it; it required no brains at all. It merely required no character.[16]

---

[13]Rohde, *Endgame,* 281–82.

[14]While some argue, drawing upon quantitative and semantic reasons, that ethnic cleansing fails to match the character of what genocide is, I argue that the term "genocide" falls short of describing ethnic cleansing. "Sociocide"—to kill society—is perhaps a more accurate term than "genocide" to describe the character and consequence of ethnic cleansing.

[15]Gustave Le Bon, *The Crowd: A Study of the Popular Mind* (Marietta, Ga.: Larlin Corporation, 1982), 3. "The age we are about to enter will in truth be the ERA OF CROWDS" (LeBon, *The Crowd,* xv).

[16]Maass, *Love Thy Neighbor,* 209.

Western leaders and UN officials appease nationalist Serb leaders year after year and meeting after meeting because Western leaders and UN officials lack an adequate understanding of why ethnic cleansing is occurring. Western leaders and UN officials had detailed reports from the CIA and the State Department on the manner and degree to which ethnic cleansing was occurring, but they lacked an objective understanding of why ethnic cleansing was occurring. Like the media, they accepted the seemingly rational accounts provided by the actors engaged in ethnic cleansing. They accepted that the aim, purpose, and goal of ethnic cleansing was to drive apart two ethnic populations and radicalize a third. Western leaders and UN officials granted the rationality of ethnic cleansers too much significance and failed to recognize what the result of ethnic cleansing was. Western leaders and UN officials are seduced by the rationality of the ethnic cleansers in part because the rationality of ethnic cleansers also implicitly informs and dominates the conduct and activities of Western leaders and UN officials.[17]

The conscious motivation for ethnic cleansing, however, fails to explain why this social conduct was necessary from the viewpoint of the actors engaged in ethnic cleansing. The manifest function, that is, the need to drive apart two ethnic populations and to radicalize a third, is insufficient to explain what compelled the gruesome conduct and sustained it over the course of so many years. The manifest function is insufficient to explain why the activity continued unchecked for so long in Kosovo and grew in magnitude. To construct an adequate account of the activity, it is necessary to understand why, from the viewpoint of the actors involved, ethnic cleansing was necessary.

Upon reflection, the manifest function for ethnic cleansing is not as rational as it purports to be. Bosnia is now partitioned. The end of ethnic cleansing can be said to have been achieved. Why, then, does ethnic cleansing persist? In northwest Bosnia, ethnic cleansing took place even during the signing of the Dayton Accord, a document that accepted and practically endorsed the political consequence of ethnic cleansing in Bosnia. If the end of ethnic cleansing was achieved and even sanctioned by world leaders with the signing of the Dayton Accord, why would the activity need to persist? What need, however perverse and dysfunctional, does the activity really serve? Is this other need perhaps greater than the manifest goal of the activity? In accepting at face value the political purpose of ethnic cleansing and in pandering to the nationalist leaders who brazenly promote this purpose, Western leaders and UN officials become implicated in the way that Bosnian Serbs are implicated.

The latent function of ethnic cleansing has grown in significance in part

---

[17]To draw upon Ferdinand de Saussure's distinction between significance and value, Western leaders and UN officials understand the significance of ethnic cleansing but not the value of ethnic cleansing.

because the latent function has not been recognized. The latent function of ethnic cleansing enlarges as the activity increases, and as the latent function increases in significance, the activity intensifies.

The need on the part of those engaged in ethnic cleansing to gain the complicity of not only Bosnian Serbs but also leaders of Western nations as well as UN officials becomes overwhelming. To give an example, the manifest function of the fall of Srebrenica and Žepa, two UN designated safe havens, was to make negotiations possible and to complete the seemingly inevitable process of partition. "Impartial" UN officials like Gen. Bernard Janvier openly advocated this position with world leaders.[18] The latent function of the fall of Srebrenica and Žepa, however, was to humiliate Western leaders and UN officials, and this latent function determined the activity to a far greater degree than the manifest function. The latent function of the fall of Srebrenica and Žepa, from the viewpoint of those engaged in the atrocity, was to show that the moral integrity of Western leaders and UN officials was no different from the moral integrity of nationalist Serb leaders. Even nationalist Serb leaders are surprised by how easily they could establish this point and succeed in this endeavor.

Western leaders and UN officials do not understand why, after being exposed in the world media by journalists, ethnic cleansing not only persisted but intensified. They do not understand why exposure in the world media increased rather than diminished the excesses of ethnic cleansing. They do not understand the now barely hidden logic that fuels ethnic cleansing. In other words, they do not understand human nature and what it is. They do not recognize the strong need on the part of national Serb leaders to win the tacit endorsement of Western leaders and UN officials for their hideous process misleadingly labeled ethnic cleansing. While Western leaders and UN officials verbally condemned ethnic cleansing, they behaviorally endorsed it by failing to confront it decisively.

Charles Horton Cooley makes the following point about human nature and its place in society:

> Human nature in this sense is justly regarded as a comparatively permanent element in society. Always and everywhere men seek honor and dread ridicule, defer to public opinion, cherish their goods and their children, and admire courage, generosity, and success.[19]

Do those engaged in sociocide exemplify an absence of human nature? Do they not seek honor and dread ridicule, albeit in perverse and self-destructive ways?

---

[18]Bianca Jagger, "The Betrayal of Srebrenica," *The European* (September 25–October 1, 1995), <http: //www.haverford.edu/rlg/sells/srebrenica/BiancaJagger1.html>, [accessed November 25, 1998].

[19]Charles Horton Cooley, *Social Organization: A Study of the Larger Mind* (New York: Schocken Books, 1962), 30–31.

Western leaders and UN officials assume that human nature is absent in the conduct of ethnic cleansing. How could human beings, they reason, do the things that ethnic cleansers did? Western leaders and UN officials forget that human nature is a permanent element of society even as human nature destroys the society upon which it depends. If human nature were understood as a permanent element of society, Western leaders and UN officials would have known better how to confront the human nature engaged in sociocide and mimicked by others.

Chapter 4

The Croat-Muslim War:
An Inconvenient Fact

The primary task of a useful teacher is to teach his students to recognize "inconvenient" facts—I mean facts that are inconvenient for their party opinions. And for every party opinion there are facts that are extremely inconvenient, for my own opinion no less than for others.

—Max Weber
"Science as a Vocation"

The war between the Muslims and the Croats marked the end of moderate warfare, the end of decency. People began to say the kind of things about one another that everyone had previously been saying only about the Serbs. They began to believe they would be saved if they just did the same as the others, that the world and God would offer them a chance to survive.

—Miljenko Jergović
Sarajevo Marlboro

RECOGNIZED WIDELY AS a modern scholar, Max Weber nevertheless preserves the Socratic tradition. "The primary task of a useful teacher," Weber says, "is to teach his students to recognize 'inconvenient' facts." This pedagogy resonates with the manner in which Socrates would raise difficult qualifications to the arguments and positions being developed in a conversation. Plato used the gadfly analogy to describe this attribute of Socratic inquiry. While annoying and seemingly destructive, for Socrates the task is to encourage critical reasoning. The task, Weber notes, is not a mere intellectual one; it represents a moral practice.[1]

The Croat-Muslim war, which emotionally and unpredictably began in Bosnia in April 1993, is an inconvenient fact for those who believe in and know, not the ideal, but the reality of the multiethnic tradition in Bosnia. After the vicious and successful Serbian campaign of ethnic cleansings throughout Bosnia, the Croat-Muslim war became an inconvenient fact for those who wished simply to demonize the Serbs. The war that broke out between Bosnian Croats and Bosniaks and the consequences of this violence for Bosnian society matched the destruction that the nationalist Serbs inflicted upon the Bosnian people. For example, a year after Serbian death camps were discovered in Bosnia and reported in the world media, nationalist Croats created their own Nazi-like concentration camps in which Bosniaks, who had been neighbors as well as fellow soldiers in the fighting against Serbian aggression, were tortured and maltreated. How and why did these events occur?

In their excellent book, *Yugoslavia: Death of a Nation*, Laura Silber and Allan Little report this anecdote from Stipe Mesić, the Croatian representative on the federal presidency of the former Yugoslavia and a trusted advisor of Franjo Tudjman, the first president of independent Croatia.

> In Zagreb, Mesić later recalled that he was first told of the camps by Jozo Primorac, an HDZ [Croatian Democratic Union] activist.
>
> *He said: "Listen Stipe, I'm surprised, I was just in Herzegovina (he had a brother there). They have camps down there. They look like in the Nazi times, even worse they don't get food and water, and are abused."*
>
> *I asked who the people in the camps were, and he said they were former neighbors, from the same villages and towns, and their only fault was that they were Muslims. Another big group there were Muslim HVO soldiers disarmed overnight and sent there. He was very surprised, especially by the treatment there.*
>
> *I used this information, and told Tudjman. He answered that the others had camps as well.*[2]

When Mesić tells Tudjman about the concentration camps in Bosnia in which Bosnian and Croatian Croats, with the support of Tudjman's political party and advisors, torture and mistreat Bosniaks, Tudjman replies, "Others had camps as

---

[1]"I believe the teacher accomplishes more than a mere intellectual task if he compels his audience to accustom itself to the existence of such facts. I would be so immodest as even to apply the expression 'moral achievement'" (From *Max Weber: Essays in Sociology*, tran., ed., and with an introduction by H. H. Gerth and C. Wright Mills [New York: Oxford University Press, 1958], 147).

[2]Laura Silber and Allan Little, *Yugoslavia: Death of a Nation* (New York: TV Books, 1996), 299. This discussion is indebted to the detailed and balanced discussion in this important work and, in particular, the chapter titled "Beware Your Friend a Hundredfold."

well." There is evidence now to demonstrate that Tudjman secretly collaborated with Slobodan Milošević in the destruction and partition of Bosnia. Like Milošević, Tudjman was an outsider who was a destroyer of Bosnia.[3]

Nationalism is a form of collective identity that suffers from an absence of doubt. For instance, when informed that Bosnian Croats had built concentration camps in Bosnia as a means to achieve the political ends that Tudjman himself promoted, Tudjman failed to consider his responsibility in the matter and question the problem it presented. Tudjman suffered from an absence of doubt, a matter that led Mesić eventually to distance himself from Tudjman. Paulo Freire formulates the problem reflected in Tudjman's response to Mesić's information when he writes, "For the oppressors, 'human beings' refers only to themselves; other people are 'things.' For the oppressors, there exists only one right; their right to live in peace, over against the right, not always even recognized, but simply conceded, of the oppressed to survival."[4] Tudjman showed no care for the people tortured and abused in the camps run by nationalist Croats. In his eyes, these people were not Croats; he saw them not as people but as things. As a nationalistic leader, Tudjman focused exclusively on his isolated right, and he denied the rights of others, even to survive.

While the Croat-Muslim war is an inconvenient fact for those who know the multiethnic history of Bosnia, it is a "convenient" fact for the Balkan leaders who instigated interethnic violence. Speaking on the Croat-Muslim enmity, the Bosnian Serb Gen. Ratko Mladić commented, "I will watch them destroy each other and then I will push them both into the sea."[5]

The Croat-Muslim conflict is also a convenient fact for Western leaders. During the Croat-Muslim war, which was eventually stopped in 1994 with U.S. intervention, Western leaders pointed to the conflict as a reason not to intervene in Bosnia given the complex and seemingly irresolvable problems in the area. The Croat-Muslim war provided Western leaders with an easy excuse not to become involved in Bosnia. The common refrain that politicians would voice was that as long as these people insist upon killing each other, there is nothing that can be done.

Thus, the Croat-Muslim war appeared to support the frequently stated opinion that the violence in Bosnia was historically determined and reflected the collective hatreds of people in the region. Silber and Little, though, make this observation.

---

[3]For a good, insider account of this matter, see anonymous author, "Further Adventures of Hjvoje Sarinić in the Land of the Serb Aggressor," *Bosnia Report*, no. 9–10 (April–July 1999): 32–37.

[4]Paulo Freire, *The Pedagogy of the Oppressed*, trans. Myra Bergman Ramos (New York: Continuum, 1989), 43.

[5]Silber and Little, *Yugoslavia*, 295.

The Croats of Bosnia fall into two distinct camps, geographically and politically. One-third of the Bosnian Croats lived in western Herzegovina, a notorious hotbed of extreme rightwing nationalism, where Croats formed close to a hundred percent of the population—at least in the countryside. Many western Herzegovinians had fought in the Croatian war, and in 1992 returned bloodied by their experience and ready for the war in Bosnia. But the majority of Bosnia's Croats lived in central and northern Bosnia, in towns and communities where all three nationalities lived. These central Bosnian Croats were, by tradition, much less nationalistic and much more inclined to live in a multiethnic Bosnian state than to seek its partition into ethnically pure units.[6]

The Croat-Muslim war did not happen automatically; there were cultural barriers within Bosnian society that hindered the outbreak of this conflict. Consider, for example, the documentary *We Are All Neighbors,* narrated by the anthropologist Tone Bringa. The documentary chronicles the destruction of a Bosnian village near Sarajevo; it records the murder of a *gemeinshaft*, the killing of a close-knit community. The village consisted of about two-thirds Bosniaks and one-third Bosnian Croats. When the Croatian army attacked the village and took control, Bosniaks were murdered and the Bosniak population was forced to relocate. Just a few weeks before this violence, people in the village were saying, "We all get along because we all have to live together. Bosnia could never be any other way." People confirmed that viable social bonds held them together. After this violent event, people were saying, "We can't live with them any more after what they've done."[7] Nationalist Croats entered the village and forced the Bosnian Croats to turn against their neighbors and friends and destroy all their homes. The documentary captures the shame and humiliation of the once healthy community. The event mimicked the ethnic cleansing that the Serbs had done throughout Bosnia the year before and continued to do for several more years.

After the Croat-Muslim war in 1993, some Bosnian Muslims, who now identify themselves as Bosniaks, began to model the nationalistic practices and xenophobic ideology of their enemies. The rationale for this development is easy to understand. Consider this comment after the outbreak of the Croat-Muslim war.

> A Sarajevo psychiatrist, called Lijiljana Oruč, kept her sense of humor throughout the siege. In the summer of 1993 she described the Bosnian capital as one vast psychiatric laboratory. Sarajevans had suffered, she said, from a collective psychotic delusion—the delusion that the world would, eventually, rescue them and their country. This delusion persisted, she continued, despite all the objective evidence to the contrary. It was, therefore, a kind of inverse paranoia: a persistent belief that everything is going to turn out all right in the end even though

[6]Silber and Little, *Yugoslavia*, 293.
[7]Tone Bringa, *We Are All Neighbors* [Video] (Chicago: Public Media, 1993).

by all rational judgement, it clearly is not. "This collective psychosis left us in May 1993," Dr. Oruč insisted. "After that, we knew we were on our own."

Here we witness a twofold sense of betrayal. Not only did the world fail to stop the sociocide that was being attempted in Bosnia, but Bosnians themselves began to engage in the sociocide that was occurring. Nationalist Serbs exemplified an evil and racist nationalism, and other groups began to mirror this nationalism as a way to defend one's community, as a way to ensure one's own survival. The normative orientation that expected Europe and the United States to intervene and save the people in Bosnia came to be perceived as delusional, as delusional as paranoia. The delusion's content, though, was inverted. The delusion was that others were motivated to help you rather than that others were motivated to harm you. After the Croat-Muslim war, the question became how do Bosnians sustain their normative orientation and commitment to mutual tolerance based on the principle of goodwill when this principle is denigrated by the world's relation to Bosnia? After Bosnians witnessed the world's betrayal of Bosnia, they were faced with the possibility of betraying themselves.

The recognition by Bosnians that "we were on our own" took different forms. For some, the task became a matter of moral education. Political leaders, academics, and citizens took on the formidable task of educating the incorrigible leaders of the world on their moral responsibility for events in Bosnia and the consequences of failing to intervene.

During the war it was easy for journalists to find morally compelling stories. For others, the task became a matter of rejecting Bosnia's relation to Europe and becoming, to some degree, the political image that Bosnia's enemies ascribed to Bosniaks. Consider, for example, the following development after the start of the Croat-Muslim war.

> In Zenica, the heartland of Muslim Bosnia, a new force altogether appeared— the Seventh Muslim Brigade. This was explicitly Muslim, rather than Bosnian, in its orientation. Its officers were hostile to Westerners, wore Islamic insignia, long beards, and greeted each other with the Arabic "al–sallam aliekum" (peace be with you). For the first time, a strident, xenophobic Muslim nationalism was being articulated in Bosnia: the politics of multiethnic tolerance, the officers of the Seventh Muslim Brigade argued, had led to the destruction of the Muslim people. It was time for Muslims to take matters into their own hands, not as Bosnians, but explicitly as Muslims.

After the start of the Croat-Muslim war, nationalism seemed to some the only viable way to preserve one's community. The event that best captures the tragedy of the Croat-Muslim war for the Bosnian society is the destruction of the Mostar bridge over the Neretva River.

The bridge—and Mostar itself—came to symbolize the very idea of Bosnia-

Herzegovina, a place where Catholic, Orthodox, and Muslim peoples lived distinctively, but all together and in mutual tolerance. It was despised by many Croat nationalists for whom it represented a lasting reminder of Turkish influence in what they viewed as their Christian land. It survived the fall of the Ottoman Empire. It survived two world wars. But on November 9, 1993 (four years to the day after the tearing down of the Berlin Wall) under a sustained artillery battering by Bosnian Croat forces, its beautiful arch collapsed into the deep blue river pool below. In a war in which multiethnicity was itself the enemy, the destruction of the bridge appeared to mirror that of the multiethnic ideal of Bosnia—a place almost defined by bridge-building—between communities, between nationalities, between faiths. For Bosnians there was no stronger image of the country they were trying to build. The Bosnian government declared a day of mourning.[8]

Weber states that inconvenient facts do not hinder sociological understanding; instead, they are opportunities to strengthen sociological inquiry and its grasp of reality. It is important, therefore, to address the Croat-Muslim war and examine its significance for an adequate account of events in Bosnia as well as Kosovo. For instance, the racism in Croatian nationalism matched the racism in Serbian nationalism. Dario Kordić, a deputy to Mate Boban, the leader of the nationalist Croats in Bosnia, asserted that the Muslims in Bosnia "did not constitute a separate nation. They were Croats of Islamic faith."[9]

Muslim nationalism at a collective level was born as a reaction to the enmity of Serbian and Croatian nationalism. It did not exist at a collective level before suffering the violence and rejection of Serbian and Croatian nationalism. It became a matter of fighting fire with fire, and the fire, no matter who carried it, destroyed communities and the families within them. Albanians in Kosovo are now experiencing the same political and social development after having been unconscionably victimized by Serbian nationalism and dismayed by the continuation of the Belgrade regime under Milošević's leadership. It is difficult for Albanians not to adapt the methods of their Serb victimizers when the attempted genocide of Albanians in 1999 goes unpunished and when the unconscionable murder of thousands of Albanians is ignored.

Paulo Freire best describes the political trap into which nationalistic Croats and others in Bosnia as well as Kosovo fall. The mistake that the victims of oppression make is to mirror the methods and rationalization of the oppressor. Defending oneself from oppression is different from becoming an oppressor. To refrain from becoming an oppressor is different from capitulating to an oppressor. Sadly, Western leaders interpreted the efforts of the Bosnian people as well as the Kosovars to defend themselves against Serbian oppression as another instance of oppression. Many Bosnians, however, especially in Sarajevo,

---

[8]Silber and Little, *Yugoslavia*, 291.
[9]Silber and Little, *Yugoslavia*, 294.

defended themselves against aggression in a principled way. As the journalism of Roy Gutman, David Rodhe, Roger Cohen, and several others testifies, many recognized the difference between defending themselves from oppression and becoming an oppressor. Freire describes the temptation that was soundly rejected by many Bosnians during the war.

> But almost always, during the initial stage of the struggle, the oppressed, instead of striving for liberation, tend themselves to become oppressors, or "sub–oppressors." The very structure of their thought has been conditioned by the contradictions of the concrete, existential situation by which they were shaped. Their ideal is to be men; but for them to be men is to be oppressors. This is their model of humanity. This phenomenon derives from the fact that the oppressed, at a certain moment of their existential experience, adopt an attitude of "adhesion" to the oppressor. Under these circumstances they cannot "consider" him sufficiently clearly to objectivize him—to discover him "outside" themselves.[10]

Nothing pleased the nationalist leaders more than when their victims copied their unhealthy ideology and antihuman practices. Nothing displeased the nationalist leaders more than when their victims considered the actions of the nationalist leaders clearly, objectively, and independently of themselves and refused to internalize the grotesque images of humanity that the nationalists leaders promoted.

What, then, triggered and structured the antipathy toward humanity that Freire calls the fear of freedom? In *Microsociology: Discourse, Emotion, and Social Structure,* Thomas J. Scheff provides one concept to explain the trap into which the enraged victims of shameful oppression could fall. Scheff calls the concept the shame-rage spiral. On this deadly form of emotional entrapment, Scheff says, "Since he views himself only from the point of view of his oppressors, he must seek a pretext for violence which falls within their system of etiquette."[11] Consider a telling comment from Peter Maass that describes this dynamic and its destructive consequences within Bosnia.

> Feeling betrayed by America and Europe, the Muslim leadership in Bosnia began turning away from Western notions of pluralism, and focused on Muslim

[10]Freire, *Pedagogy,* 29–30.

[11]Thomas J. Scheff, *Microsociology: Discourse, Emotion, and Social Structure* (Chicago: University of Chicago Press, 1990), 130. For a more detailed development of the destructive consequences of shame and rage within social relations, see Thomas J. Scheff, *Bloody Revenge: Emotions, Nationalism, and War* (Boulder: Westview Press, 1994). Scheff addresses the social-psychological reasons for the culture of silence among the oppressed, which Freire explicates and critiques. From a symbolic interactionalist perspective Scheff pursues Georg Simmel's unique insight on social conflict: "The deepest hatred grows out of broken love.... Here separation does not follow from conflict, but, on the contrary, conflict from separation" (Scheff, *Bloody Revenge,* 2).

nationalism. It was the cruelest of self-fulfilling prophecies: The Western world viewed them as Muslims, not Europeans, so they became Muslims, tough Muslims. They had little choice.[12]

The Croat-Muslim war is an inconvenient fact for those who wish to demonize the Serbs and assert that the Serbs alone engaged in the destruction of Bosnia. The painfulness of the Croat-Muslim war is that some of the victims of Serbian aggression became self-victimizing. Some of the victims could not resist internalizing the pathos of Serbian aggression. Some of the victims became self-victimizing in the same way that the Serbs were self-victimizing, especially in their relation to others.

The inconvenient fact of the Croat-Muslim war, however, supports the argument in this book that the destructive events in Bosnia were more than a matter of genocide. The concept of genocide does not fully encompass the significance of events in Bosnia, although it does encompass one aspect of these events. The events in Bosnia reflected an act of sociocide, the attempted killing of a viable and functional society. The more successful this sociocide became, the easier it was to enlist the participation of others, regardless of their ethnicity or civic identity. A lament by Maass captures our fear in witnessing this development.

> After a year of warfare, the virus of nationalism, carried by Serbs and Croats, was infecting Muslims and eating away at the multinational society they once belonged to. How far would it spread?... A year after the war started, well-educated liberals with connections outside Bosnia began leaving in greater numbers, thereby letting less tolerant militants get a stronger grip on the hearts and minds of those who remained behind. This is perhaps the saddest part of Bosnia's tragedy, that its unique mosaic of nationalities, held together by civic tolerance, may disappear forever.... It would be a true pity for Bosnia, which has lost so many lives already, to lose its soul.[13]

The world has a duty to Bosnia and to itself to prevent this possibility from becoming a reality. If Bosnia were to lose its soul (and I do not fear that it will), it is difficult to imagine how the world would not also lose its soul. The chapters that follow seek to demonstrate this argument.

---

[12]Peter Maass, *Love Thy Neighbor: A Story of War* (New York: Vintage Books, 1997), 240–41.

[13]Maass, *Love Thy Neighbor*, 241–42.

Chapter 5

The Ritual of Shame and the Western Response to Bosnia

Metaphysical guilt: There exists a solidarity among men as human beings that makes each co-responsible for every wrong and every injustice in the world, especially for crimes committed in his presence or with his knowledge. If I fail to do whatever I can to prevent them, I too am guilty. If I was present at the murder of others without risking my life to prevent it, I feel guilty in a way not adequately conceivable either legally, politically, or morally. That I live after such a thing has happened weighs upon me as indelible guilt.

—Karl Jaspers
The Question of German Guilt

UNDERSTANDING THE VIOLENCE of ethnic cleansing is formidable. The world watches as politicians and intellectuals in the Belgrade regime plan and establish an apartheid state. The dignity of not just thousands but millions of human beings is unconscionably assaulted; many in Bosnia and Kosovo have lost their right to speak, work, own property, worship, and live.

There is much official documentation of these events, and this documentation touches upon issues that sociologists examine. Few sociologists, however, have taken up or contributed to this documentation. From a sociological point of view, ethnic cleansing makes little sense. While it is easy to identify the political motive (to create a Greater Serbia), it is more difficult to identify the sociological motive. The costs are too high, not only for the victims, but also for the victimizers. The victimizers destroy, not only the homes, communities, and lives of other people, but also the social fabric upon which the victimizers themselves depend. To what logic, then, does ethnic cleansing conform? Can we, drawing upon the sociological tradition, account for the significance of these activities, and, after doing so, critique the conduct?

In 1956 Harold Garfinkel, a notable American sociologist, published a short essay in *American Journal of Sociology* entitled "Conditions of Successful Degradation Ceremonies." Degradation ceremonies, Garfinkel says, are "any communicative work between persons, whereby the public identity of an actor is transformed into something looked on as lower in the local scheme of social types."[1]

Ethnic cleansing is an attempted degradation ceremony. With sadistic violence and unconscionable aggression, ethnic cleansers assert that they are making a point. Their motive is to transform the public identities of individuals and a community. Nationalist Serbs seek to transform the public identities of Bosniaks (Bosnian Muslims) and Kosovar Albanians into something looked on as lower in the local scheme of social types. First this activity occurred in the state media and intellectual circles of former Yugoslavia. Then militia from Serbia and Montenegro, with the support of the Yugoslav Peoples Army, entered Bosnia and methodically engaged in genocidal activities. The activity repeated itself in Kosovo; the repetition was predictable, unbelievable, and redundant.

For a degradation ceremony to be successful, "The identities referred to," Garfinkel stresses, "must be 'total' identities. That is, these identities must refer to persons as 'motivational' types rather than as 'behavioral' types, not to what a person may be expected to have done or to do...but to what the group holds to be the ultimate 'grounds' or 'reasons' for his performance." In other words, "The transformation of identities," Garfinkel writes, "is the destruction of one social object and the constitution of another.... It is not that the old object has been overhauled; rather it is replaced by another. One declares, 'Now, it was otherwise in the first place.'"[2]

Just One Example

In his book, *Love Thy Neighbor: A Story of War,* Peter Maass reports a painful

---

[1]Harold Garfinkel, "Conditions of Successful Degradation Ceremonies," *American Journal of Sociology* 61 (March 1956): 420–24, cite on p. 420. Think of negative campaigning during elections in the United States as another example of the status degradation ceremony. In their campaign ads, politicians attempt to denounce and shame their opponents as successfully as possible to win the election.

[2]Garfinkel, "Degradation Ceremonies," 421–22. This formulation of a "total identity" is central to Garfinkel's analysis. The formulation draws upon the metaphysical realm and represents Garfinkel's distinct contribution to social inquiry as an empirical scientist. "The man at whose hands a neighbor suffered death becomes a 'murderer.' The person who passes on information to enemies is really, i.e., 'in essence,' 'in the first place,' 'all along,' 'in the final analysis,' 'originally,' an informer."

event, one that was typical of the way in which ethnic cleansing was carried out.[3]

> You can, for example, barge into a house and put a gun to a father's head and tell him that you will pull the trigger unless he rapes his daughter or at least simulates rape. (I heard of such things in Bosnia.) The father will refuse and say, I will die before doing that. You shrug your shoulders and reply, Okay, old man, I won't shoot you, but I will shoot your daughter. What does the father do now, dear reader? He pleads, he begs, but then you, the man with the gun, put the gun to the daughter's head, you pull back the hammer, and you shout, Now! Do it! Or I shoot! The father starts weeping, yet slowly he unties his belt, moving like a dazed zombie, he can't believe what he must do. You laugh and say, That's right, old man, pull down those pants, pull up your daughter's dress, and do it![4]

The gunman wants to debase the father. Does the activity, however, say anything substantive about the father, what we hold to be the ultimate grounds or reasons for his conduct? Does the event, orchestrated by the gunman, touch upon either the father or the daughter's "total identity"? Does the gunman really perform a status degradation ceremony?

In narrating this event, Maass employs the second person pronoun. To win the indignation of the reader, Maass puts his reader in the place of the gunman. Maass's assumption is that, by putting his reader in the role of the gunman, the reader will be repulsed and seek distance from the activity of the gunman. Yes, the reader will seek emotional distance from the activity of the gunman, but, by default, the reader will also seek distance from the gunman's victims, which, in part, is the gunman's aim. To counter this possibility, the following discussion puts you in the place of the father. The purpose is to encourage you to identify with the father and his daughter so as to win your empathy for them and draw you closer to them.

If the gunman tells you that your daughter will be killed unless you have intercourse with her and if you know that the gunman is capable of murdering a

---

[3]In the documentary *Killing Memory: Bosnia's Cultural Heritage and Its Destruction*, we see that ethnic cleansing was an assault, not just against people and their lives, but against historical buildings and cultural monuments. Andras Reidlmayer says, "When a person dies, it is that person's life, that person's family that's affected. When a culture is killed, it forecloses the future and it destroys the memory of the past. Even if the people to whom those monuments and documents belong survive, they've lost their anchor, their connection to who they are, of how they belong to a particular place.... I think that you cannot separate the sufferings of people from the destruction of monuments of culture. The killing of memory is as great a tragedy as the killing of people" (Andras Riedlmayer, *Killing Memory: Bosnia's Cultural Heritage and Its Destruction* [Haverford, Pa.: Community of Bosnia Foundation, 1994]).

[4]Peter Maass, *Love Thy Neighbor: A Story of War* (New York: Vintage Books, 1997), 51–52.

human being, how can you not comply? You state first that you will die before you do what the gunman asks. The gunman responds that, unless you do what he asks, he will kill your daughter. For the sake of your dignity, you are willing to sacrifice your life, but it is not your life that the gunman wants. It is your dignity that the gunman wants. The gunman wants to degrade you. Why is your degradation more important to the gunman than your life?

You comply, but what is the nature of your compliance? You comply because you are a father. The gunman's conduct, in other words, does not transform you into a nonfather. Your "total identity," the first principle of what it is to be a father, is left untouched because the ultimate grounds for your conduct are clear. You cherish the life of your daughter. Since you cherish the life of your daughter, you cannot bear to watch her being murdered. While, for the sake of your dignity, you are willing to sacrifice your life, you are not, for the sake of your dignity, willing to sacrifice your daughter's life. Your daughter's life is more important than your dignity. If you had sacrificed your daughter's life for the sake of your dignity, you would have lost your dignity.

The gunman has power over you not because of his gun. The gun alone signifies no power at all. One aspect of the gunman's power is the absence of any normative constraint regarding the gunman's use of coercive force. Another and more important aspect of the gunman's power over you is your need not to see your daughter murdered. The gunman has power over you because you cherish your daughter. Your need makes you dependent upon the gunman. The gunman has power over you because he recognizes your need and the dependence upon him that it creates. Neither the gun nor the gunman's anomic use of the gun explains the gunman's power over you. It is your normative need not to see your daughter murdered and your steadfast relation to this need.[5]

In coercing you to have intercourse with your daughter, the gunman confronts your first principles as a father, your dignity. The motive of the gunman is to attempt a status degradation ceremony. Here is the logic that governs the gunman's behavior, and here is the pathos of ethnic cleansing throughout Bosnia and Kosovo. Although some of the individuals who are engaged in ethnic cleansing shun the role of denouncer and seek surreptitiously to help the victims and former friends, for many the role of denouncer guides the activity.[6] The better we understand this role, the better we are able to understand the character of ethnic cleansing. The better we understand the character of ethnic cleansing, the better we are able to readdress its consequences.

Notice the assumptions that the gunman must make to gain whatever per-

---

[5]On the social construction of power, see Peter Blau, *Exchange and Power in Social Life* (New York: John Wiley and Sons, 1964), 118–25.

[6]On how some individuals shunned the role of denouncer, consider this account: "The best of all the guards was Željko, also known as Džigi; he was forty years old and a partner in a gas station at Omarska. He never once hit anybody. His post was under the window

verse pleasure he does from his activity. First, the gunman must assume that you are willing to do whatever you can to save your daughter's life. Second, the gunman assumes that you abhor the idea of raping your daughter. The gunman recognizes you as a father. Without these assumptions with respect to your ultimate values, the gunman's conduct is unintelligible.

The gunman knows you, not in a particular way, but in a general way. He knows that you are a father and he knows what it means to be a father. In other words, there is a "We-relation" between you and the gunman. If there were not this "We-relation, the possibility of a degradation ceremony would not be present. The phenomenologist Alfred Schutz writes,

> He and I, we share, while the process lasts, a common vivid present, our vivid present, which enables him and me to say: We experienced this occurrence together. By the We-relation, thus established, we both—he, addressing himself to me, and I, listening to him—are living in our mutual vivid present, directed toward the thought to be realized in and by the communicating process.[7]

It is painful to acknowledge this We-relation between you and the gunman because the substance of the We-relation is nothing except the gunman's negation of the We-relation. The We-relation perpetuates itself simply through the denial of its own existence.

To understand the significance of the gunman's action, we need to identify the motive with which the gunman acts. To assess the motive, we need to formulate the motive as oriented toward some normative expectation. What normative resources exist in this interaction that provide the background for this conduct?

The character of evil is not its unintelligibility. Innocence imagines that evil is unintelligible. For the innocent, evil makes no sense. Such, perhaps, is the perspective of U.S. president Bill Clinton toward the genocide and crimes against humanity in Bosnia and Kosovo. From the viewpoint of innocence, if evil makes

---

of Djemo's dorm. He often threw a piece of bread or a freshly picked plum through the window. Djemo knew him from before; they had even been friends. On his first day as a guard at Omarska, Džigi had called to Djemo and said openly, in front of all the prisoners, 'Djemo, you're the prisoner and I'm the guard, but you were my friend before, and that's how you'll stay.' As he said it, he gave Djemo a firm handshake. 'I'll do whatever I can, just don't expect any miracles.' Djemo thought he saw a tear roll down Džigi's unshaven face" (Rezak Hukanović, *The Tenth Circle of Hell: A Memoir of Life in the Death Camps of Bosnia,* trans. Colleen London and Midhat Ridjanovic with a foreword by Elie Wiesel [New York: Basic Books, 1996], 78).

[7]Alfred Schutz, "On Multiple Realities," *Philosophy and Phenomenological Research* 5 (June 1955): 543.

no sense, it does not exist. If it does not exist, it does not have to be dealt with. Innocence, whether the innocence of an adult or a child, believes that evil is grounded in nothingness. In contrast, a sociological formulation of evil focuses on evil's parasitic relation to what does make sense, to what is intelligible, and to what is.

"It is proposed," Garfinkel writes, "that only in societies that are completely demoralized, will an observer be unable to find such ceremonies, since only in total anomie are the conditions of degradation ceremonies lacking."[8] An opinion frequently stated by journalists was that the situation in Bosnia was one of total anomie, a place where self-interest and self-interest alone ruled, a pure, concrete example of the Hobbesian jungle. The situation in Kosovo also became one of total anomie. Hobbes, though, argues that this presocial state of nature never existed and never will. For Hobbes, the presocial state is an ideal type. Hobbes reasons that the Hobbesian jungle is too painful, too nasty and brutish, to last for any period of time. He, in fact, uses the idea of a presocial state, for heuristic purposes, to explain the origins of society.[9]

While popular, the Hobbesian account of what happened in Bosnia is an innocent one. While descriptively the account seems accurate, if it were true, the conditions for degradation ceremonies would be lacking and observers would be unable to witness them. Degradation ceremonies, however, were witnessed in Bosnia and Kosovo; they were witnessed in the media clearly and repeatedly. These degradation ceremonies occurred at every level, between civilians, soldiers, political leaders, and diplomats. Although each story was particular, each shared a common thread. The world was gripped by these stories and fixated to the ritual they dramatized.

Rather than stipulate, as many pundits do, that the situation was one of total anomie, a better track to take is to ask what conditions were present that allowed observers to witness degradation ceremonies? What features in the organization of the society prevailed such that degradation ceremonies were attempted? The more ethnic cleaning persists, the more of a ritual it becomes. The substance of the ritual, moreover, is neither political nor psychological. Here is why politicians found it difficult to stop the conduct. As events in Kosovo show, ethnic cleansing was self-perpetuating; ethnic cleansing fueled itself independently of its political motive.

Let us return to the example from *Love Thy Neighbor*. Recall the two conditions present for the gunman to attempt a degradation ceremony. The gunman sees two things. One, you are willing to do whatever you can to save your daughter's life. Two, you abhor the idea of intercourse with your daughter. Without

---

[8]Garfinkel, "Degradation Ceremonies," 420.
[9]Thomas Hobbes, *Leviathan,* ed. C. B. MacPherson (Middlesex, England: Penguin, 1968), 187.

these dual assumptions, the gunman lacks the resources with which to shame you. Because you are a father, you must do what he tells you. Because you are a father, you must not do what he tells you. The assumptions are contradictory but interrelated. Here is the perverse logic that guides the gunman's activity.

Notice that, if your normative expectations were not real, if the ultimate principles that ground your conduct were not authentic, the conditions for a status degradation ceremony would be absent. Moreover, if the gunman did not himself recognize your normative orientations, if he did not himself see that your normative orientations were real, not only to you, but also to the world, he would lack the resources with which to attempt a degradation ceremony.

The mere presence of these necessary conditions, however, does not guarantee the success of a degradation ceremony. "Indeed, the question is: Starting from any state of a society's organization, what program of communicative tactics will get the work of status degradation done?"[10] Certain strategies and communicative tactics must be followed to ensure a successful degradation ceremony. A degradation ceremony is a construction. If the criteria are not adequately met, the degradation ceremony fails. At this point, Garfinkel introduces the role of the witness in the status degradation ceremony and the relation of the witnesses to both the denouncer and the denounced. Degradation ceremonies occur only if there are witnesses.[11] The denouncer and the denounced do not alone constitute a degradation ceremony (unless viewed from a strict psychological viewpoint). To induce shame, a denouncer needs to convince the witnesses to view the event in a special way. "The paradigm of moral indignation," Garfinkel says, "is 'public' denunciation. We publicly deliver the curse: 'I call upon all men to bear witness that he is not as he appears but is otherwise and in essence of a lower species.'"[12] Here is the task of the denouncer, and it involves considerable work.

Garfinkel accounts for the methodology that must be followed. First, the denouncer needs to demonstrate to witnesses that the denouncer and witnesses

---

[10]Garfinkel, "Degradation Ceremonies," 421.

[11]This point is as empirical as it is theoretical. From the viewpoint of analytical realism, which Garfinkel inherits from Talcott Parsons, the distinction between empiricism and theoretical understanding disappears. "The rape victim, age twenty-nine, reported to Human Rights Watch that the police took her away from the house where she was being held and brought her to another house. There she was placed in a room and forced to strip naked. One after the other, five members of the Serb forces entered the room to look at her body, but it was only the last man who raped her, she said. While he was assaulting her, the other four entered the room and watched. The woman also stated that someone had placed a walkie-talkie under the bed in the room, and that throughout the ordeal the Serbian forces shouted at her via the walkie-talkie to scare her. In all, she was held in the room for about half an hour" (*Kosovo Human Rights Flash no. 31*, "Rape of Ethnic Albanian Women in Kosovo Town of Dragacin" [Human Rights Watch, 1999]).

[12]Garfinkel, "Degradation Ceremonies," 421.

share values. Moreover, the values that are shared need to be fundamental. Second, the denouncer needs to demonstrate that the denounced does not share these values. The denouncer needs to show that the reason the denounced does not share these values is based on choice rather than conditions. Moreover, while the denounced may seem to hold the shared values of the community, the denounced, the denouncer needs to show, does not and never really did. "The work of the denunciation," Garfinkel asserts, "effects the recasting of the objective character of the perceived other: The other person becomes in the eyes of his condemners literally a different and new person. It is not that the new attributes are added to the old 'nucleus.' He is not changed, he is reconstituted."[13]

To return to the example from *Love Thy Neighbor*, the gunman's motive is to depict you as a nonfather, to depict you as not being who you are, and as never having been who you seem to be, namely, a father.

In a starkly objective manner, Garfinkel accounts for the communicative steps that are followed for a degradation ceremony to be successful. Let us finish reviewing this complicated blueprint. The denouncer must show as well that he or she is a legitimate and objective spokesperson for those values that the denouncer and witnesses share and from which the denouncer claims that the denounced are estranged. To repeat, if the degradation ceremony is to be successful, the denouncer must show that the denounced chose to be estranged from the values that the denouncer and witnesses share, not because of unfavorable conditions or unfortunate circumstances, but because it is the choice of the denounced. Degradation ceremonies, Garfinkel insists, can only be successful if they meet all of these social criteria.[14] If the denouncer falls short of any of these criteria, the degradation ceremony misses its mark and at best achieves partial success.

In attempting a degradation ceremony, the gunman falls short. It is important to address the reasons why the gunman fails. First, the gunman fails in his attempt to debase you because the gunman cannot be a legitimate spokesperson for the values he claims to share with his witnesses when he himself flagrantly violates these values from which he claims, you, the denounced, are estranged. This event is the gunman's idea, and you, the father, are the object of the gunman's projection. Your selection is arbitrary; it has no relation to you as a particular person. Your motive, your intention as a social actor, your agency as a member of society, is irrelevant from the viewpoint of the gunman.

To construct a degradation ceremony, however, the denouncer must expose your motive clearly. The denouncer must unmistakably show that your motive is the only thing that is relevant in your behavior. To demonstrate that you (your character, your soul) are the causal reason for the denounced action, the

---

[13]Garfinkel, "Degradation Ceremonies," 421.

[14]"[T]he characteristics of denunciatory communicative tactics…tell us not only how to construct an effective denunciation but also how to render denunciation useless" (Garfinkel, "Degradation Ceremonies," 424).

denouncer must expose your motive so that it can be clearly known. Here is why, in postmodern times, it is so difficult to achieve a successful degradation ceremony. From a postmodern perspective, motives and the social schemata for judging motives are the least relevant aspects of social life.[15] The gunman cannot denounce you if the conduct for which you are being denounced is coerced by him with the threat of violence. These factors short-circuit the gunman's attempted degradation ceremony, although they do not detract from the gunman's will to enact one.

It is important to address why, from the viewpoint of the gunman, his activity seems at least partially successful. If the gunman sees himself as successfully constructing a degradation ceremony, what conditions exist that allow him to think this way? In Bosnia and Kosovo, the world watches. The world plays the role of witness to ethnic cleansing. In Bosnia, the UN forces in particular played this role.[16] In this manner, the gazing world becomes a sustaining component of the system that perpetuates ethnic cleansing. Nationalist Serbs play the role of denouncers; the others, whether Bosnians, Bosnian Muslims, or Kosovar Albanians, are the ones denounced; and the world is the witness to the ritual. As long as nationalist Serbs sustain this triadic structure and as long as witnesses allow nationalist Serbs to sustain this triadic structure, ethnic cleansing persists and grows. By insisting on their "simulated" privilege to assume the role of denouncer, nationalist Serbs block those whom they degrade from denouncing

---

[15]Even if all members of a group simultaneously attempt to perform a degradation ceremony, these efforts would be futile without the necessary social organization. Imagine a world in which everyone acted like Jay Leno; there would be no laughter. Leno needs both his audience and the normative expectations they represent to constuct his derogatory jokes qua status degradation ceremony. The schemata for judging motives, for making a laugh, involve a dichotomy and a tension within this dichotomy, although the dichotomy itself can be conditional and historical. "The features of the mad-dog murderer reverse the features of the peaceful citizen. The confessions of the Red can be read to teach the meanings of patriotism. There are many contrasts available, and any aggregate of witnesses this side of a complete war of each against all will have a plethora of such schemata for effecting a 'familiar,' 'natural,' 'proper,' ordering of motives, qualities, and other events" (Garfinkel, "Degradation Ceremonies," 423). Today postmodernism argues that we are no longer on this side of a complete war of each against all. Instead, we are inside of a complete war of each against all. That is, this plethora of schemata carries no necessary significance, either intellectually or morally.

[16]Here is why, after the grotesque spasm of sadistic and murderous ethnic cleansing in Kosovo, which Milošević initiated and led, Milošević now wants the UN rather than NATO troops to police Kovovo. In Bosnia the UN troops played the role of witness well. In Kosovo NATO troops might do more than play the role of witness. They might become denouncers of the genocide.

them for executing genocide. Nationalist Serbs exemplify a "reaction forma-tion."[17] To avoid becoming the subject of a renunciation, nationalist Serbs seize upon their simulated right, based on bogus history, to engage in renunciation.[18]

For the gazing world, the role of witness to the ritual of ethnic cleansing becomes problematic. Serving as witness to evil becomes untenable. The role creates dissonance. With whom do the witnesses identify and align themselves— the denouncers, who confess the Christian faith as Orthodox Serbs, or the denounced, who follow the Islamic faith? Nationalist Serbs exploit this variable, which gives them status and so an advantage in the American and European news media whose viewers are predominately Christian.

As time passes, it becomes more and more unclear who are the objects of the degradation ceremony called ethnic cleansing. It is no accident that during their activity ethnic cleansers would select to be present the weakest individuals from their victims and then release these individuals assuming that they would be too degraded to tell the world what happened to them. Consider the following account from a survivor:

> One of the Serb soldiers came into the room and turned to me and started to beat me, especially on my head and spine, and I fainted. Two days later, I had my first epileptic seizure. When the Serbs from the camp heard about this, they took me to watch them torture others. They were sure I was going to die. I was very weak; my weight was down to 36 kilos, and I could only walk with difficulty. One night, two soldiers came in and took me to an area where they hung people. I saw one man hung through his back on the hook of the lift for a lorry. He was still alive and screaming. And yet the Serbs went on beating him. On the floor was another man whose skin was split; he was dead…. Throughout the night they ordered me to watch the torture, while they laughed. When I returned to the room, I had another epileptic seizure.[19]

Ethnic cleansers designate the role of witness because it is an essential compo-nent of their activity. It is a necessary component of their activity from their own point of view. Ethnic cleansing is not a natural phenomenon; it is social.

The world itself does not volunteer for this role. Indeed, whenever the world tries to disassociate itself from this relationship, ethnic cleansers simply increase

---

[17]"They 'stand it on its head'; they exalt its opposition; they engage in malicious, spiteful, 'ornery' behavior of all sorts to demonstrate not only to others, but to themselves as well, their contempt for the game they have rejected" (Albert K. Cohen, *Deviance and Control* [Englewood Cliffs, N.J.: Prentice-Hall, 1966], 205).

[18]"To simulate is to feign to have what one hasn't" (Jean Baudrillard, *Jean Baudril-lard: Selected Writings*, ed. with an introduction by Mark Poster [Stanford, Calif.: Stan-ford University Press, 1988], 167).

[19]Sabahudin Mešinović, *Bosnia: Testament to War Crimes as Told by Survivors,* ed. with an introduction by Alijah Gordon (Malaysian Sociological Research Institute, 1993), 6.

their brutality and violence so as to make it impossible for the gazing world to distance itself. The more the world is implicated in the process of ethnic cleansing, the more nationalist Serbs coopt the world into its project. Eventually, the world becomes, not only a witness, but also an object of the degradation ceremony.

The gunman, for instance, is not just trying to shame you; he is trying to shame your relation to the world, the fact that you and the world share values, fundamental values such as fatherhood, from which the gunman himself is estranged. The more estranged the gunman is from the world, the more the gunman wants to estrange you from the world and the world from itself. The more estranged the gunman is from you and the world, the more the gunman estranges himself from himself and his relation to the world.

Only in this way can the gunman, in these postmodern times, presume to be a legitimate spokesperson for the world. As long as the world stands for nothing, the gunman becomes the legitimate spokesperson for the world. The gunman comes to represent the world. As Garfinkel says, "The denouncer must make the dignity of the supra-personal values of the tribe salient and accessible to view, and his denunciation must be delivered in their name."[20] If the dignity of the world is to stand for nothing, then the gunman speaks for the world and the world's relation to you, that is, the world's rejection of you and itself.

Soon you begin to see that the world, even more than you, is being denounced. Your role at this point changes. You become not the one being denounced, but the witness to the denuciation of the world. You become the witness to the denunciation of the witnesses to your denunciation. You see that the world rather than you is being denounced, and you begin to pity the world. You become, as it were, a martyr. In this way, Bosnia and now Kosovo are the centers of the world because they are where we witness the denunciation of the world. When the world gazes upon Bosnia and Kosovo, it sees itself as the object of denunciation, which is why the world is riveted to the conduct of ethnic cleansing.

At first, the logic that fuels ethnic cleansing is to bind Bosnian Serbs with a band of collective guilt. As ethnic cleansing becomes more and more sadistic, this logic becomes insufficient. The more the world watches, the more the world is included in this band of collective guilt, which is initially meant only to bind together Serbs.

The food that fuels the ego of the nationalist Serbs is their ability to bully the world's ego. The food that fuels the ego of nationalist Serbs is their ability to submit the world's ego to their will, their ability to force the world's ego to repress its conscience, its superego, to the same degree and in the same manner that nationalist Serbs repress their conscience, their superego. As ethnic cleansing

---

[20]Garfinkel, "Degradation Ceremonies," 423.

persists, the ways in which the gunman and the world are alike become more and more important, and the ways in which the gunman and the world are not alike become less and less important.[21] In turn, as ethnic cleansing persists, the ways in which you and the world are alike become less and less important, and the ways in which you and the world are not alike become more and more important.[22]

This disassociation, which can never be completely achieved in reality given the character of our species-being, is the objective of ethnic cleansing, which is what makes ethnic cleansing evil. The purpose of evil is to destroy our species-being. The way in which evil achieves this purpose is by claiming, not just that one person is of a lower species, but that our species-being itself is of a lower species. Our species-being then is no longer capable of making us whole and one with each other.

A Postscript for Sociologists

As a social scientist, Garfinkel explains as objectively as he can the way moral indignation is socially constructed. Garfinkel successfully formulates the grammar that organizes and makes meaningful moral indignation as a social affect. In this sense, Garfinkel's account is interpretive and causal.[23] When we apply this sociology to the subject of ethnic cleansing, however, the subject strains the scientific commitment within Garfinkel's sociology.

Garfinkel, for example, does not judge whether it is right to perform a degradation ceremony. Moral indignation is a social reality. It exists as a necessary and ubiquitous feature of social life. We see it and experience it whether in a brothel

---

[21]Here is the moral ambiguity of the Dayton Peace Accord. The ways in which the nationalist Serbs and the world are alike are more important than the ways in which the nationalist Serbs and the world are not alike. In turn, the ways in which the Bosnian government and the world are alike are less important than the ways in which the Bosnian government and the world are not alike.

[22]The refusal of NATO forces to arrest the most important indicted war criminals exemplifies this point. It shows that the way in which the aggressors and the world are alike is more important than the way in which the aggressors and the world are not alike.

[23]"Sociology (in the sense in which this highly ambiguous word is used here) is a science that attempts the interpretive understanding of social action to arrive at a causal explanation of its course and effects [author's parenthesis]" (Max Weber, *The Theory of Social and Economic Organization*, trans. A. M. Henderson and Talcott Parsons [New York: Free Press, 1964], 88). Notice how this definition for many sociologists is tantamount to an oxymoron. How can sociology, without the use of experimental methodology, arrive at a causal explanation of social action? How can sociology, with the use of interpretive understanding, arrive at causal explanations? The means that Weber promotes belie the end that he proposes. Is Weber's definition of sociology a blessing or a curse? Here is the double-bind from which sociology has still to emancipate itself.

or a seminary. For Garfinkel, the scientific responsibility of the sociologist is simply to account for the process through which indignation comes to exist as a feature of social life.

The question Garfinkel does not ask is when moral indignation is appropriate. For Garfinkel, this question is not a matter of sociological inquiry; for this discussion, it is. For example, the indignation one feels toward those engaged in ethnic cleansing is different from the indignation that ethnic cleansers feign toward their victims. From an empirical point of view, however, the two seem to be more alike than unalike. How, then, do we distinguish between the two? We focus on the normative orientation that animates and gives meaning to each appearance of moral indignation. We focus on the teleology that each normative orientation draws upon for its weight and significance. One, the moral indignation that one feels toward those perpetuating ethnic cleansing, is based on a recognition of the importance of justice; the other, the moral indignation that ethnic cleansers feign toward their victims, is based on self-interest wrongly understood.

Sociology, Garfinkel shows, explains the path that each must follow to exist as an instance of moral indignation; sociology as it is now configured, however, is not able to address the question of when moral indignation is appropriate and when it is not. Sociology, as it is now configured, is not able to distinguish the two instances of indignation. Why? The question involves addressing issues that are nonempirical but, at the same time, necessary features of social understanding. Parsons explains this paradox in the following manner.

> The voluntaristic theory of action, recognizing that the specific "social" element involves reference to the "ideal" but thought of in its relation to action, while it at the same time involves a reference beyond its logical formulations to the nonempirical aspects of reality, avoids these intolerable consequences. It leaves room for an epistemology of a genuine realist nature, but involving nonempirical elements which are also nonsociological. For "society" to be the object of an explanatory science, it must participate in empirical reality. But such participation does not preclude significant relations outside it.[24]

At this point, it is useful to review the epistemology that legitimates and limits the use of ideal types in sociological inquiry since Garfinkel's analysis of degradation ceremonies is based, afterall, on the construction of an ideal type. Weber writes on the use of ideal types in sociological inquiry:

> In no case does it [the theoretically conceived pure type of subjective meaning attributed to the hypothetical actor or actors in a given type of action] refer to an objectively "correct" meaning or one which is "true" in some metaphysical

---

[24]Talcott Parsons, *The Structure of Social Action: A Study in Social Theory with Special Reference of a Group of Recent European Writers* (New York: Free Press, 1968), 448.

sense. It is this which distinguishes the empirical sciences of action such as sociology and history, from the dogmatic disciplines in that area such as
jurisprudence…, which seek to ascertain the "true" and "valid" meanings associated with the objects of their investigation.[25]

On what basis does Weber distinguish the empirical sciences of action from
the dogmatic discipline of jurisprudence? Weber says that sociology is not a dogmatic discipline in that, in using "pure types" for theoretical analysis, it does not
seek to ascertain the "true" or "valid" meanings associated with the objects of its
investigation. If sociology were to seek to ascertain the true or valid meanings
associated with the objects of its investigation, it would be no different from
jurisprudence. But the question is, if sociology does not seek to ascertain the true
and valid meanings associated with the objects of its investigation, what then
does sociology seek to ascertain? "Have we thrown the baby of explanation out
with the bath water of teleology?"[26]

How is the meaningfulness of "the theoretically conceived pure types of subjective meaning," which Weber, as a theoretical sociologist, seeks to ascertain,
distinct from the true and valid meaning, which jurisprudence seeks to ascertain?
Weber's recommendation for the development of sociology as an empirical science of action hinges upon this distinction, but it is exceedingly difficult to surmise the basis for this distinction with respect to a teleology or, more correctly,
the absence of teleology for the empirical sciences of action. Here is how Talcott
Parsons laments the problem:

> [T]he only positive characterization of the ideal type that Weber gives is that it is
> a construction of elements abstracted from the concrete, and put together to
> form a unified conceptual pattern. This involves a one-sided exaggeration
> (*Steigerung*) of certain aspects of the concrete reality, but is not to be found in it,
> that is, concretely existing, except in a few very special cases, such as purely
> rational action. It is a Utopia.[27]

Parsons suggests that Weber wants it both ways and yet, at the same time,
neither way. The ontology for the use of the ideal types in sociological inquiry
(the empirical sciences of action) is neither "metaphysical truth" nor "empirical
objectivity." At the same time, the ontology that supports the use of ideal types in
theoretical sociology is somewhat like metaphysical truth and somewhat like
empirical objectivity. Parsons oberves, "It is a Utopia."[28]

[25]Max Weber, *The Theory of Social and Economic Organization,* Talcott Parsons, ed.,
A. M. Henderson and Talcott Parsons, trans. (New York: Free Press, 1964), 89–90.

[26]Stephen P. Turner and Regis A. Factor, *Max Weber: The Lawyer as Social Thinker*
(London: Routledge, 1994), 120.

[27]Parsons, *Structure of Social Action,* 603.

[28]Consider the postmodern turn on this issue: "Representation starts from the principle

Here are the difficult questions for appreciating Weber's discussion of the place of ideal types in theoretical sociological inquiry: What is the ontology that the ideal type puts the sociologist in touch with? How is it that only the ideal type can put the sociologist in touch with this ontology? How important is this ontology to the development of sociological understanding? How is this ontology, which is central to the development of sociological knowledge, distinct from a Utopia-like knowledge?

Here is the position that I recommend: As Garfinkel and other successful sociologists show, sociology needs ideal types to explicate the social world. The social world is greater than the sum of its parts. This is not to say that the ideal type that is employed to explicate the social world is itself the whole. The social world is greater than the sum of its parts, including the part that is the ideal type whose purpose is to explain the relationship of the parts.

To conclude, I cite a comment by Garfinkel in which he seems to disclose his teleological attitude toward the subject of degradation ceremonies, an attitude that stands independently of his scientific account but nevertheless informs his scientific account.

> Quarrels which seek the humiliation of the opponent through personal invective may achieve degrading on a limited scale. Comparatively few persons at a time enter into this form of communion, few benefit from it, and the fact of participation does not give the witness a definition of the other that is standardized beyond the particular group or scene of its occurrence.[29]

The social knowledge of a person that one gains from a degradation ceremony is situational and parochial; it lacks a necessary relation to what is essential or intrinsicially significant to the subject per se. In a postmodern world, the gunman entertains the thought that his degradation of you may have a chance of success because the teleology that informs the world's normative orientations is difficult to surmise. In a postmodern world, teleology is present only through its conspicuous absence, and social life withers. "And in all the seriousness of truth, hear this: without *It* man cannot live. But he who lives with *It* alone is not a man."[30]

---

that the sign and the real are equivalent (even if this equivalence is Utopian, it is a fundamental axiom). Conversely, simulation starts from the Utopia of this principle of equivalence, *from the radical negation of the sign as value*, from the sign as reversion and death sentence of every reference. Whereas representation tries to absorb simulation by interpreting it as false representation, simulation envelops the whole edifice of representation as itself a simulacrum [Baudrillard's italics]" (Baudrillard, *Selected Writings*, 170).

[29]Garfinkel, "Degradation Ceremonies," 424.

[30]Martin Buber, *I and Thou*, trans. Ronald Gregor Smith (New York: Macmillan, 1987), 34.

Chapter 6

On the Dialectic of the Scapegoat in Kosovo

Following our view of sadism, we should say that the destructive component had entrenched itself in the super-ego and turned against the ego. What is now holding sway in the super-ego is, as it were, a pure culture of the death instinct, and in fact it often enough succeeds in driving the ego into death, if the latter does not fend off its tyrant in time.

—Sigmund Freud
The Ego and the Id

The biggest hope for Kosova Albanians, especially those in its northern part, is the belief that in the meantime Kosova leaders will succeed in organizing methods of defense to protect them from genocide. Another hope is that the current situation could become a trap for Milošević, a trap where the region around Trepça including Mitrovica would be the bait, but not the scapegoat.

—Nexhmedin Spahiu
"Another Serbian Aim: The Partition of Kosova"

EVERY PLATONIC DIALOGUE shows that the most decisive concerns in social discourse are moral concerns, and, insofar as social science fails to address the moral concerns of social discourse, then it in turn fails to be a decisive social science. In the preceding chapter ethnic cleansing was examined from a sociological rather than political or psychological point of view. Ethnic cleansing was formulated as an attempted degradation ceremony, and a critique was put forth. An empirical study was employed in a paradoxical way for the purpose of moral commentary. This is how Harold Garfinkel raises the issue of the manner in which sociology examines seemingly nonempirical subjects:

> While constructions like "substantially a something" or "essentially a something" have been banished from the domain of scientific discourse, such constructions have prominent and honored places in the theories of motives, persons, and conduct that are employed in handling the affairs of daily life. Reasons can be given to justify the hypothesis that such constructions may be lost to a group's "terminology of motives" only if the relevance of socially sanctioned theories to practical problems is suspended. This can occur where interpersonal relations are trivial (such as during play) or, more interestingly, under severe demoralization of a system of activities.[1]

Constructions like "substantially a something" or "essentially a something" endow a subject with moral character; they point to the metaphysical content of a subject. What are the reasons that such constructions cannot be lost to a group's terminology of motives? Why are such constructions required? Rather than say, "Reasons can be given to justify the hypothesis that such constructions may be lost to a group's 'terminology of motives' only if the relevance of socially sanctioned theories to practical problems is suspended," it would be better to be direct and say that such constructions must be used to make sense of everyday life. Even positions opposing this argument make use of constructions like "substantially a something" or "essentially a something." We "should" not use "should." The negation positively employs what it negates.

Constructions like "substantially a something" or "essentially a something" are always critical to accounting for the practical affairs of social life.[2] This point is an empirical fact for Garfinkel, not a metaphysical claim. While Garfinkel may seem to betray the epistemology of empiricism, he is not guilty. When scientific discourse ignores "a group's terminology of motives," it cannot study the seriousness of social life. During times of triviality or total anomie, the vitality of social life is lost.

Thus, questions from the preceding chapter still linger. There is a shadow of ambivalence as to whether ethnic cleansers are qualified spokespersons for the values from which degradation ceremonies can be constructed. The relation between ethnic cleansers and the observing world is unclear. For example, when the media focuses on the Orthodox Easter celebrations during the NATO bomb-

---

[1]Harold Garfinkel, "Conditions of Successful Degradation Ceremonies," *American Journal of Sociology* 61 (March 1956): 422.

[2]Garfinkel, "Degradation Ceremonies," 422.

ing of Serbia and Kosovo, with whom does the observing world identify? The Orthodox Serbs doing ethnic cleansing? Or the Muslim Albanians being murdered and driven from their homes? To what degree do the prejudice and racism in the activity of ethnic cleansing mirror the prejudice and racism of the observing world?

These questions cannot be adequately examined from a strictly empirical epistemology. Garfinkel points to a source that invigorates the sociological study of such matters. The work of Kenneth Burke in social theory is infrequently recognized in sociology.[3] For this study, Burke's distinctive reading of the "scapegoat mechanism" is helpful. Burke formulates the scapegoat mechanism in psychoanalytic rather than behavioristic terms.[4] In doing so, he stresses the role of the superego in the scapegoat mechanism. Burke's dramatistic formulation cuts through the indeterminacy of the relation between the ethnic cleansers and their victims and dissolves the ambiguity of the relation between the ethnic cleansers and the world. While events in Kosovo in the spring of 1999 are examined, the character of these events do not differ from the ones that preceded them in Bosnia.

Nationalist Serbs have forced Bosnians and Kosovars into the scapegoat role. Despite incisive objections and morally compelling resistance, Bosnians and Kosovars were entrapped in the scapegoat mechanism. It is important to understand this role in a deep rather than a superficial manner. By providing a psychoanalytical rather than behavioristic account of the scapegoat mechanism, Burke provides such an opportunity, and his account leads to unexpected conclusions.

What is the scapegoat mechanism? Burke first says, "[T]he scapegoat is 'charismatic,' a vicar."[5] Burke uses these terms in a specific and seemingly theological sense. A charismatic figure may be benign or malign.[6] In either case, its value is otherworldly. The scapegoat serves as a substitute through whom

---

[3]Burke's dramatistic method of inquiry has influenced the work of such sociologists as Erving Goffman, Harold Garfinkel, Talcott Parsons, and C. W. Mills. For a particular discussion of Burke's influence on sociology, see Keith Doubt, "The Untold Friendship of Kenneth Burke and Talcott Parsons," *Social Science Journal* 34 (1997): 527–37.

[4]See C. Allen Carter, *Kenneth Burke and the Scapegoat Process* (Norman: University of Oklahoma Press, 1996). I am grateful to David Williams for sharing generously his knowledge and expertise on Kenneth Burke.

[5]Kenneth Burke, *A Grammar of Motives* (Berkeley: University of California Press, 1969), 406.

[6]"He becomes 'charismatic' (if we may incongruously extend this word beyond the purely 'benign' category into the 'malign' category)" (Kenneth Burke, *On Symbols and Society*, ed. with an introduction by Joseph R. Gusfield [Chicago: University of Chicago Press, 1989], 294).

transference occurs. For Burke, the scapegoat is a vicar endowed with charismatic value.

In what sense are Bosnians and Kosovars vicars? For whom and for what do they serve as substitutes? Why do they lose the right to represent themselves? For clergy this ascetic role is a pious vocation (a vicar substitutes for the bishop, a bishop for Christ), but within the social realm the role can be unjust. To be forced to represent another is to lose the right to represent oneself.

The tacit expectation that Bosnians and Kosovars should become like sacrificial animals reflects a prejudice within the Christian community toward non-Christians. For instance, it is difficult to see how NATO countries, during the bombing of Kosovo, did not see the civilians being killed as scapegoats. What, then, is this role? In a transcript of a testimony to Human Rights Watch, a twenty-one-year-old woman reports her harrowing experiences during her expulsion from Kosovo.

> The Serbs arrived late in the evening during the Muslim celebration of Bajram, on March 26 or 27. There were about fifty of them. Some of the Serbs were giving loud orders. Their voices were so loud that they scared the children. By this point, Izbice had become like a base for Albanians from all the villages in the area. These refugees began arriving after the NATO bombing began, because the Serbs started shelling neighboring villages when the bombing started.
>
> When we saw the Serbs coming we didn't dare stay in our houses. We went by tractor to a nearby field—me, my mother and father, my brother, my sister, her family, and her mother-in-law—a total of ten people. We joined the rest of the people from the village in the field, all the other families. Families had started leaving their houses at about 4 A.M. By 10 A.M. everyone was in the field. There were thousands of people, almost all women, children, and old people. Only about 150 men were among us.[7]

To formulate the dialectic of the scapegoat, Burke stresses the following point:

> As such, it [the scapegoat] is profoundly consubstantial with those who, looking upon it as a chosen vessel, would ritualistically cleanse themselves by loading the burden of their own iniquities upon it. Thus the scapegoat represents the principle of division in that its persecutors would alienate from themselves to it their own uncleanlinesses. For one must remember that a scapegoat cannot be "curative" except insofar as it represents the iniquities of those who would be cured by attacking it.[8]

---

[7]"Witness to Izbice Killings Speaks: Possibly Largest Massacre of Kosovo War," *Kosovo Human Rights Flash* 39 (May 19, 1999), <http: //www.hrw.org/hrw/campaigns/kosovo98/flash6.htm#39>.

[8]Burke, *Grammar of Motives*, 406.

Is it an accident that Serb soldiers entered the village during the Muslim celebration of Bajram? Was it an accident that in Sarajevo in 1992 nationalist Serbs started shelling the city during the festival of Bajram? Bajram is the most important feast in the Islamic calendar. The feast is a commemoration of Abraham's sacrifice of the ram releasing him from his promise to sacrifice his son. When Abraham showed absolute obedience to God, a ram was provided as a substitute for the son. While the son is not named in the Koran, it is accepted in Islamic faith that the son to be sacrificed is Abraham's first son, Ishmael. In the Old Testament, which Jews and Christians read, Isaac, Abraham's second son, is named as the son who is to be sacrificed. Abraham is the patriarch of Islam and Judaism. Islam, Judaism, and Christianity are consubstantial religions.

Albanian Kosovars become vicars for the iniquities of those doing ethnic cleansing. For Kosovars, leaving Kosovo means carrying with them the sins of the Serbs. When they leave Kosovo, they carry with them the iniquities of the Serbs and display them to the world. This role is forced upon the Kosovar Albanians. It is designated. The violence and sadism against Kosovar Albanians seems really to have no other purpose. Yes, it is possible to rationalize the violence and sadism as part of a military strategy to ethnically cleanse an area. Yes, it is possible to intellectualize the violence and sadism in terms of political gains, for instance, establishing solidarity among the aggressors and dividing the victims from the aggressors. A stronger account, however, encompasses the sociological motive guiding the conduct. The pain and horror of ethnic cleansing tempts us to forget to ask why ethnic cleansing is happening. Denial brings partial relief. Not understanding ethnic cleansing, however, makes it harder to confront and stop the activity.

Consider the following report from the young woman forced to flee Kosovo:

> At the field everyone got off their tractors and huddled together. We had chosen the field because we wanted to be together. We were too scared to stay alone in our houses; it would be too easy for the Serbs to kill us there. From the field, we could see the Serbs setting our houses on fire. They were shooting in the air and yelling loudly; insulting us and scaring the children.
>
> They told us: "Give us money if you want to survive." They said it cost 1,000 German Marks (DM) to save your family and 100 DM to save your tractor. Everyone paid, each man paying for his own family. My father paid 1,100 DM.
>
> After the Serbs got the money, they shot out the tires of everyone's tractors, and then burned all our belongings, which were bundled up on the tractors. They also set fire to the school.
>
> At about 11 A.M. they separated the women from the men. We asked them why they were doing this and they told us, in a very scary voice: "Shut up, don't ask, otherwise we'll kill you." The children were terrified. The Serbs yelled: "We'll kill you and where is the United States to save you?" All the women had covered their heads with the handkerchiefs out of fear of the Serbs, hiding their

hair and foreheads. The Serbs called us obscene things, saying "Fuck all Albanian mothers," and "All Albanian women are bitches."

They took the men away and lined them up about twenty meters away from us. Then they ordered us to go to Albania. They said: "You've been looking for a greater Albania, now you can go there." They were shooting in the air above our heads. We followed their orders and moved in the direction we were told, walking away from the men. About 100 meters from the place we started walking, the Serbs decided to separate out the younger boys from our group. Boys of fourteen and up had already been placed with the men; now they separated out boys of about ten and up. Only very small boys were left with us, one old man who had lost his legs, and my handicapped brother, who can't walk because of spinal meningitis.

So they took the ten to fourteen-year-olds to join the men. The boys' mothers were crying. Some even tried to speak to the Serbs, but the Serbs pushed them. We were walking away very slowly because we were so worried about what would happen to our men.

We stopped moving when we heard automatic weapon fire. We turned our heads to see what was happening but it was impossible to see the men. We saw the ten- to fourteen-year-olds running in our direction; when they got to us we asked them what was happening. They were very upset; no one could talk. One of them finally told us: "They released us but the others are finished."

We stayed in the same place for some twenty minutes. Everyone was crying. The automatic weapon fire went on non-stop for a few minutes; after that we heard short, irregular bursts of fire for some ten minutes or so. My father, my uncle and my cousin were among the men killed.[9]

The Serbs' selection, segregation, and release of the young boys between ten and fourteen are not arbitrary. Neither are they a matter of trained incompetence. Nor are they a self-conscious activity on the part of the Serbian militia murdering civilians. The Serbian soldiers need the young boys in a particular way. They are vicars who carry the Serbs' iniquities to the surviving victims. The young boys are sacred vessels who seem vainly to return the lives of the murdered men back to their surviving families. They represent how it could have been otherwise; they represent how it is not otherwise. Idealization and reality are co-present. Why do the Serb soldiers need these vicars?

Not killing the young boys creates the illusion that the Serb soldiers have limits. There is something they won't do. Sending the young boys back to their mothers and sisters creates the illusion that the Serbs soldiers are in control of themselves. Sending the young boys back seems to suggest that there is a limit to what they can do and that their superego plays some sort of strange role in the conduct of ethnic cleansing. The superego, after all, is what sets limits for the ego, even when the ego is unhealthy.

---

[9]"Witness to Izbice Killings," *Kosovo Human Rights.*

The Serb militia, however, cannot give back the lives of the murdered men. They cannot undo what they have done. Not killing the boys does not exemplify the superego that the Serb militia would like to have it exemplify. Releasing the young boys, however, does exemplify the work of the superego within the pathological ego of the Serb militia.

The Serb militia needs the young boys as scapegoats. At first, the young boys represent "the original state of merger" between the family members. They represent as well the Serbs' memories of themselves as boys. The Serb soldiers see themselves in the boys—they see what they no longer are, and they see that to which they no longer have a relation. Next, the boys represent "the principle of division." They are separated from their mothers. Symbolically, the boys become men. The boys are not men; the boys are men. Then, the boys represent "a new principle of merger," which Burke calls "vicarious atonement." The men become boys again, children whose innocence has been cruelly and unconscionably destroyed.[10]

Review Burke's formulation of the scapegoat mechanism:

> For one must remember that a scapegoat cannot be "curative" except insofar as it represents the iniquities of those who would be cured by attacking it. In representing *their* iniquities, it performs the role of vicarious atonement (that is, unification, or merger, granted to those who have alienated their iniquities upon it, and so may be purified through its suffering).[11]

The following questions must now be asked. To what degree is ethnic cleansing fueled by the anger of the Serbs' superego that the world continues to permit them to carry out their massacres and dwell in their culture of death? To what degree is ethnic cleansing driven by an unconscious desire to recover, through sheer negativity, the lost foundation upon which social order is created?

Sending the young boys back to their mothers is a feeble attempt on the part of the Serb soldiers to atone for their murders. Burke calls it vicarious atonement. The superego in the egos of the Serb soldiers wants to be released from its murderous activity. Selecting, segregating, and then releasing the young boys discloses a sense of guilt on the part of the Serb soldiers. The release of the young boys corresponds with the desire of the Serb soldiers to be released from what they do. "For the alienating of iniquities from the self to the scapegoat amounts to a *rebirth* of the self."[12]

---

[10]On the three divisions that occur here, Burke writes, "All told, note what we have here: (1) an original state of merger, in that the iniquities are shared by both the iniquitous and their chosen vessel; (2) a principle of division, in that the elements shared in common are being ritualistically alienated; (3) a new principle of merger, this time in the unification of those whose purified identity is defined in dialectical opposition to the sacrificial offering" (Burke, *Grammar of Motives*, 406).

[11]Burke, *Grammar of Motives*, 406.

[12]Burke, *Grammar of Motives*, 407.

The futility of the scapegoat mechanism is that it does not result in a rebirth of the self. It only deepens the pathology of the crime and increases the dependency of the Serbs upon their scapegoat. The Serbs' decision in May 1999 to stop allowing Kosovar Albanians to flee Kosovo was treated in the media as unintelligible. What was its political purpose? What was the Serbs' strategy behind the closing of the borders? The mechanism of the scapegoat perhaps provides the best explanation. Given the pathology of their crimes, the Serbian soldiers panic at the possibility that eventually there will be no scapegoats upon whom they can project and transfer their iniquities. Given the depth of their iniquities and depravity, the Serbian soldiers cannot bear the pain of not having a scapegoat upon whom to release their sins. The Serbian soldiers are dependent upon the Kosovar Albanians in a sinister way. The Serbs are "consubstantial" with their scapegoat, and this dependence discloses a thread of superego that remains in the egos of the Serbs.

As the Serbs flee Kosovo when NATO forces enter, it is reported that the Serbs burn their own homes. The explanation that the Serbs give reporters is that they do not want Albanians to occupy and live in their homes. Another explanation for this behavior is that the Serbs wish to show that they are consubstantial with the Albanians. The Serbs now do to themselves what they did to their neighbors. This is what Burke calls vicarious atonement. After having forced the Albanians into the scapegoat role, Serbs fleeing Kosovo assume the role for themselves. By embracing the scapegoat role, the Serbs in Kosovo disclose an unconscious recognition that, even after their violence, they are consubstantial with the Albanians in Kosovo and still wish to be. Serbs mimic against themselves their victimization of Albanians. "We have decided not to leave, at least for now," one Serb man said. "But for those who have decided to go, they are burning their own houses as revenge against the Albanians."[13]

Both the Serbian priest, Father Sava, and the Albanian, Miss Lokaj, confirm and disavow the scapegoat role.

> Sincere diplomacy could have solved the problem without war, Father Sava said, and if the unarmed monitors of the Organization for Security and Cooperation in Europe had remained in Kosovo, but in larger numbers, "nothing like this would have happened." The problems here "would not have been easy to resolve," Father Sava said. "But it could have been done. And now we've ethnically cleansed Kosovo and destroyed it and produced enormous suffering on all sides."
>
> Miss Lokaj [an Albanian woman whom Father Sava had found and protected] had worked for the security organization in Pec. She, too, speaks fluent English, and she, too, is very angry. "When the OSCE left, they told us they

---

[13]Anonymous correspondent, "Leaving in Flames and Tears," Institute for War and Peace Reporting, *Balkan Crises Report* 46 (June 14, 1999), <www.iwpr.net>.

would be back in two weeks and everything would be the way we wanted it," she said bitterly. "We hoped so, but after three days, everything changed. When NATO started bombing, the police and the paramilitaries started destroying everything that was Albanian."

The Serbs "made a war against civilians, against people with empty hands," she said. "There was no KLA in Decani or in Pec, and they had no right to do what they did. This is a catastrophe. And the world saw this, it saw everything, and the world is too late. I know the world felt it had the best intentions, but there is a fatality about good intentions, and they always come too late."

She turned away, brushing her brown hair from blazing eyes. "I hate the words, 'I'm sorry,'" she said. "The world always says, 'I'm sorry,' and it's always too late. The British said, 'Be patient. You have the sympathy of the world.' Well, the ground burned under our feet, and the world says we have its sympathy."

Miss Lokaj stopped again, and then said, keeping her voice slow and even: "Don't ever be sorry about the people who are still alive. Just be sorry for the dead."[14]

The reluctance on the part of the Clinton administration to commit ground troops to the war in Kosovo was based in part on the assumption that U.S. soldiers would be captured and turned into scapegoats. Clinton, for instance, worried that what happened in Somalia, the situation in which the dead bodies of U.S. soldiers were paraded in public, would likely happen in Kosovo. To prevent U.S. soldiers from falling into the scapegoat role, Clinton seemed to expect the Kosovars to play this role.

It is unlikely, though, that U.S. soldiers would become scapegoats in Kosovo; there was not the required identification between the Serbs and the U.S. soldiers. As former-Yugoslavs, the Kosovar Albanians fulfill this first requirement of the scapegoat mechanism. Serbs and Albanians lived together for a long time; they were familiar. U.S. soldiers and Serbs lack the intimacy that would allow the U.S. soldiers to fulfill the scapegoat role. This perhaps is why the Belgrade regime released the three U.S. soldiers they kidnapped in Macedonia. The Serbian leadership discovered that the consubstantial relation between Serbia and the United States was missing, and the three U.S. soldiers were inadequate vicars for Serbia's transgressions.

[14]Steven Erlanger, "Refuge for Kosvars in Serbian Monastery, After the Burning," *New York Times* (June 16, 1999).

Chapter 7

Feminism and Rape as a Transgression of Species-Being

Journalists and human rights activists only lately came to understand the scale of the atrocities. Few realized that the systematic use of rape as a means of ethnic cleansing and gaining military advantage—as practiced during the Bosnian war—was being repeated in Kosovo.

> —Gordana Igrić
> "Kosovo Rape Victims Suffer Twice"

There is nothing about being "female" that naturally binds women.... Gender, race, or class consciousness is an achievement forced on us by the terrible historical experience of the contradictory social realities of patriarchy, colonialism, and capitalism....

The theoretical and practical struggle against unity-through-domination or unity-through-incorporation ironically not only undermines the justifications for patriarchy, colonialism, humanism, positivism, essentialism, scientism, and other unlamented -isms, but *all* claims for an organic or natural standpoint.

> —Donna Haraway
> "Cyborg Manifesto and Fractured Identities"

I WOULD LIKE TO PRESENT a problem regarding conversation, and I will do so in two ways. I will present the problem abstractly and concretely or theoretically and practically. Whether presented abstractly or concretely, we are still, I believe, facing the same problem, and problems guide research, whether in the social sciences, the humanities, or the natural sciences.

I will begin abstractly. Is there such a thing as a privileged speaking position? How do we distinguish between authentic and inauthentic talk? Is it possible for me to speak of another's experience in a way that is faithful to the character of the other's experience? Is the particularity of the experience a barrier to such a possibility? Is gender a barrier? What constitutes a genuine representation of another's experience? Is to simulate rather than represent the experience of one who is neither myself, nor even of the same gender the best that I can do?

On this question, postmodern feminism argues that irony is the strongest relation that one can have to another. Consider, though, the way irony is formulated by the feminist Donna Haraway: "Irony is about contradictions that do not resolve into larger wholes, even dialectically, about the tension of holding incompatible things together because both or all are necessary and true."[1] For postmodernism irony is positive because it does not violate the necessity and truth of the other or oneself. Postmodern irony, though, does not resolve contradictions or transform tensions into larger wholes, which is what Platonic irony does.

Let me now present the problem concretely. However the problem is presented, we are still facing the same questions. In *Rape Warfare*, Beverly Allen points out the problem in its practical form.

> One instance of story manipulation stands out in particular. In October 1993, a book entitled *Violentate* (which would translate as "raped women") was published in Italy. The author's name, "Ehlimana Pašić," indicated that she was a Bosnian-Herzegovinian Muslim woman. The stories inside, implicitly the inside stories, in fact, were apparently those of herself and other survivors of genocidal rape, women who had confided in her as a sister victim. In fact, no such woman as Ehlimina Pašić exists. This book is a compilation of survivors' testimonies retold as stories by two male journalists from the Sarajevo newspaper *Oslobodjenje* who evidently assumed that their words would have greater right of truth if they appeared to come directly from a survivor than if they revealed their own presence as transcribers, or even as rewriters.[2]

The actions of the journalists reflect a matter of doing what is effective. First-person accounts are perceived as more authentic and so more persuasive. Given the events, the use of a pseudonym is intelligible. The literary device is not uncommon. What ethic, though, would stop the journalists from doing what they did? Allen addresses this question:

---

[1] Donna Haraway, "The Cyborg Manifesto and Fractured Identities," in *Social Theory: The Multicultural and Classic Readings*, ed. Charles Lemert (Boulder, Colo.: Westview Press, 1993), 597.

[2] Beverly Allen, *Rape Warfare: The Hidden Genocide in Bosnia-Herzegovina and Croatia* (Minneapolis: University of Minnesota Press, 1996), 33–34.

Their book leaves me very uneasy. I understand and empathize with the urgent need to tell the world about genocidal rape, about Serb rape/death camps, about ongoing atrocities. Yet I feel sad and angry that these men, whatever their intentions, took the words from the real survivors, made them over into a writing that was theirs, and then presented them as if they belonged not to a real woman but to an invented one. There are enough real women who have suffered genocidal rape not to have to invent a fictive one. Anonymity can be preserved in other ways. A more honest approach would have been for the journalists to identify themselves and state how they had obtained their information. My unease turns to outrage.[3]

What rule of representation did the journalists violate? What grammar did they transgress? From what principle of authentic talk did they deviate?

Upon reflection, one wonders why the male journalists decided to conceal their identities. Did they think that they were unqualified to represent this story? If so, why? Why did the journalists simulate rather than represent the accounts of the rape victims when the accounts were real and when they spoke for themselves? Allen indicates that *Violentate* stands as a simulacra, an image of the original that is fractured from and destructive toward the original—an image that no longer mimes the original but only itself. As Donna Haraway writes, "The cyborg skips the step of original unity, of identification with nature in the Western sense."[4] Did the journalists' invention represent nothing but themselves?

The journalists felt that they lacked the original unity with their subjects from which to represent their stories authentically. To compensate for this lack, the journalists invented an identification with the subject that was not true. Not only did this simulation belie what it purported to represent, but it also concealed the original unity from which the journalists do have the right to represent the events. In choosing to simulate a woman's identity, the journalists accepted their apparent lack of identification and concealed the reason they wanted to tell another's story and tell it authentically.

On the foundation of privileged speaking, Haraway presents the postmodern understanding: "In a sense, the cyborg has no origin story in the Western sense—a 'final' irony since the cyborg is also the awful apocalyptic *telos* of the 'West's' escalating dominations of abstract individuation, an ultimate self untied at last from all dependency, a man in space."[5] The journalists accept the false assumption that they are untied to their subjects. They conceal their interdependency with the women who were raped. To overcome the postmodern assumption, the journalists compensate in a way that confirms the false assumption and belies the truth.

[3] Allen, *Rape Warfare*, 34.
[4] Haraway, "Cyborg Manifesto," 598.
[5] Haraway, "Cyborg Manifesto," 598.

Haraway says that, for the purpose of strong critique, postmodern feminism selects blasphemy. What position, then, does postmodern feminism profane? Haraway writes, "Cyborg feminists have to argue that 'we' do not want any more natural matrix of unity and that no construction is whole."[6] Consider the debunked and dismissed position within Haraway's postmodern theorizing, namely, the notion of species-being:

> Man is a species-being not only in the sense that he makes the community (his own as well as those of other things) his object both practically and theoretically, but also (and this is simply another expression for the same thing) in the sense that he treats himself as the present, living species, as a *universal* and consequently free being.[7]

For Marx there is a dialectical relation between universality and freedom; through human labor, universality and freedom develop. Each, as it were, in dialectical relation to the other, makes us whole. Capitalism, Marx argues, alienates us from our species-being. Capitalism is a form of sociocide.

While committed to liberation, Haraway rejects the notion of species-being and replaces it with the unnatural idea of the cyborg.[8] For Haraway the cyborg is a positive image for humanity. Haraway writes, "It is no accident that the symbolic system of the family of man—and so the essence of woman—breaks up at the same moment that networks of connection among people on the planet are unprecedentedly multiple, pregnant, and complex."[9] In postmodern feminism, the notion of species-being is profaned, and so it is important to recollect what the notion is. Marx writes, "Conscious life activity distinguishes man from the life activity of animals. Only for this reason is he a species-being. Or rather, he is only a self-conscious being, i.e., his own life is an object for him, because he is a species-being. Only for this reason is his activity free activity."[10]

Not all feminists reject Marx's notion of species-being. Audre Lorde's theorizing vis-à-vis bourgeois feminism creatively and critically affirms the idea of species-being. The notion is positively embraced.

> Difference must be not merely tolerated, but seen as a fund of necessary polarities between which our creativity can spark like a dialectic. Only then does the necessity for interdependency become unthreatening. Only within that interde-

---

[6]Haraway, "Cyborg Manifesto," 602.

[7]Karl Marx, "Alienated Labor," in *Seeing Ourselves: Classic, Contemporary, and Cross-Cultural Readings in Sociology,* John J. Macionis and Nijole V. Benokraitis, eds. (Upper Saddle River, N.J.: Prentice Hall, 1989), 266.

[8]"A cyborg is a cybernetic organism, a hybrid of machine and organism, a creature of social reality as well as a creature of fiction" (Haraway, "Cyborg Manifesto," 597).

[9]Haraway, "Cyborg Manifesto," 604.

[10]Marx, "Alienated Labor," 266.

pendency of different strengths, acknowledged and equal, can the power to seek new ways of being in the world generate the courage and sustenance to act where there are no charters.[11]

According to Marx and Lorde, the journalists did have the grounds upon which to represent the events their subjects report. Species-being is the foundation upon which the journalists are not simply male but human. It is the foundation upon which they are self-conscious and interdependent with the rape victims and from which they represent an original unity. Species-being is the source of self-consciousness, and it represents an organic and natural standpoint.

A Sociology of Rape

The rapes that occurred in Bosnia and Kosovo were assaults on individuals' bodies and selves.[12] The purpose was not just to harm a woman or young girl's body, although here was one purpose. The purpose was also to destroy the person's sense of self, of being an autonomous, self-conscious person. The damage that rape does to the self, while sometimes invisible, takes longer to heal than the damage done to the body, although both the harm to the body and the harm to the self are crimes and acts of injustice.[13]

In Bosnia and Kosovo, rape had an even more wretched significance. The purpose was to destroy the person's relation to her family and community, in part by provoking her family and community to reject her. The rapes sought to destroy the person's sense of identity and connectedness to those whom she loved. Rape was done knowing that it would likely lead to the person being rejected by her parents or husband. In a word, rape was an attack against the person's species-being and an attempt to destroy the person's interconnectedness with others. Rape was an attempt to turn a person into an animal and take from the person what distinguishes one's humanity from an animal. "The animal is one with its life activity. It does not distinguish the activity from itself. It is *its activ-*

---

[11]Audre Lorde, "The Master's Tool Will Never Dismantle the Master's House," in *Social Theory: The Multicultural and Classic Readings*, Charles Lemert, ed. (Boulder, Colo.: Westview Press, 1993), 486.

[12]The work of George Herbert Mead distinguishes between the body and the self, stressing that the self, not the body, is the true subject of social inquiry.

[13]Here is a quantitative report on this subject: "A while back a European Commission of Inquiry headed by Dame Anne Warburton made a study in the former Yugoslavia and reported that 20,000 women had been raped. *New York Times* correspondent John Burns puts the number at 50,000. Michigan law professor Catharine A. MacKinnon, who is representing Bosnian victims pro bono, puts the total at "more than 50,000" women and girls raped, and another 100,000 women and children killed" (Grace Halsell, "Women's Bodies: A Battlefield in War for 'Greater Serbia,'" *Washington Report on Middle East Affairs* 11, no. 9 [April/May, 1993]).

ity. But [the human being] makes…life activity itself an object of [one's] will and consciousness. [The person] has a conscious life activity."[14]

Consider now the testimonies of persons who were raped. The painfulness of the testimonies is based on the physical harm done to the person and the damage to the person's sense of interdependency that is the social life of the person. The painfulness is based on our species-being and sense of connectedness with the person who was raped.

> A doctor from my same town was prisoner here. One day the Serbian guards called for this doctor. They wanted him to sew up a ten-year-old girl they had raped. She was torn apart. Seeing the mutilated child, the doctor forgot he was a prisoner, and that he was in a concentration camp. He cursed the Serbs, telling them, "You are not human!" According to Issa, the guards left the child bleeding on the table and assaulted the doctor. Issa said that when she again saw the doctor, "He was barely alive."[15]

The rapists, to achieve their purpose, sever their relation to their species-being. They lose their self-consciousness, often through drinking. The doctor's curse was a reminder to the rapists of their species-being, a reminder that the rapists could not tolerate.

Consider another testimony:

> Refugees from Srebrenica thought the worst was over when they reached a UN base at Potocari, two miles north of the fallen safe haven. But it was there, despite the presence of Dutch peace keepers, that Ms. Turković says Bosnian Serbs chose a young victim from among the sleeping refugees. "Two took her legs and raised them up in the air, while the third began raping her," Ms. Turković said. "Four of them were taking turns on her. People were silent, no one moved. She was screaming and yelling and begging them to stop. They put a rag into her mouth and then we were just hearing silent sobs coming from her closed lips. "When they finished, the woman was left there," she said.[16]

The assault on this young person is unconscionable in and of itself. But it is also a direct assault against her family and community and an attempt to destroy the bonds of care that hold the girl and her community together. The timing and place of the rape are utterly obscene and unconscionable.

Bosnian Serbs created rape camps.

> We had to cook for them, and serve them, naked. They raped and slaughtered

[14]Marx, "Alienated Labor," 266.
[15]Halsell, "Women's Bodies," 16.
[16]Snježana Vukić, "Refugees Tell of Woman Singled Out for Rape," *The Independent* (July 18, 1995).

some girls right in front of us. Those who resisted had their breasts cut. One night Željka's brother helped twelve of us escape.... Sometimes I think I will go crazy. Every night in my dreams I see the face of Stojan, the camp guard. He was the most ruthless among them. He even raped ten-year-old girls, as a "delicacy." Most of those girls didn't survive. They murdered many girls, slaughtered them like cattle. I want to forget everything. I cannot live with these memories. I will go insane.[17]

In the rape camps, a person's species-being was assaulted and denied, if not seemingly destroyed. The rape camp was designed to force the person to give up her species-being because retaining it seemed to be the source of horror and pain. Witnessing these brutalities against others and oneself was like poison to the person's species-being.

In Kosovo rapes took on a specific, equally horrific turn.

But Serb paramilitary forces have used rape to target the families of supporters of Kosovo Liberation Army (KLA), fully aware of the devastating effect the rapes have on the fighters and their home communities. For a year or more before the onset of the NATO air offensive, Serb forces were routinely detaining women family members of men suspected of separatist activity.[18]

Rape is a war crime because it is an attempt to destroy a community and sever the bonds of interdependency within a community based on care and trust. Such bonds hold communities and families together. The premeditated and methodic use of rape to attack and destroy the foundation of a society is evil; the evil started in Bosnia in 1992 and has continued in Kosovo through 1999. It is an insidious form of sociocide.

An exceptional documentary on this subject is "Calling the Ghosts."[19] It is exceptional because it shows that the species-being of the people apprehended and abused was not destroyed. The species-being of the people survived up to the point of death for those who perished and beyond the unspeakable experiences for those who survived. Witnessing the moments of care and self-consciousness on the part of the people who lived through a social hell is a testimony to humanity qua species-being. People remembered their universality based on their connectedness to others and the world. This universality exemplified their freedom even during their most unfree moments. The willingness of the people who suffered in Bosnia and Kosovo to share their self-consciousness is something that

[17]Mirsada, "Testimonies of Rape," *Women for Women in Bosnia: Testimonies,* <http://www.embassy.org/wmn4wmn/personal.html>, [accessed December 15, 1997].

[18]Gordana Igrić, "Kosovo Rape Victims Suffer Twice," *Balkan Crises Report* 48 (June 18, 1999), <http://www.iwpr.net>, [accessed June 19, 1999].

[19]Women Make Movies, "Calling the Ghosts" (New York: Bowery, 1996), Videocassette.

the world must listen to and be grateful for. The people who suffered in Bosnia and Kosovo bear witness to the indestructible character of human beings *qua* species-being. The world will be impoverished if it does not accept this gift from the people who were victims of rape. Here is one such gift from Hasiba Haram-bašić as recorded in "Calling the Ghosts."

> You see a friend who has several cuts on his throat. His collar bone is broken and his arm is hanging limp. He is all beaten up, in bruises—I get chills when I think of him and how he looked—bloody, torn, full of lice, a mess. Everyone had dysentery, so everyone stunk. It was suffocating. But that man, truly a gentleman, at that moment when he passes us by, he makes sure that his shirt collar is closed. He holds it with his hand so we don't see his wounds, so we are less afraid. Can you imagine what that looks like? Scenes like that were going on twenty-four hours a day.[20]

---

[20]Transcribed from "Calling the Ghosts."

Chapter 8

The Iron Cage of Rationality in Bosnia: Max Weber and the UN

But it is still important to try to understand why the UN acted in the way that it did. And while it might be comforting to attribute the policy to some inherent organizational malignity, the truth is that the people who run United Nations peacekeeping are, as a rule, among the most intelligent and sophisticated civil servants in the world, and tend to be more sensitive, not less, to the slaughter house that our world really is. In reality, it was the gap between the sensitivity with which many UN officials, both in the former Yugoslavia and in New York and Geneva, apprehended what was going on and their insistence that the slaughter had to be allowed to go on that was so shocking to outsiders.

—David Rieff
Slaughterhouse: Bosnia and the Failure of the West

We criticize Americans for not being able either to analyze or conceptualize. But this is a wrong-headed critique. It is we who imagine that everything culminates in transcendence, and that nothing exists which has not been conceptualized. Not only do they care little for such a view, but their perspective is the very opposite: it is not conceptualizing reality, but realizing concepts and materializing ideas, that interests them.

—Jean Baudrillard
America

MAX WEBER'S SOCIOLOGY of bureaucracy is tedious. We have before us, however, an opportunity to revisit Weber's sociological account of modern bureaucracies in a vigorous way. During the war in Bosnia, people were cruelly
victimized, not only by the violence of ethnic cleansing, but also by the iron cage
of rationality within which the United Nations and the world entrapped them.
The impartiality exemplified by UN officials dehumanized Bosnians as much as
the violence of ethnic cleansing did. If sociologists do not begin to address this
subject, they risk the viability of their discipline and the seriousness of their intellectual traditions.[1] By examining the conduct of the UN in Bosnia, sociologists
can revisit Weber's work in a pointed way, identify the particular character of UN
conduct, and address what troubles many journalists writing on the subject.

To account for the development of bureaucracy in modern societies and to
explain its significance to the growth of capitalism, Weber formulates an ideal
type that typically informs bureaucratic social structure. As members of a modern
bureaucracy, UN officials employ this ideal type to explain the significance of
their conduct and defend its legitimacy. On this use of ideal types in social
inquiry, Weber states the following:

> It is necessary for the sociologist to formulate pure ideal types of the
> corresponding forms of action which in each case involve the highest possible
> degree of logical integration by virtue of their complete adequacy on the level of
> meaning. But precisely because this is true, it is probably seldom if ever that a
> real phenomenon can be found which corresponds exactly to one of these ide-
> ally constructed pure types. The case is similar to a physical reaction which has
> been calculated on the assumption of an absolute vacuum.[2]

On the one hand, the ideal type formulated by Weber to account for bureaucratic conduct does not exist in reality. On the other hand, the ideal type informs
the reality and meaningfulness of bureaucratic conduct. While UN officials use
Weber's ideal type to make sense of their activities and make them accountable
to others and the world, the UN is not itself this ideal type. While the UN may be

---

[1] For an informative application of Weber's work on bureaucracy to the Holocaust, see
Richard L. Rubenstein, *The Cunning of History: The Holocaust and the American Future*
(New York: Harper and Row, 1975). For a distinctive and critical discussion of the UN,
see Shirley Hazzard, *Countenance of Truth: The United Nations and the Waldheim Case*
(New York: Viking, 1990).

[2] Max Weber, *The Theory of Social and Economic Organization*, trans. A. M. Henderson and Talcott Parsons, ed. with an introduction by Talcott Parsons (New York: Free
Press, 1964), 110. In a footnote to this citation, Parsons warns readers on "the difficulty of
maintaining the position Weber here takes" (Weber, *Social and Economic Organization*,
110). For Weber, the task is to advise readers on the difficulty of not maintaining the position he here takes. The use of ideal types in sociological inquiry is critical to the growth of
sociology. For Parsons, however, Weber's nonempirical epistemology borders on heresy.

an exceptional model of bureaucratic organization, it is not its reification. The ideal type is calculated on the assumption of an absolute vacuum, and this assumption, Weber says, guides the interpretative methodology known as *verstehen*.

Formal Rationality versus Substantive Justice

In 1994 *Balkan War Report* published a special issue on the UN in Bosnia. The bulletin, published by the Institute for War and Peace Reporting, informs the international debate on conflict and provides support for voices of moderation caught in war. One of the authors, David Rieff, accuses the UN of complicity in the ethnic cleansing that occurred in Bosnia.[3] In response, a "long-serving" member of the UN writes a rebuttal, which *Balkan War Report* subsequently published. In his rebuttal, the UN official states, "And success should be measured in light of the goals that the organization sets itself, not by unassigned tasks ascribed by the international *glitterati* feeding off the energy of this war's injustices."[4]

How do bureaucratic officials measure success? On this question, Weber writes, "There is the principle of fixed and official jurisdictional areas, which are generally ordered by rules, that is, by laws or administrative regulations." Weber

[3]David Rieff, "Accomplice to Genocide," *War Report* 28 (September 1994): 35–40.

[4]Anonymous author, "A Partial Reply to UNPROFOR's Critics" *War Report* 30 (December 1994/January 1995): 18. Writing in a personal capacity, the long-serving UN official decided not to sign his or her name. This practice exemplifies the impersonality that bureaucratic officials strive for. When seeming to act outside of the author's official role, the author chooses to remain anonymous because he or she does not want to compromise the character of his or her vocation in the UN. Bureaucratic work is ideally abstract in that it does not reflect the personal sentiments of the bureaucratic official. To share one's personal sentiments in a public forum is to violate this rule. Thus, the UN official believes that he or she must write anonymously. In this rebuttal, we see the official as an individual, but not as a person.

Consider another example of this impersonal orientation. The former UN Special Envoy to former Yugoslavia, Yasushi Akashi, in an interview in 1998, argues, "Yes, we negotiate even with devils, demons. But you are not allowed to involve your own judgment." The Dutch journalist Robert van de Roer asks, "Did you loathe Karadžić?" Akashi responds, "I never disclose my personal feelings about the parties I negotiate with. Mladić, Milošević, Silajdžić, they are not normal people." Van de Roer then asks, "You cannot call the former Muslim prime minister Haris Silajdžić a war criminal, can you?" Akashi evades the question by answering the pointed question with a question, "And how about the Croatian president Tudjman?" (Yasushi Akashi, "Muddling on Is an Achievement," *Bosnet Digest* 6, no. 1,036 [November 2, 1998]. The exchange shows that the impartiality UN officials claim to sustain is unsustainable in serious social interaction. With a certain poetic but tragic justice, the Bosnian government, even before the fall of Srebrenica, declared Yasushi Akashi "dead."

continues, "The regular activities are distributed in a fixed way as official duties." Weber adds, "The authority to give the commands is distributed in a stable way and is strictly delimited by rules concerning the coercive means."[5] In his or her rebuttal to Rieff, the UN official confirms that the UN is a bureaucracy and does what bureaucracies do. In a disciplined way the UN follows the goals that the organization sets for itself through a stable and fixed set of rules.

The UN official also asserts that the UN does not follow moral edicts "ascribed by the international *glitterati* feeding off the energy of this war's injustices."[6] The author is working closely with Weber's distinction between formal rationality and substantive justice. The goal of formal rationality is efficiency; its purpose is stability and self-perpetuation. The goal of substantive justice is moral knowledge; its purpose is to realize what is right in the here and now. Substantive justice transcends the hegemony of formal rationality; formal rationality suppresses the requirements of substantive justice.

Weber recounts this tension in the following way:

> If, however, an "ethos"—not to speak of instincts—takes hold of the masses on some individual question, it postulates *substantive* justice oriented toward some concrete instance and person; and such an "ethos" will unavoidably collide with the formalism and the rule-bound and cool "matter-of-factness" of bureaucratic administration. For this reason, the ethos must emotionally reject what reason demands.[7]

This passage from Weber, perhaps more than others, reveals Weber's ambivalence. To explicate this ambivalence, consider the following set of questions: On what basis does substantive justice reject the demands of formal rationality? When is it proper for the emotion of substantive justice to win over the discipline of formal rationality? Upon what is the emotion of substantive justice based? Is the intuition of substantive justice empirical or metaphysical? Weber indicates in the passage cited above that, for the sake of democracy, formal rationality defers to the ethos of substantive justice, "which takes hold of the masses on some concrete instance or person."[8] Why must formal rationality do so? Does substantive justice carry universal import? Is there a principle inherent in substantive justice to which formal rationality must defer? If not, there is no reason for formal rationality to defer to the ethos of substantive justice.

The UN, according to the long-serving official, cannot be derailed by the voices of substantive justice, if only because, according to the official, these

---

[5]Max Weber, *From Max Weber: Essays in Sociology*, trans. and ed. with an introduction by H. H. Gerth and C. W. Mills (New York: Oxford University Press, 1958), 196.

[6]"A Partial Reply," *War Report*, 18.

[7]Weber, *From Max Weber*, 220–21.

[8]Weber, *From Max Weber*, 220–21.

voices are disparate and random. The author makes this point in the following way:

> This war appears to be all things to all people: a moral crusade; a project of international law; a project for the Western European Union; an effort to create the new world order; a new rallying cry for the Islamic world; a crisis for NATO; a project for maintaining an American presence in Europe; a simple Byronic adventure; an opportunity to make a career in one distended bureaucracy or other. From their patterned responses, it's not clear that these occasional travelers can always feel empathy or understanding for the real people in this real war. They do listen to the feelings and uttering of politicians and others just like themselves—writers, artists, academics—who understand precisely how to speak tellingly and true.[9]

According to the official, the problem with the ethos of substantive justice is that its many voices are individually motivated and conditionally determined. According to the official, the advantage of formal rationality is that its principle is grounded in experience and rationality. Formal rationality, according to the official, has universal import, and substantive justice does not.

Notice how Yasushi Akashi, the former UN special envoy to former Yugoslavia, also employs Weber's distinction between formal rationality and substantive justice. In an interview, Robert van de Roer asks Akashi, "But do you still think you did everything right, save for that rather insignificant incident?" Akashi replies, "I did not say right. I said: I can see no other option." Akashi does not allow his conduct to fall under the scrutiny of substantive justice. Formal rationality is the measure with which he insists that his conduct be judged. "All our options were bad options; I had to choose the least bad ones."[10]

What, then, is formal rationality? To what are UN officials committed? The American sociologist George Ritzer answers the question in the following way:

> Formal rationality means that the search by people for the optimum means to a given end is shaped by rules, regulations, and larger social structures. Thus, individuals are not left to their own devices in searching for the best means of attaining a given objective. Rather, there exist rules, regulations, and structures that either predetermine or help them discover the optimum methods. Weber identified this as a major development in the history of the world: Previously, people had to discover such mechanisms on their own or with vague and general guidance from larger value systems. After the development of formal rationality, they could use rules and regulations to help them decide what to do, or, more strongly, people existed in structures that dictated what they should do. In effect, people no longer had to discover for themselves the optimum means to an end;

---

[9]"A Partial Reply," *War Report,* 19.
[10]Akashi, "Muddling."

rather, optimum means had already been discovered and were institutionalized in rules, regulations, and structures. People simply had to follow the rules, regulations, and dictates of the structure. An important aspect of rationality was that it allowed less room for individual variation in choice of means to ends. Since the choice of means was guided or even determined, virtually everyone could make the same, optimal choice.[11]

UN officials are faithful to this notion of formal rationality. Previously, people would choose the optimum means to a given end individually or with guidance from larger value systems or, perhaps more correctly, with a combination of the two. In a bureaucracy, formal rationality dominates. UN officials do not think independently of the rules, regulations, and structures of UN policy.[12] To heed the principle of substantive justice voiced by an international *glitterati* "feeding off the energy of the war's injustices" would harm the organization. Whether one agrees or not, it is important to recognize how Weber's notion of formal rationality is employed by UN officials to defend their conduct.

Shashi Tharoor, Special Assistant for Peacekeeping, likewise makes use of Weber's ideal type to defend the conduct of the UN in Bosnia. Tharoor makes the following observations in an interview in *War Report*:

> UNPROFOR has, for too long, been blamed for failing to do things it was never mandated, staffed, financed, equipped, or deployed to do. Many of its critics would have liked it to take sides in the conflict; others wanted UNPROFOR to intervene more directly on behalf of some of the war's many victims; yet others blame UNPROFOR for not ending the war. These are not the functions of a peacekeeping force. Most important, they are not, and cannot be, UNPROFOR's functions.[13]

Tharoor then adds, "If you read the Security Council's resolutions on Bosnia-

---

[11] George Ritzer, *The McDonaldization of Society: An Investigation into the Changing Character of Contemporary Social Life* (Newbury Park, Calif.: Pine Forge Press, 1993), 19. This study applies Weber's theory of bureaucracy to the gargantuan fast-food chain McDonald's so as to describe and critique its unhealthy influence on society.

[12] "And yet the more I encountered UN officials, the more it seemed to me that not only were they trapped in an organization that is probably more conformist and hierarchical than any institution except a military force, but they had grown accustomed to speaking to each other in a self-referential language that might have made sense to them but made increasingly little sense in the context of Bosnia. Surely, it was partly because of the way the UN fetishized 'the mandate' that Boutros Boutros-Ghali's report...could brush aside all significant criticism of the operation" (David Rieff, *Slaughterhouse: Bosnia and the Failure of the West* [New York: Touchstone, 1996], 170).

[13] Shashi Tharoor, "A Mandate of Impartiality," *War Report* 28 (September 1994): 24.

Herzegovina, you'll find that UNPROFOR has actually done pretty well in ful-filling the tasks it was set."[14] While critics find such talk specious, from the view-point of formal rationality, Tharoor is speaking responsibly.

The Ideal Type Employed

Can sociologists, drawing upon the ideal type that Weber formulates, explain the conduct of UN officials as objectively as UN officials? Can sociologists, through the methodology of *verstehen*, understand UN officials as well as they under-stand themselves? In turn, can sociologists, still drawing upon the ideal type that Weber formulates, critique the conduct of the UN as incisively as professional journalists like David Rieff and Ian Williams?[15] Does explanation mean aban-doning the need for criticism? Does criticism mean abandoning the responsibility of explanation? Here is Weber's distinctive but unappreciated gift to the disci-pline of sociology. The use of ideal types in social inquiry not only permits but also *requires* sociologists to use explanation and criticism simultaneously. On the one hand, UN officials implicitly employ Weber's ideal type to make their con-duct accountable to themselves and others. Sociologists can make this ideal type transparent. On the other hand, the ideal type does not provide "adequacy on the level of meaning" with respect to the UN activities in Bosnia. The ideal type itself is insufficient for grasping the significance of the social conduct.[16]

With this caveat in mind, let us return to the discussion at hand. Another well-known characteristic of bureaucracies is their hierarchical structure, but Weber formulates this characteristic in an unexpected way. Weber says, "When the principle of jurisdictional 'competency' is fully carried through, hierarchical subordination—at least in public office—does not mean that the 'higher' author-ity is simply authorized to take over the business of the 'lower.' Indeed, the oppo-site is the rule."[17] Weber's paradoxical insight is critical. On what basis does the "lower" authority take over the business of the "higher" authority? On what basis do middle- and upper-level bureaucrats take over the business of its higher body? A statement by Tharoor sheds light on this paradox:

There is a larger, more important point: no single Security Council resolution on Bosnia can be read in isolation from the others. Even in those resolutions that allowed for the use of force, the Security Council reaffirmed its previous resolu-tions on UNPROFOR; in other words it did not want UNPROFOR to abandon its existing mandates in order to undertake new ones. UNPROFOR thus had the difficult task of reconciling its authority to use force with its obligation to per-

[14]Tharoor, "Impartiality," 24.

[15]Besides Ian Williams' many essays in *War Report,* see as well Ian Williams, *United Nations for Beginners* (New York: Writers and Readers Publishing, Inc., 1995).

[16]Weber, *Social and Economic Organization,* 99.

[17]Weber, *From Max Weber,* 197.

form all other tasks mandated by the Security Council—tasks which required co-operation of, and deployment amongst, all parties to the conflict. The result has been an immensely complicated balancing act that UNPROFOR has so far carried out admirably.[18]

The imperative guiding Tharoor's statement is based on the bureaucratic principle that "The 'higher' authority...[is not] simply authorized to take over the business of the 'lower.' Indeed, the opposite is the rule."[19] For Tharoor, the UN Security Council is not authorized to take over the business of its lower authorities. Instead, the lower authorities, for instance, middle- and upper-level officials, take over the business of the higher authority, namely, the UN Security Council.

This principle is ingrained into Tharoor's thinking, and he as well as other UN officials enjoy pointing out this principle to journalists who seem ignorant of it. Reflecting on his responsibility for what happened at Srebrenica, Akashi says, "My task is not to order specific positions for the troops. That decision is for the commander at Srebrenica to make. We were not there to interfere in his movements or orders." Van de Roer asks, "What do you mean: not to interfere? You were head of the UN in Bosnia." Akashi replies, "You have obviously never been in the army." Van de Roer answers, "As a matter of fact I have, although not as a general." Akashi persists, "Such matters are not decided by generals, but by the company or battalion commander. We made decisions about strategic matters throughout the war zone, not about specific locations or movements. The manner of protecting the civilians is at the discretion of local commanders." Van de Roer, though, says, "But they, in this case the Dutchman Karemans, report to you." Akashi does not back down, "Yes, but for me it was important to be certain the troops were observing the basics of peacekeeping." Although the higher authority, Akashi insists that his relation to the lower authority in Srebrenica was rationally abstract. His discipline as the higher authority was not to take over the business of the lower authority, in this case, Dutchman Karemans. Akashi's responsibility was simply to insist that "the basics of peacekeeping" be observed.[20]

Let us consider another example of bureaucratic hierarchy and its significance. By highlighting the absence of a hierarchical order in other organizations representing the international community in Bosnia, the "long-serving" UN official points out what he or she believes to be the superiority of the UN.

---

[18]Tharoor, "Impartiality," 26.

[19]Weber, *From Max Weber,* 197.

[20]Akashi's claim that he was unwilling to micromanage those below him may be disingenuous. Criticism of the UN arises from inside as well as outside the organization. In either case, the criticism employs, whether negatively or positively, the ideal type that typically informs bureaucratic activity. It is interesting to note a criticism of the UN originating from inside the organization. Brett Lodge employs a commonsensical understanding

The international community that has traveled to the former Yugoslavia is far broader than us in the UN family. It is an array of dissimilar organizations with conflicting and confusing mandates, who are often concerned as much about institutional, political and physical survival as they are about justice.[21]

The term "family," a personal and intimate term, is a misleading but revealing way to refer to the UN's modern bureaucracy. Also, it is hypocritical for the author to suggest that the UN is less concerned with physical survival and more concerned with justice than other international organizations. Still, the key point beneath these confusions is the implication that the UN is better than other international groups because of its hierarchical authority structure. Weber says, "The decisive reason for the advance of bureaucratic organization has always been its purely technical superiority over any other form of organization."[22] Note that nothing gives bureaucracies their advantage other than their purely technical superiority.

On this subject Weber writes,

> The reduction of modern office management to rules is deeply embedded in its very nature. The theory of modern public administration, for instance, assumes that the authority to order certain matters by decree—which has been legally granted to public authorities—does not entitle the bureau to regulate the matter by commands given for each case, but only to regulate the matter abstractly.

---

of bureaucracy when he writes, "But as an organization, the UN appears incapable of sloughing off the desiccated skin of bureaucracy and coming to terms with peacekeeping missions for what they are: field operations. Genuine field operations demand flexibility in administration, dynamism, and decisiveness in execution at all levels, and a degree of autonomy from New York, which would allow those in charge in the field to exercise true leadership. Too much responsibility combined with too little authority—especially in an environment where buck-passing is endemic—leave staff reluctant to take quick decisions" (Brett Lodge, "A Culture of Buck-passing," *War Report* 28 [September 1994]: 25). In contrast to Akashi, Lodge is saying that the problem in the UN is that the higher authorities frequently do take over the business of the lower authorities. Notice, though, the conceptual ambivalence in this statement. With Weber, Lodge is that saying that it is dysfunctional within a bureaucracy for higher authorities to take over the business of lower authorities. Against Weber, Lodge is saying that this action is typical of modern bureaucracies. The advantage of applying Weber's study is that it helps us focus clearly on the problems and distinguish the competing issues.

[21]"A Partial Reply," *War Report*, 19.

[22]Weber, *From Max Weber*, 214.

> This stands in extreme contrast to the regulation of all relationships through individual privileges and bestowals of favor, which is absolutely dominate in patrimonialism.[23]

The long-serving UN official suggests that other international organizations administer their services according to individual privileges and bestowals of favor. Their structure and institutional values are more typical of patrimonialism, and, to some degree, the Bosnian society and culture have more affinities with a patrimonial rather than bureaucratic social structure.

In contrast to other international organizations, the UN administers its services impersonally. As a model of bureaucracy, the UN does not digress into its alternative. By refraining from patrimonialism, the UN maintains its bureaucratic nature. By indulging in patrimonialism, other international organizations neglect the principles and technical superiority of modern bureaucracies.

Peter Jennings on the UN

Weber's sociology is fraught with ambivalence on modern society's increasing dependence on bureaucratic organizations. Weber feared the dehumanizing aspects of bureaucracies in capitalistic economies as much as Karl Marx feared the consequences of alienated labor after the Industrial Revolution. The iron cage of formal rationality within which bureaucratic officials restrict their social action both dehumanizes the officials and entraps their subjects.[24]

An ABC special program titled "The Peacekeepers: How the UN Failed in Bosnia" provides a critical commentary on the complicity of the United Nations in the ethnic cleansing in Bosnia. The documentary hosted by Peter Jennings reviews the events that led to the creation of designated safe areas by the UN Security Council. The documentary reports the UN mandates, describes how the UN failed to follow its own mandates, and then interviews UN officials on the matter. The promises of the UN Security Council to protect civilians in these areas and to deter attacks were not kept. Officials like Sir Gen. Michael Rose and Tharoor skillfully rationalize their actions and explain away the discrepancies that Jennings points out.

As a news journalist, Jennings becomes a spokesperson for the ethos of substantive justice. As a professional soldier and a UN servant, Rose is an exemplar

---

[23]Weber, *From Max Weber,* 198.

[24]On the one hand, "Weber praised bureaucracies, and more generally formal rationality, for its many advantages over other mechanisms for discovering and implementing optimum means to ends," but, on the other hand, "Weber was painfully aware of the problems associated with bureaucracies and formal rationality; in other words, he knew of the irrationalities of formally rationalized systems. Thus, Weber described bureaucracies as dehumanizing" (Ritzer, *McDonaldization,* 20). Examining the conduct of the UN in Bosnia raises Weber's subtle but pressing concerns.

of formal rationality. For this reason, Jennings is a threat to Rose; Jennings wants to refute the moral adequacy of UN actions in Bosnia. Rose is committed to the hegemony of formal rationality as the only legitimate standard with which to measure UN conduct. Rose and Jennings reason independently of each other, and their exchanges bypass each other.

To maintain his integrity, Rose clings to the particular rigor of calculability. Calculability is the armor that Rose dons to defend himself against Jennings's one-sided representation of substantive justice. To counter the ethos of a mass media that thinks in individualistic rather than universalistic terms, Rose employs the idea of calculability as a rhetorical device.[25] Whether visiting the safe haven Goražde after an intensive bombing of the civilian population or talking to journalists, Rose remains fixated to the discipline of calculability. Following reports of severe and cruel conditions for civilians during the fighting in Goražde, Rose retorts, "I have long ceased to believe the first reports I hear in this country."[26]

Consider the following exchange between Jennings and Rose: Jennings asks, "So when they were coming to attack this United Nations designated safe area, the Bihać pocket, did you feel any compulsion to call in NATO to deal with them?" Rose answers, "Well, certainly. And we did, indeed, do that." Jennings asks, "When?" Rose replies, "I can't remember what night it was, but the first time they started to shell the town of Bihać and I think some tank fire was put in. We called in NATO to do those attacks." Rose points out to Jennings that it would be incorrect to say that the UN did nothing in the situation that Jennings mentions. Concretely speaking, the UN did do something. If the UN did do something, it can be counted. While Jennings's problem with the UN is that it did not do enough to protect the victims of ethnic cleansing and that what the UN did was of no moral consequence, Rose's retort remains factual—it cannot be said that the UN did nothing.[27]

---

[25]"When fully developed, bureaucracy also stands, in a specific sense, under the principle of *sine ira ac studio*. Its specific nature, which is welcomed by capitalism, develops the more perfectly the more the bureaucracy is 'dehumanized,' the more completely it succeeds in eliminating from official business love, hatred, and all purely personal, irrational, and emotional elements which escape calculation. This is the specific nature of bureaucracy and it is appraised as its special virtue" (Weber, *From Max Weber*, 215–16).

[26]"The Peacekeepers: How the UN failed in Bosnia," (Alexandria, Va.: ABC News, 1995). Videorecording.

[27]Van de Roer observes, "You were being criticized precisely because you kept muddling on." Akashi responds, "Muddling on is an achievement, more so than getting stuck. We were keeping nearly three million people alive, by feeding them, supplying them with gas and electricity, repairing roads and bridges, building schools and hospitals. I scored a few successes, achieved a few cease-fires. Do you know 'The Myth of Sisyphus' by Camus? Our job was comparable to Sisyphus: unappreciated work that looks hopeless, but someone has to do it. We have a moral responsibility" (Akashi, "Muddling").

Consider another exchange between Jennings and Rose. Jennings asks, "Is not part of your mandate to deter attacks on United Nations' designated safe areas?" Rose answers, "That is absolutely sound. And that is exactly what we did at the time of Goražde. We deterred the attacks that were taking place at that time." First, Rose accepts the validity of Jennings's question, but then he hides behind it. The phrase "at the time of Goražde" is not specific, but it suggests a frame, a time and space, in which an action can be identified and quantified.[28] Rose focuses on questions of "when" and "where" to evade questions of "what." By focusing on the quantifiable questions, Rose evades the qualitative questions of what was done and whether what was done had substance.

Here is another exchange that demonstrates this dynamic. Jennings asks, "When the Serbs shell a civilian population do you say, 'That's a war crime'?" Rose replies, "Of course, any shelling of a civilian population is a war crime." Jennings then asks, "Do you therefore feel when it's occurring that you have got to do something about it, that your mandate requires you to do something about it?" Rose answers, "We always do do something about it."[29] This response befuddles Jennings. In a way, Rose wins. When Jennings focuses on the moral quality of particular actions by the UN in Bosnia, Rose neutralizes this focus by reframing the issue into the concrete albeit more abstract issue of quantity.

Officials within bureaucracies do not make decisions pertaining to quality; they only make decisions pertaining to quantity. Here is why Weber fears bureaucracies and finds them dehumanizing:

> Bureaucratization offers above all the optimum possibility for carrying through the principle of specializing administrative functions according to purely objective considerations. Individual performances are allocated to functionaries who have specialized training and who by constant practice learn more and more. The "objective" discharge of business primarily means a discharge of business according to calculable rules and "without regard for persons."[30]

The key to understanding the idealized role of "calculable rules" in social action is to reflect on this illusion that there is no choice. For Rose there is no choice between quality and quantity. There is only a choice between different quantities. For Rose, quantity, however minuscule, is the exclusive representation of quality.

The issue of substance and quality is already decided. Herein lies the pathos behind Rose's commitment to calculability as the only measure of truth in his conversation with Jennings. On the one hand, Jennings cannot abide by Rose's rationalizations. On the other hand, Rose cannot abide by Jennings's moralizing. Jennings rejects the formal rationality of Rose, however crassly displayed, and

---

[28]"The Peacekeepers," ABC News.
[29]"The Peacekeepers," ABC News.
[30]Weber, *From Max Weber*, 215.

Rose rejects the substantive justice of Jennings, however objectively stated.

By continuous practice, Rose has learned. He knows what he is doing in his exchanges with Jennings. Speaking about Goražde, Rose says, "We have been through the hospital records. We know exactly the number of people who were operated on. And we know the number of deaths that were recorded. And whereas people were talking in terms of 2,000 casualties, civilian and military, I think you'll find those figures closer to 100, mostly soldiers." Jennings says to Rose, "We went back to see Dr. Begović [head of hospital in Goražde] at the hospital and we told him your figure of 100 casualties and he laughed and he said, 'Did he mean 100 a day?'" Rose replies, "Well, I didn't say 100 casualties. I merely said the number, the operations that took place in that hospital under anesthetic conditions were of that order." Jennings then says, "We visited the hospital, we have interviewed the aid workers, and everybody appears to stand by the figures they reported at the time which is approximately 2,000 wounded and 700 dead. What is the evidence that you have that has consistently proven them wrong?" Rose then rescues himself with this remark: "Well, either you can prove, as I say, one side right or one side wrong. Possibly the truth lies somewhere in between. As I say, you'll never get to the bottom of the truth."[31] Rose's strict use of calculable rules forces Jennings to abandon the voice of substantive justice and converse with Rose on his terms. Once Rose has forced Jennings to focus on issues of calculability, Rose wins by default. Restricting the discussion to the issue of calculability encapsulates the conduct of the UN from criticism since there is little of substance to calculate.

One of the most vexing problems is the UN's commitment to impartiality. Tharoor states the following:

> Peacekeeping requires impartiality as you or I require oxygen: the only way peacekeepers can work is by being trusted by both sides, being clear and transparent in their dealings, and keeping lines of communication open. The moment they lose this trust, the moment they are seen by one side as the "enemy," they become part of the problem they were sent to solve. This is axiomatic in "traditional peacekeeping." But I can understand why the value of impartiality is questioned when it seems to involve tolerating, even cooperating with killers, ethnic cleansers, and so on. The problem remains that the criticism is addressed to a totally inappropriate party. UNPROFOR is not an army that has been sent to make war and has failed to fight with sufficient vigor; it is a peacekeeping and aid-escorting force whose modus operandi requires frequent and active contact and cooperation with all parties.... For such a vulnerable force to take sides, as you suggest, might be morally gratifying—at least briefly—but it would also be militarily irresponsible.[32]

---

[31]"The Peacekeepers," ABC News.

[32]Tharoor, "Impartiality," 24, 26. Akashi provides the same rationalization for impartiality

For Tharoor, impartiality is the optimum means to a particular end; it is the most rational way for the UN to win the goodwill of the aggressor. Its efficiency is what makes it right. Here, though, is the critical question: How far can the process of formal rationality depart from the principle of justice without becoming irrational? At some point, the antinomy between formal rationality and substantive justice needs to be resolved. Substantive justice with no relation to reason is mob psychology based only on emotion and intuition. Formal rationality with no relation to substantive justice is an accomplice of evil.

Tadeusz Mazowiecki, the former prime minister of Poland, who had been appointed by the UN as envoy for human rights and advocated the establishment of safe areas, resigned after the fall of Srebrenica. In his letter of resignation, he made the following statement:

> One cannot speak about the protection of human rights with credibility when one is confronted with the lack of consistency and courage displayed by the international community and its leaders…the very stability of international order and the principle of civilization are at stake over the question of Bosnia. Crimes have been committed with swiftness and brutality and, by contrast, the response of the international community has been slow and ineffectual.[33]

For Mazowiecki the antinomy between substantive justice and formal rationality was so severe and untenable that he had to resign.

Consider Akashi's negative assessment of Mazowiecki's action and the reasons that Akashi believes that he took a superior course of action. Van de Roer asks, "Why did you not go to the Security Council and tell them, 'I...'" Akashi interjects, "And feel good, yes?" The interviewer continues, "cannot take responsibility for this; if you decline to take control, I shall resign?" Akashi replies, "That is what Mr. Mazowiecki of Poland did. He resigned as Special Rapporteur on Human Rights in Bosnia. That's very easy! Anybody can resign! But it requires some courage to stay on and persevere under great pressure from criticism and denunciations."[34]

---

when he says, "The man you bomb today is the same man whose cooperation you may require tomorrow for the passage of a humanitarian convoy" (Akashi, "Muddling").

[33] Cited in Bianca Jagger, "The Betrayal of Srebrenica," *The European* (September 25–October 1, 1995).

[34] Akashi, "Muddling."

Chapter 9

Charismatic Authority: Mladić in Bosnia

In order to do justice to their mission, the holders of charisma, the master as well as his disciples and followers, must stand outside the ties of this world, outside the routine occupations, as well as outside the routine obligations of family life.

—Max Weber
"The Sociology of Charismatic Authority"

I don't see it that way. I did what everyone else has done, to defend my own people.

——Ratko Mladić
"Pariah as Patriot"

PERHAPS THE MOST interesting way to study Max Weber's theory of bureaucracy is through its dialectical relation to its opposing form of authority. Weber's sociology of bureaucracy stands in sharp opposition to his sociology of charisma. In Weber's discussion, there is a dialogical relation between the two forms of authority. In Bosnia, the conflict between bureaucratic and charismatic authority paralyzed the community. On one extreme, the UN represented an extreme model of formal rationality—foreign, detached, and calculating. On the other extreme, nationalist leaders represented an almost pure form of charismatic authority.

Yasushi Akashi, the UN Special Envoy to former Yugoslavia during the war, recognizes the charismatic foundation of the nationalist Serb leaders. Akashi was asked, "About Karadžić: Can you give an example of something he said or thought that surprised you?" Akashi responds in the following way:

He is a man of the past, captivated by history and the glory of the Serbian nation. I tried to direct his eyes to the future, to the outer world, to the consequences of his military actions. But he is a headstrong man. Some Bosnian Serbs are almost suicidal, comparable to the Massad psychology [named after the rock where Jewish rebels in A.D. 73 chose to commit suicide rather than surrender to the Romans]. It is impossible to penetrate their minds. I told them: you are a minority, condemned and isolated by the international community. But they did not care.[1]

Akashi laments the legitimacy that Karadžić has as the Bosnian Serb leader, a legitimacy based solely on the principle of charisma. Karadžić's authority runs counter to Akashi's notion of bureaucratic authority. Indeed, if Ratko Mladić, as the military commander of the Bosnian Serbs, had more power than Karadžić, it was because Mladić was more charismatic. Even Karadžić recognizes this fact when he says, "Maybe we went a little bit too far with General Mladić: we have made a legend of him."[2] To have authority over the Bosnian Serbs, both needed to "stand outside the ties of this world." To defer to the logic of modern rationality was impossible for both of them.

Why, then, was it difficult for Akashi to penetrate their minds? Weber helps answer this question when he formulates the foundation of charismatic authority.

The charismatic holder is deserted by his following, however, (only) because pure charisma does not know any "legitimacy" other than that flowing from personal strength, that is, one which is constantly being proved. The charismatic hero does not deduce his authority from codes and statutes, as is the case with the jurisdiction of office; nor does he deduce his authority from traditional custom or feudal vows of faith, as is the case with patrimonial power.

The charismatic leader gains and maintains authority solely by proving his strength in life.... Above all, however, his divine mission must "prove" itself in that those who faithfully surrender to him must fare well.... The genuinely charismatic ruler is responsible precisely to those whom he rules.[3]

---

[1]Yasushi Akashi, "Muddling on Is an Achievement," *Bosnet Digest* 6, no. 1,036 (November 2, 1998).

[2]Karadžić cited on August 4, 1995 (Robert Block, "The Madness of General Mladić," *New York Review of Books* [October 5, 1995]: 8). Block also reports the following: "On Friday, August 4, 1995, with 100,000 Croatian regular forces being mobilized for attack against Serb-held areas in the Krajina, Karadžić announced that he was removing Mladić as Bosnian Serb military commander and assuming personal command of the army himself. Karadžić blamed Mladić for the loss of Grahovo and Glamoc, two key towns in western Bosnia populated entirely by Serbs.... It turned out to be one of the most unsuccessful military reshuffles in recent history. Mladić refused to go, calling the move 'unconstitutional.' 'I entered the war as a soldier and that is how I want to leave.... I shall remain...as long as our fighters and people support me'" (Block, "The Madness," 8–9).

[3]Max Weber, *From Max Weber*, trans., ed., and with an introduction by H. H. Gerth and C. Wright Mills (New York: Oxford University Press, 1958), 248–49.

Consider the various ways Mladić exemplifies these attributes as described in various news reports. An essay on Mladić in *People* opens this way: "He is stocky, gruff and shy of publicity. When he does speak to the press, he tends to stress how unremarkable he is. 'I am not a legend,' he said recently. 'I am just a common man who defends his own people.'"[4] Notice the double-voiced discourse here. On the one hand, Mladić is unremarkable. He is a common man. On the other hand, he lives for his people and because he lives for his people, his people live for him. This point is frequently echoed in other commentaries. What guides Mladić are not codes or statutes. What guides him are his loyalty to his people and their reciprocal and dutiful loyalty to him. These loyalties are the foundations of Mladić's power.

Weber says that "The charismatic leader gains and maintains authority solely by proving his strength in life."[5] Consider the anecdotes regarding Mladić. David Binder reports the following story:

> Then, in August 1991, Mladić led troops to liberate a Serb army barracks near Vrlika. The road was blocked by a bus rigged with more than 70 pounds of explosives. An engineering unit was unable to defuse the bombs. But Mladić, watched by reporters and cameramen, entered the bus and cut the detonator wires.

It is worth citing another example of Mladić's seemingly god-like invincibility:

> In the Croat-Serb fighting of 1991 Mladić moved with a combination of audacity and guile that astonished his opponents. Before new uniforms and insignia made the various sides distinguishable, he traveled across the lines in mufti, using identification papers of Croat officers he had known. Once, when he was posing as Col. Stjepan Fazlijan, a Croatian militiamen spotted his large ring and stopped him saying, "You're not Stjepan. You're Col. Ratko Mladić. You're dangcrous. We should liquidate you."
>
> "I was uncomfortable," Mladić recalls. He flashed an identity card belonging to Fazlijan and persuaded the militiaman he was the Croat. "I told him Mladić was really dangerous and ought to be liquidated."[6]

Mladić's reputation in Croatia caught the attention of the Bosnian Serb nationalists, and they soon had him transferred to Bosnia and named commander of the Bosnian Serb forces. Mladić was called by the nationalist Serbs. Because the nationalist Serbs called him they were expected to follow him. Weber's writing keenly captures the particular character of Mladić's leadership and the basis of his power among the Bosnian Serbs.

---

[4]Bill Hewitt et al., "A Bloody Crusade," *People* (June 13, 1994): 109.

[5]Weber, *From Max Weber*, 249.

[6]David Binder, "Pariah as Patriot: Ratko Mladić," *New York Times* (September 4, 1994): 28.

Charisma knows only inner determination and inner restraint. The holder of charisma seizes the task that is adequate for him and demands obedience and a following by virtue of his mission. His success determines whether he finds them.
His charismatic claim breaks down if his mission is not recognized by those to
whom he feels he has been sent. If they recognize him, he is their master—so
long as he knows how to maintain recognition through "proving" himself. But
he does not derive his "right" from their will, in the manner of an election.
Rather, the reverse holds; it is the *duty* of those to whom he addresses his mission to recognize him as their charismatically qualified leader.[7]

The actions of a charismatic leader like Mladić fell outside the cognitive
scope of a bureaucratic leader like Akashi. Akashi could not read Mladić's mind
because Mladić represented his antithesis. The advantage that Mladić had over
UN officials is that he understood his alter egos and their nature better than his
alter egos understood Mladić's exemplification of charismatic authority. In this
context, consider the comments of George Kenney, a former Bosnia expert at the
State Department: "Mladić is vicious. He doesn't seem to have any internal inhi-
bitions, which is one reason they put him in charge."[8]

Weber says, "If they recognize him, he is their master—so long as he knows
how to maintain recognition through 'proving' himself." By seizing Srebrenica
and Žepa in the heinous and sadistic manner that he did, Mladić was proving himself to be a divine and undefeatable figure to the Bosnian Serbs. This is what the
nationalist Serbs wanted from Mladić, and this is what Mladić gave them. Nothing, Mladić sought to show, constrained him. The more he hated himself for what
he did, the more he needed this unwavering support. The more he did what he
had to do to keep this support, the more he hated himself. Mladić himself was
conscious of this orientation:

After the fall of Žepa, when the UN rushed to conclude a civilian evacuation
deal with the Bosnian Serbs, Mladić, before television cameras, boarded a bus
carrying civilians from Žepa to Sarajevo and announced, "I am General Mladić.
You have probably heard of me. Has anyone here been raped by Bosnian
Serbs?" When the cameras were switched off, he told the group, "No Allah, no
UN, no NATO can save you. Only me."[9]

Weber writes, "Genuine charismatic domination therefore knows of no
abstract legal codes and statutes and of no 'formal' way of adjudication. Its
'objective' law emanates concretely from the highly personal experience of
heavenly grace and from the god-like strength of the hero."[10] One reason Mladić,

[7]Weber, *From Max Weber*, 246–47.
[8]George Kenney cited in Hewitt, "A Bloody Crusade," 110.
[9]Block, "The Madness," 8.
[10]Weber, *From Max Weber*, 250.

who is now an indicted war criminal by the International Tribual at The Hague, was not apprehended by NATO forces is that Western leaders still fear the charismatic power that they believe that Mladić continues to possess.[11]

Let us review the foundation of authority for a modern bureaucracy, for the purpose of contrast. Bureaucracies exemplify four elements of rationality: efficiency, control, predictability, and calculability. Each element is interconnected.[12] The more strongly the bureaucracy exemplifies these four elements, the more authoritative the bureaucracy is, especially within a capitalistic economy. According to Akashi, the UN was hampered by the fact that three of these elements—efficiency, control, and predictability—were painfully missing in their work. According to Akashi, the UN lacked efficiency primarily because the Security Council was "totally divided" and "The UN's resolutions were often ambiguous, contradictory, and inconsistent." The UN also lacked control because "Sometimes generals were tormented by conflicting interests." Akashi adds, "It affected our efficiency. It weakened the team spirit and the unity of conduct."[13] According to Akashi, predictability was also lacking in the work of the UN in Bosnia. Akashi is asked, "Don't you feel responsible for having underestimated the chances the Bosnian Serbs would overrun the enclave?" Akashi responds, "Underestimated or not, none of us thought the Bosnian Serbs were

---

[11]It is worth noting another feature of Mladić's charismatic nature. Weber writes, "But charisma, and this is decisive, always rejects as undignified any pecuniary gain that is methodical and rational. In general, charisma rejects all rational economic conduct" (Weber, *From Max Weber*, 247). Along this line Block writes, "In a land where politicians and warlords have grown rich from the trade in war booty, Mladić is considered an ascetic. He leads a humble, some would say Spartan, existence.... His dislike of war profiteers is said to be intense" (Block, "The Madness," 7).

[12]George Ritzer, *The McDonaldization of Society: An Investigation into the Changing Character of Contemporary Social Life* (Newbury Park, Calif.: Pine Forge Press, 1993).

[13]To compensate for this lack of efficiency, control, and predictability, the UN could only focus on the one other element of rationality—calculability, which it could still do. UN soldiers, for example, were assigned the task of counting ordinances exploded in the beseiged towns. Akashi uses a revealing example to make his point that the UN lacked control. Akashi is asked, "According to a senior UN officer, Janvier was passed by his own Government in the recapture of the Vrbanja bridge near Sarajevo. Serbs dressed like French UN soldiers had captured the bridge. But in the counterattack [by French UN soldiers], Paris gave direct orders to its own tactical commander. Was Janvier vexed by this?" Akashi responds, "I am unaware of this. Janvier acted like a good and honourable UN general and he may not always have been a good French general. If there is a loyalty conflict between your country and the UN, we in the UN are required to follow UN rules." In this situation, as a UN general, Janvier was not in control of his UN troops who were French soldiers. The French government was. Janvier himself would not have ordered the retaking of the Vrbanja bridge near Sarajevo because it cost lives. When Paris took control, it violated the principle of hierarchical order and also the mandate of the UN to be a

going to be so reckless as to capture Srebrenica. Who could have foreseen those massacres? No one could read Mladić's mind."[14]

Many make the opposite assertion. Given the pattern of ethnic cleansing in Bosnia for several years, anyone could foresee the horrific and unconscionable massacres that occurred after the fall of the Srebrenica enclave. How, then, could Akashi not read Mladić's mind? Akashi persists, "But perhaps Mladić was so stupid as to think he could take Srebrenica. But political leaders like Karadžić should have foreseen the devastating public opinion consequences."[15] It is worth pausing to ask what is it for Akashi to characterize Mladić as stupid and what is it for Akashi to expect Karadžić to know better? Where is Akashi coming from? What is it about Mladić and Karadžić that Akashi does not see? As much as Akashi is an extreme example of a bureaucratic leader, Mladić and Karadžić are extreme examples of its antinomy. In Bosnia, the world watched as the latter trounced the former. What Akashi characterizes as stupidity, Weber would characterize as socially intelligible, however irrational or nonrational it appears to be from the viewpoint of formal rationality.

The conflict in Bosnia became a conflict of competing versions of social authority, and the people in Bosnia were caught between the two extremes. As charismatic authority became more and more charismatic, bureaucratic authority became more and more bureaucratic. Each type of authority drove the other to take its extreme form. If this dichotomy had been grasped, its destructive antinomy could have been confronted. An objective point of view could have formed with respect to how each type of authority was responsible for the extreme posturing of its adversary.

Once one recognizes Mladić's power basis, it is possible to anticipate Mladić's moves. It is also possible to undermine his power base—either show that he is not invincible or that he is not as loyal to his people as his people think he is. Failure, for example, would have gone a long way to undermine Mladić.

Negotiations between nationalist Serb leaders and Western diplomats, however, were guided by the assumption that, at some point, the nationalist Serb

---

"peace-keeping" rather than a war-making military force. The UN, Akashi is saying, could do nothing about these "individualistic" deeds on the part of different nations. As a UN official, Akashi is committed to the formal rationality of bureaucratic authority and opposed to the political acts of particular nations, when they are governed by an ethos of substantive justice that simply inflames the emotions of the masses. Paris, according to Akashi, was enraged, not objective. He and Janvier, as UN officials, remained objective and impartial (Akashi, "Muddling").

[14]Akashi, "Muddling."
[15]Akashi, "Muddling."

leaders would see the light of reason. The weight of modern rationality was over-valued, and Karadžić's parasitic relation to the assumptions of Western leaders was recognized but not addressed. Negotiations were guided by an assumption that Karadžić would honor whatever codes or statutes were established through discussion. Nationalist Serb leaders, however, repeatedly broke whatever "social contract" was tentatively drawn up. The reality was recognized and lamented, but the logos of the reality was not explicated. The only authority that the national Serb leaders recognized and depended upon was charismatic. It was to their advantage to act in bad faith. By acting in bad faith, nationalist Serbs treated the talks as an occasion to strengthen the legitimacy upon which they relied. They could not be controlled by the world, and this demonstration is all they needed to control their own people and keep their loyalty.

To the question, Do you feel responsible for what happened after Srebrenica? Akashi says, "No, What decision could one have made under the circumstances? Please! We could not have foreseen this, and even if we had foreseen it, we would have been powerless to do anything." The fall of Srebrenica symbolized the overpowering of bureaucratic authority with charismatic authority. Mladić lifted the world out of modern history.

> Pure charisma does not know any "legitimacy" other than that flowing from personal strength, that is, one which is constantly being proved.... His power rests upon this purely factual recognition and springs from faithful devotion. It is devotion to the extraordinary and unheard-of, to what is strange to all rule and tradition and which therefore is viewed as divine. It is a devotion born of distress and enthusiasm.[16]

The detailed accounts of Mladić and his troops' behavior at Srebrenica in David Rohde's *Endgame* and Jan Willem Honig and Norbert Both's *Srebrenica: Record of a War Crime* confirm this attribute of Mladić's action. Mladić's success is intelligible because it is oriented. It was a logical consequence of what the charismatic figure must do to retain legitimacy.

For example, of all the European nations, the Dutch were Mladić's greatest enemies. Honig and Both make this interesting observation:

> By July 1995, the general seemed on a perpetual high. He had repeatedly humiliated the international community over the course of the war.... He clearly believed he could not go wrong and that he could get away with anything, including murder. As for Srebrenica, it was an especially attractive target for rubbing the humiliation in even deeper, because of the presence of Dutch peacekeepers. Mladić harboured a particular resentment towards the Dutch, whose

---

[16]Weber, *From Max Weber,* 248–49.

successive governments had consistently called for tougher action against the Serbs since the beginning of the war.... Mladić was out to teach the international community, and the Dutch in particular, a lesson.[17]

More than the other European countries, the Dutch took the moral high ground. Their politics and efforts based on moral principles provoked Mladić and, in part, motivated him to do what he did in Srebrenica.

Sadly, Honig and Both record Mladić's success and promote Mladić's perspective; they wrote, "As with no other country, the Dutch were cruelly caught out and the terrible hollowness of their 'principled course' was exposed."[18] At another point, they make this comment:

> The fundamental flaw with the Dutch decision-making process regarding the deployment of combat units to Bosnia was that it was driven almost exclusively by moral outrage. The public, parliament, and the government all wanted to do something about the war. But few considered carefully whether something that was actually *useful* could be achieved.[19]

Honig and Both themselves endorse Mladić's cynical attitude toward the Dutch government and its moral outrage about events in Bosnia. Like Mladić, Honig and Both resent the distinctive way in which the Dutch government responded to the war in Bosnia. Mladić's purpose, the authors indicate, was to teach the Dutch that morality has no place and no use in international politics. To a surprising degree, Honig and Both endorse Mladić's lesson, although obviously not his means. They suggest that, by taking the moral high ground, the Dutch brought the situation upon themselves as well as the Bosnian Muslims in Srebrenica. Clearly, it is time to take up a critical examination of journalism in Bosnia.

[17]Jan Willem Honig and Norbert Both, *Srebrencia: Record of a War Crime* (Middlesex, England: Penguin, 1996), 179–80.

[18]Honig and Both, *Srebrenica*, 184.

[19]Honig and Both, *Srebrenica*, 125.

Chapter 10

Journalism and Modern Ethics: Tim Judah and Roy Gutman in Bosnia

There is a method to presenting the reality of war in *Times* style, a restrictive method but a perfectly valid one just the same. It focuses mainly on institutions and political leaders and their duties and decisions, while leaving the common folk to exemplify trends, to serve as types: a fallen soldier, a screaming mother, a dead baby—literal symbols.... This method is described by various terms: detachment, disinterestedness, dispassion, distancing, and others with negative prefixes engineered to obliterate any relationship between observer and observed. When I went to Bosnia to work, I used to imagine I had entered a great grassland teeming with life. "I build a tower hundreds of feet high," I told one of my friends. "I climb it every morning and observe the wildlife devouring one another and struggling to survive down below. And from that distance, I write about what I see, send my story, have something to eat, and go to sleep."... I once saw soldiers unload babies crushed to death in the back of a truck and immediately ran off to interview their mothers. I accidentally killed an eighteen-year-old man who raced in front of my car on a bike; his head was smashed; I held the door when they loaded him into the backseat of the automobile that carried him to the emergency room of Sarajevo's main hospital. I expressed my condolences to his father; then I got a tow back to my hotel, went to my room, and sent that day's story to New York.

—Chuck Sudetic
Blood and Vengeance: One Family's Story of War in Bosnia

IN HIS ESSAY, "Politics as a Vocation," Weber says that journalists play an important role in modern politics. They are tantamount to moral educators. While most journalists would not describe their vocation in this way, they nevertheless articulate the ethical persuasions and moral viewpoints through which people understand world events.

> The journalist belongs to a sort of pariah caste, which is always estimated by "society" in terms of its ethically lowest representative. Hence, the strangest notions about journalists and their work are abroad. Not everybody realizes that a really good journalistic accomplishment requires at least as much "genius" [*Geist*] as any scholarly accomplishment, especially because of the necessity of producing at once and "on order," and because of the necessity of being effective, to be sure, under quite different conditions of production. It is almost never acknowledged that the responsibility of the journalist is far greater, and that the sense of responsibility of every honorable journalist is, on the average, not a bit lower than that of the scholar, but rather, as the war has shown, higher.[1]

Today journalists play an even more important role in politics than the one Weber describes, because political leaders, perhaps more than before, belie the role of moral persuasion in politics; they shirk the task of articulating the moral reasoning for this or that political action. Bill Clinton pretended to play this role to win his election in 1992, but once elected, Clinton abandoned this role and spoke against the moral reasons for intervening in Bosnia.[2] Given the weaknesses of political leaders today, journalists fill the gap. It has become the responsibility of journalists to articulate the moral imperatives through which to view events in Bosnia and Kosovo.

Journalists, however, are caught in a paradox. They report as objectively as they can the murders, violence, rapes, and genocidal activities that occur. They

[1] Max Weber, *Politics as a Vocation,* trans. H. H. Gerth and C. Wright Mills (Philadelphia: Fortress Press, 1965), 21.

[2] It is worth citing two journalistic references to Clinton's change of heart on Bosnia: "Clinton...promised a very different policy on the campaign trail. 'I know that ethnic divisions are one of the strongest impulses in all of society all over the world,' he said, 'but we've got to take a stand against it.' The Bush administration, he charged, was immoral 'for turning its back on violations of basic human rights,' and needed to show 'real leadership.' When the Clinton administration dithered, unlike the Bush administration, it did so in defiance of its promises" (Warren Bass, "The Triage of Dayton," *Foreign Affairs* 77, no. 5 [September/October 1998]: 98). "In the campaign of 1992, the governor of Arkansas, thinking that he could embarass the incumbent president, proclaimed that a Clinton administration would act to end the killing. America, he intoned, would not be party to an agreement that rewarded ethnic cleansing by supporting any partition plan that seemed to ratify Serb gains" (David Rieff, "Almost Justice," *The New Republic* [July 6, 1998]: 30). If a moral position against ethnic cleansing helped Clinton defeat Bush, why abandon this moral position after winning the election to retain popularity?

report as objectively as possible the reasons that political leaders give for not intervening to stop these activities. Journalists, however, find that they cannot report these events without at some point referring to the normative expectations that would require intervention. They cannot report these matters without formulating the ethical persuasions through which events in Bosnia need to be understood. Thus, journalists become the bridges over which people interested in and concerned about Bosnia must cross. It is important, then, to examine what girds and buttresses these bridges.

Tim Judah and Roy Gutman are two notable journalists who worked extensively in Bosnia. To examine the ethical persuasions that inform their work, it is helpful to draw upon Weber's work. Weber stipulates that "all ethically oriented conduct may be guided by one of two fundamentally differing and irreconcilably opposed maxims: conduct can be oriented to an 'ethic of ultimate ends' or to an 'ethic of responsibility.'"[3] According to an ethic of ultimate ends, there are moral principles that support society and buttress its intelligibility. Embedded in the normative orientations of a society are truths that give character and substance to social life. One such truth is the principle of justice.

An ethic of ultimate ends is uncommon among modern academics and skeptically denounced by postmodern intellectuals; still, it is worth considering a clear, eloquent statement on its behalf.

> The whole is a stable equilibrium of all the parts, and each part a spirit in its native element, a spirit which does not seek its satisfaction beyond itself, but has the satisfaction within itself for the reason that itself is in this balanced equipoise with the whole. This condition of stable equilibrium can, doubtless, only be living by inequality arising within it, and being brought back against to equipoise by Righteousness and Justice. Justice, however, is neither an alien principle (Wesen) holding somewhere remote from the present, nor the realization (unworthy of the name of justice) of mutual malice, treachery, ingratitude, etc., which, in the unintelligent way of chance and accident, would fulfill the law by a kind of irrational connexion without any controlling idea, action by commission and omission, without any consciousness of what was involved.[4]

Hegel's account of justice as neither an alien principle remote from reality nor the realization of mutual malice provides an operational definition of what justice is and how it serves society.[5]

The ethic of responsibility, Weber says, is fundamentally opposed to the

---

[3]Weber, *Politics*, 46.

[4]G. W. F. Hegel, *The Phenomenology of Mind*, trans. with an introduction and notes by J. B. Baillie (New York: Humanities Press, 1977), 480.

[5]It is worth citing another example of a strong commitment to the ethic of ultimate ends. Socrates says in his contentious exchange with Callicles: "We are told on good authority... that heaven and earth and their respective inhabitants are held together by the bonds of society and

ethic of ultimate ends. Drawing upon reason and experience, an ethic of responsibility anticipates the consequences of a political action and orients accordingly. To realize one's values in politics, it is necessary to act independently of moral imperatives. Machiavelli was an early teacher of the ethic of responsibility.[6] On the one hand, Weber distances himself from the radicalness of Machiavelli's position. On the other hand, Weber makes more palatable the rationalizations that support Machiavelli's political advice.[7] Weber, in a way, civilizes Machiavelli's argument.[8]

Wolfgang Schluchter, a leading Weber scholar, observes that today there is widespread preference for the ethic of responsibility.[9] Little, if any, respect is given to the ethic of ultimate ends.[10] In most circles, the ethic of ultimate ends

---

love and order and discipline and righteousness, and that is why the universe is called an ordered whole or cosmos and not a state of disorder and license" (Plato, *Gorgias*, trans. with an introduction by Walter Hamilton [Middlesex, England: Penguin, 1960], 117–18).

[6]"A man who wishes to make a profession of goodness in everything must necessarily come to grief among so many who are not good. Therefore it is necessary for a prince, who wishes to maintain himself, to learn how not to be good, and to use this knowledge and not use it, according to the necessity of the case" (Niccolò Machiavelli, *The Prince* [New York: New American Library, 1952], 84).

[7]See also Leo Strauss *What Is Political Philosophy? and Other Studies* (Westport, Conn.: Free Press, 1959).

[8]Weber himself is ambivalent on the dialectical relation between these two opposing and seemingly irreconcilable maxims. On the one hand, Weber suggests that it is important not to dichotomize the two positions: "This is not to say that an ethic of ultimate ends is identical with irresponsibility, or that an ethic of responsibility is identical with unprincipled opportunism" (Weber, *Politics*, 46). On the other hand, Weber suggests that it is quite difficult to synthesize the two positions: "An ethic of ultimate ends and an ethic of responsibility are not absolute contrasts but rather supplements, which only in unison constitute a genuine man—a man who *can* have the 'calling for politics'" (Weber, *Politics*, 54).

[9]See Wolfgang Schluchter, "Value-Neutrality and the Ethic of Responsibility" in *Max Weber's Vision of History: Ethics and Methods* (Berkeley: University of California Press,1979), 65–114 and Wolfgang Schluchter, *Paradoxes of Modernity: Culture and Conduct in the Theory of Max Weber*, trans. Neil Solomon (Stanford, Calif.: Stanford University Press, 1996), 48–50.

[10]"Morality must be universal; politics cannot be. As people have been saying since Max Weber, the 'ethics of responsibility' is a politics, not an ethics. Now a humanitarian politics is in a sense a contradiction in terms" (Tzvetan Todorov, *On Human Diversity: Nationalism, Racism, and Exoticism in French Thought*, trans. Catherine Porter [Cambridge: Harvard University Press, 1993], 207). Todorov reduces the distinction to a polemic. For Weber, the ethic of responsibility is an ethic. It is not "unprincipled

has become "a term of abuse."[11] Commenting in *Time* magazine on his perception of Clinton's foreign policy in Kosovo, Charles Krauthammer makes this remark.

> Proving simply that highfalutin moral principles are impossible guides to foreign policy. At worst, they reflect hypocrisy; at best extreme naiveté.... The Clinton Doctrine aspires to morality and universality. But foreign policy must be calculating and particular.[12]

Events in Bosnia and Kosovo confront the hierarchy of values that privileges an ethic of responsibility above an ethic of ultimate values. More strongly, Bosnia and Kosovo, as social entities, make a farce of this intellectual understanding of the role of ethics in politics.[13] Events in Bosnia and Kosovo and the world's response to these events require that we readdress the popularity of today's intellectual positions based on this well-known but misleading dichotomy.

Tim Judah and Roy Gutman worked extensively in Bosnia. They are significant, not just because of the important information they reported, but also because of the ethical persuasions they articulated to frame their information. Whether consciously or not, Judah and Gutman engaged in moral persuasion.[14] The weaker Western leaders were, the more important and influential journalists became. In telling the story, the storytellers became a part of the story.[15]

The ethical persuasion that informs the narrative in Judah's work is what Weber calls the ethic of responsibility. Judah's stories highlight the unpredictable

---

opportunism," and here is the essential point. What is the sense of ethics that informs the ethic of responsibility?

[11]"Who would not place himself on the side of reason and experience in spite of the danger of being reproached by adherents to an ethic of conviction as being a mere realpolitiker?" (Schluchter, *Paradoxes*, 49).

[12]Charles Krauthammer, "The Clinton Doctrine," *Times* (April 5, 1999): 88.

[13]"Dayton dispenses with moral handwringing over tainted interlocutors and instead treats all sides—invader and invaded, democrat and demagogue—equally with pragmatism and *raison d'état*" (Bass, "The Triage," 105).

[14]Gutman is open and reflective on this matter. "The norms are not out there, in the sense that our governmeents are not telling us what they are, and yet here's a preexisting set of norms, international treaties, and conventions. We, the press, have a need, we the media have a need, to find some norm to refer the public and ourselves to so that we know what we're reporting" (Roy Gutman, "Conversation with History," <http://globetrotter.berkeley.edu/conversations/Gutman>, 1997).

[15]Consider this timely comment, "Nobody believes that the discretion of any able journalist ranks above the average of other people, and yet that is the case" (Weber, *Politics*, 21).

significance of practical events. They identify the arbitrary consequences of political decisions and analyze the results of decisions by power elites from an everyday point of view rather than a larger or morally principled point of view.[16] In contrast, the ethical persuasion that guides Gutman's work is what Weber calls the ethic of ultimate ends. The principle of justice and the notion of universal human rights are underlying concerns in Gutman's journalism.[17]

Judah and the Ethic of Responsibility

The success of Judah's writing is based on his ironic affinity with the ethic of responsibility and his superior understanding of this ethic. Judah's narrative often reflects a sardonic tone.[18] The point of his sardonic tone is to make readers aware of what Weber calls the sober demands of the day. To understand the world as it really is, to comprehend the world objectively on its own terms, one needs to acknowledge and accept the ethical irrationality of the world.[19] The pedagogy behind Judah's sardonic tone is to give readers the impression that he is a critical rather than cosmic realist.

While the ethical irrationality of the world may be glaringly evident in the Balkans, it exists, Judah knows, in every political arena.[20] Judah's lesson is that what happens in the Balkans is not different from what happens in any part of the world. Weber makes the point this way:

[16]See Tim Judah, *The Serbs: History, Myth, and the Destruction of Yugoslavia* (New Haven: Yale University Press, 1997).

[17]Roy Gutman, *A Witness to Genocide* (New York: Macmillan Publishing Company, 1993).

[18]See, for example, Judah's review of Noel Malcolm's book, *Kosovo: A Short History* in the *New York Review of Books*. Judah writes, as if a snide retort stands as an adequate refutation, "In setting out his view, Malcolm is rather like someone claiming that the May-flower sailed from America to Britain or that Ellis Island had little to do with immigration to the United States" (Tim Judah, "Will There Be a War in Kosovo?" *New York Review of Books* [May 14, 1998]: 36).

[19]"The proponent of absolute ends cannot stand up under the ethical irrationality of the world. He is a cosmic-ethical 'rationalist'" (Weber, *Politics*, 48).

[20]Here is a typical example of an event in Bosnia and the way in which Judah reported it: "On 15 July notices were posted on the town hall announcing that buses would be leaving for Croatia.... The buses took them to a rendezvous point where the cleansed were decanted into UN trucks. The UNHCR has briefly agonized about doing this sort of job. Some argue that, by agreeing to help Muslims and Croats leave, the UN would become an accomplice to Serbian ethnic cleansing. Bosanski Novi was a relatively civilized affair, however, by this time it was becoming clear that far worse things were happening, that psychopaths as opposed to brutal political extremists were on the loose [What is the difference?]. In these circumstances, saving lives was the priority. Debates on the ethics of the matter faded into the background" (Judah, *The Serbs*, 228).

As a political ethic the ethic of responsibility is, in the first instance, critical insofar as it not only takes account of the ethical irrationality of the world but also recognizes that the peculiar dilemma of realizing values in politics consists in using power and force as means and therefore in leading to "a pact with diabolical powers." In a specific sense, the ethic of responsibility is realistic.[21]

What is meant by the ethical irrationality of the world? What insight informs the ethic of responsibility in relation to the ethical irrationality of the world? In politics, it is necessary, Weber argues, to employ force in realizing one's values.[22] Pacifism is unrealistic as a political commitment. The point, however, is that whenever force is employed (and pacifism recognizes this fact), no matter how good the intentions behind the use of force, bad results follow or evil consequences occur.[23] For example, NATO's bombing of the Chinese embassy in Belgrade in May 1999 is a case in point. After the bombing that killed several people in the embassy, both the Belgrade regime and the Chinese government used the event to degrade the ethic of ultimate ends that seems to support NATO's bombing of Serbia. The argument that was made is that the more committed a political group is to an abstract concept with universal pretensions, the more likely local instances of injustice will occur as a result of this commitment. While, from a universal point of view, the bombing may appear just, the resulting deaths of Chinese citizens in their own embassy is not.

Weber calls this the paradox of consequences, and the Belgrade regime as well as others use the paradox of consequences to discourage the ambivalent world from supporting strong military action as morally appropriate. Weber states this problem in the following way:

> No ethics in the world can dodge the fact that in numerous instances the attainment of "good" ends is bound to the fact that one must be willing to pay the price of using morally dubious means or at least dangerous ones—and facing the possibility or even the probability of evil ramifications. From no ethics in the world can it be concluded when and to what extent the ethically good purpose "justifies" the ethically dangerous means and ramifications.[24]

The inverse idea is equally true, although Machiavelli more than Weber stresses this anterior point.[25] Actions whose motives are inherently evil can lead

---

[21]Schluchter, "Value-Neutrality," 88.

[22]"The decisive means for politics is violence" (Weber, *Politics*, 47).

[23]"If an action of good intent leads to bad results, then, in the actor's eyes, not he but the world, or the stupidity of other men, or God's will who made them thus, is responsible for the evil" (Weber, *Politics*, 47).

[24]Weber, *Politics,* 47.

[25]"How laudable it is for a prince to keep good faith and live with integrity, and not with astuteness, every one knows. Still the experience of our times shows those princes to

to good results. For example, reporting on the hostage crises in 1995 when UN troops were seized and used as human shields by Bosnian Serb forces, Judah observes, "Three years ago, when hundreds of thousands of Bosnian Muslims and Croats were being driven from their homes by Serbian forces, it was a commonplace to revile Mr. Milošević as the Butcher of the Balkans." Now, Judah points out, "Western foreign ministers regularly come to pay court to him and the hostage affair has only served to boost his prestige." Judah focuses on the positive upshot of the hostage affair.

> Not only has the hostage affair meant that cold relations between Pale and Belgrade have warmed but it has reopened diplomatic channels. British and French diplomats among others have been in contact with the Bosnian Serbs and their discussions have ranged over the whole peace process.[26]

Here is a tale that Judah loves recounting as specifically as possible. Just as good deeds can lead to negative results, so can bad deeds lead to positive outcomes. Unanticipated but constructive gains can arise from actions whose motives are evil. Such is the ethical irrationality of the world.

The cutting edge of the ethic of responsibility is its critique of the ethic of ultimate ends, which is either indifferent to or ignorant of the irrational ways of the world.[27] Think here of the loaded term "mission creep." The persuasiveness of this term is its ability to refer to the unspecified but inevitable and impossible consequences of righteous but practicially naive actions. Given the irrationality of the world, it is naive for a politician to assume that from good comes good and from evil, evil follows. Practical reason and experience teach that this enchanting idea does not correspond to the ways of the world.[28] Such have been the frequent

---

have done great things who have had little regard for good faith, and have been able by astuteness to confuse men's brains, and who have ultimately overcome those who have made loyalty their foundation" (Machiavelli, *The Prince*, 92).

[26]Tim Judah, "Another Long, Hot Bosnian Summer," *The Herald (Glasgow)* (June 15, 1995): <http://www.lexis-nexis.com>.

[27]Daniel Bell observes, "Such were Weber's personal complaints against Georg Lukács. 'I suddenly realized that it was Lukács whom Weber had had in mind in those closing pages of 'Politics as a Vocation'; that when he had written, 'The proponent of an ethic of absolute ends cannot stand up against the ethical irrationality of the world,' it was Lukács' decision that had prompted Weber's anguish" (Daniel Bell, "First Love and Early Sorrows," *Partisan Review* [1981]: 547).

[28]"The ethic of ultimate ends apparently must go to pieces on the problems of the justification of means by ends" (Weber, *Politics*, 48).

complains of Western politicians against President Izetbegović.[29]

Like Weber, Judah devalues an ethic of ultimate ends. The irony, according to Weber and Judah, is that in politics believers in an ethic of ultimate ends become the real antagonists.[30] Believers in an ethic of ultimate ends must at some point use violence to achieve their ends, and, whenever they do, the paradox of consequences, of course, occurs. Consider the particular way in which the widely read pundit Noam Chomsky advises us to sidestep this problem.

> A standard argument is that we had to do something: we could not simply stand by as atrocities continue: That is never true. One choice, always, is to follow the Hippocratic principle: "First, do no harm." If you think of no way to adhere to that elementary principle, then do nothing. There are always ways that can be considered. Diplomacy and negotiations are never at an end.[31]

With this advice, Chomsky idealistically collapses the tension between an ethic of responsibility and an ethic of ultimate values. His ultimate value, "First do no harm," is tantamount to a perfect exemplification of an ethic of responsibility. The two ethics simulataneously become one ethic.

For Weber, the superiority of an ethic of responsibility is that, before acting, it takes into account the paradox of consequences and acts accordingly.[32]

---

[29]"I found that Izetbegovic''s deepest feelings became apparent from time to time when he openly agonized...over whether to accept the compromises in various peace settlements. He had two loyalties, to multi-ethnic Bosnia and his own Muslim party, but it was religion that gave him an inner certainty and composure.... My favorable appraisal of Izetbegović is not shared by others who have also spent long hours negotiating with him. Some feel he is the most difficult of all the people they had to deal with in the former Yugoslavia" (David Owen, *Balkan Odyssey* [New York: Harcourt Brace and Company, 1995], 38). In the same vein, Holbrooke reports that at a critical junction during the Dayton negotiations, Warren Christopher said to Izebegović, "Mr. President, I am truly disappointed...at the fuzzy, unrealistic, and sloppy manner in which you and your delegation have approached this negotiation. You can have a successful outcome or not, as you wish" (Richard Holbrooke, *To End a War* [New York: Random House, 1998], 305). Owen and Christopher, whose political practices represent primarily a commitment to the ethic of responsibility, are exasperated by Izebegović's commitment to an ethic of ultimate ends, which the media typically translated as fundamentalism.

[30]"In the world of realities, as a rule, we encounter the ever-renewed experience that the adherent of an ethic of ultimate ends suddenly turns into a chiliastic prophet. Those, for example, who have just preached 'love against violence' now call for the use of force for the *last* violent deed, which would then lead to a state of affairs in which *all* violence is annihilated" (Weber, *Politics*, 48).

[31]Noam Chomsky, "The Current Bombings: Behind the Rhetoric," <http://www.zmag.org/current_bombings.htm>.

[32]"However a man who believes in an ethic of responsibility takes account of precisely the average deficiencies of people; as Fichte has correctly said, he does not even

In contrast, the ethic of ultimate ends takes into account only the logic of the ultimate end that is pursued.[33] Here is an example from Judah's reporting:

> But the "problem" of the siege of Sarajevo was not humanitarian aid.... It was about winning and losing a war. The siege became the strangest in military history. After Mitterrand's visit, the UN and its refugee agency, the UN High Commissioner for Refugees (UNHCR), opened the city for emergency aid. Up to 4 January 1996 and despite many airport closures, the UNHCR was to fly 12,951 aid flights, which literally kept the city alive. In this way Sarajevo was saved from defeat and thus, in a hideous paradox, the war could go on for over three more years.... This is not to say that the UN should not have done what it did, because Sarajevo was the victim of aggression driven by the SDA and plotted by Serbia and the JNA's most senior officials. It is only to point out that the haphazard western response to the war helped to fuel it and prolong it.[34]

Here is the reasoning guiding Judah's analysis: however good the intentions of the humanitarian aid and however righteous this action is, it nevertheless contributed the prolonging of the war, where, in reality, the only issue is winning or losing. Judah degrades political actions based on an ethic of ultimate ends vis-à-vis his perception of realities based on an ethic of responsiblity.

The ethic of responsibility has constantly set powerful limits on what politicians would and would not do in Bosnia and now Kosovo. It is the reasoning that politicians used to block military intervention in Bosnia. It is the reasoning that politicians articulate to prohibit the use of ground troops in Kosovo. It is the reasoning that NATO leaders express to discourage the arrest of indicted war criminals. For example, it is argued that, while it may serve justice to arrest the indicted war criminals, it is not responsible from a practical or realistic point of view. It is not fair, for instance, to the soldiers who risk their lives in such an endeavor or to the innocent victims of the anticipated reprisals. Why, believers in the ethic of responsibility ask, stir up the now relatively complacent nationalist Serbs by arresting their charismatic leaders? The practical consequences would

---

have the right to presuppose their goodness and perfection. He does not feel in a position to burden others with the results of his own action so far as he was able to foresee them; he will say: these results are ascribed to my action" (Weber, *Politics*, 47).

[33]"The believer in an ethic of ultimate ends feels 'responsible' only for seeing to it that the flame of pure intentions is not quenched: for example, the flame of protesting the injustice of a social order. To rekindle the flame ever anew is the purpose of his quite irrational deeds, judged in view of their possible success. They are acts that can and shall have only exemplary value" (Weber, *Politics*, 47).

[34]Judah, *The Serbs*, 213.

not be worth the moral rewards, which are abstract and remote from reality.

The paradox of consequences is also the logic that nationalist Serbs employ to educate Western political leaders. Judah brings this point to his readers attention in this way:

> Outraged, or rather embarrassed at their impotence, western leaders felt the pressure to "do something" but exactly what they did not know. They certainly did not want their young men to die fighting the Serbs, but at the same time an intense debate was taking place in Washington and between Washington and European capitals about whether to launch air strikes against Serbian positions. As the siege began, aerial photos clearly showed where these were, but the U.S. military and the CIA were terrified of being sucked into a new Vietnam. The psychiatrist in Radovan Karadzic knew this and fed the American paranoia: "If there is armed intervention over Sarajevo, Bosnia will turn into a new Vietnam. This not an ideological but a civil war. We shall fight to the death."[35]

Despite the best intentions of believers in an ethic of ultimate values, bad consequences will still follow whenever they resort to forceful action.[36] To avoid these bad consequences, many of which can be anticipated, it is necessary to adapt an ethic of responsibility. When political actions are examined from the viewpoint of an autonomous and value-free practical science, irresponsible actions can be reduced, if not avoided. Such is the political wisdom that Weber, Judah, and other contemporary pundits seek to impart.

Notice another component of an ethic of responsibility. Given the ethical irrationality of the world, political leaders, to realize their values, must make pacts with diabolical powers. Angels, for example, must shake hands with devils. Journalists were keen to focus on whether U.S. politicians would shake hands with Milošević and other Bosnian Serb leaders at Dayton and when or when not they were willing to do so.[37] Not only must angels shake hands with devils, but angels also must dance with devils. Holbrooke is an American hero in this regard.

[35] Judah, *The Serbs*, 212–13.

[36] The point is prevalent in everyday life as well. Residents of Belgrade tell jokes during the bombing of Serbia, and here is one that plays upon the paradox of the consequences for its pun: "'Why will Bill Clinton become the next President of Yugoslavia?' The answer: 'He's succeeded in uniting the Serbs and destroying the Albanians'" ("Serb's Dark Humor Finds Many Targets," *New York Times* [May 24, 1999]: <http://www.nytimes.com>).

[37] "Here, at long last, was a diplomat who did not comport himself like Owen, Vance, Toltenberg, Akashi, and the rest. Here was a diplomat who recognized a moral difference between the Serb aggressors and the Bosnian victims. Mladić and Karadžić, he said bluntly, in public and in private, were evil. He told members of his delegation that if they did not want to shake the Bosnian Serb leaders' hands, he would not force them to do so" (Rieff, "Almost Justice," 33).

He danced with Milošević.[38]

Weber says that the conditions of the world are disenchantment. It is not only vain, but also irresponsible for politicians to act with righteousness. Given the ethical irrationality of the world, morally principled action causes more harm than good and sometimes even more harm than action whose motivation is not good. This logic that Weber forumulates discourages decisive intervention in either Bosnia or Kosovo.

Gutman and an Ethic of Ultimate Ends

Just as the ethical persuasion that informs Judah's work is the ethic of responsibility, the ethical persuasion that governs Gutman's work is the ethic of ultimate values, in particular, the ultimate value of justice. Gutman is what Weber would call a true believer. Notice, though, that many admire and respect Gutman's work. This fact suggests that the world is perhaps not as disenchanted as Weber and Judah would have us think. Why does Gutman's work win admiration and gain respect? It is because his work exemplifies as best as it can an ethic of ultimate values. This feature of Gutman's work is what people find, not just enchanting, but also inspiring.

During an interview in a series called "Conversation with History" at the Institute of International Studies at University of California, Berkeley, Gutman states that he believes in the principle of human rights. The Helsinki agreement in the 1970s, he says, led to peaceful revolutions in Eastern Europe. Notice Gutman's logic—from good comes good. Dissidents in Eastern Europe gained the understanding and knowledge that they needed to fight for freedom of expression and human rights. A commitment to justice empowered people and helped build communities. The Helsinki agreement, Gutman argues, produced a body of principles and agreements that today are as good a character as we could have of the

---

[38]Weber describes the modern principle of moral persuasion that Holbrooke employs in his presentation of himself to his American readers in *To End a War:* "However, it is immensely moving when a *mature* man—no matter whether old or young in years—is aware of a responsibility for the consequences of his conduct and really feels such responsibility with heart and soul. He then acts by following an ethic of responsibility and somewhere he reaches the point where he says:'Here I stand; I can do no other.' That is something genuinely human and moving. And every one who is not spiritually dead must realize the possibility of finding himself at some time in that position" (Weber, *Politics*, 54). Here is the very manner in which Holbrooke seeks to move his readers: "Through Tom Donilon, we were aware of Washington's ambivalence about our efforts. Lake had also told us the previous day that 'not everyone in Washington wants you to succeed.' This neither surprised nor alarmed me; every Administration contains different points of view. The responsibility for failure or success rested with us, and this was no time to worry about Washington's ambivalence" (Holbrooke, *To End a War*, 307).

international system.[39]

Gutman is a rationalist in terms of a cosmic rather than critical ethic. Gutman believes that moral principles exist that bear upon political action in necessary ways. He believes that the normative knowledge of a healthy society is grounded in moral truths. This normative knowledge, moreover, makes possible a permanent hierarchical order of values and practically neutralizes the paradox of consequences. Gutman is aware of but not deferent toward the ethical irrationality of the world.

Like many people in the post-World War II generation, Gutman believed that the Holocaust was supposed to be a one-time event, that it could not happen again, and that it should not happen again. When Gutman first visited a concentration camp in Bosnia, he said that he would not describe his feeling as outrage. He said that he would describe his feeling as white rage, a totally contained rage. Gutman knows that crime, massive crimes by states, upset the world environment, and degrade the lives of everyone in the world.

Gutman also knows that from evil follows more evil. What a realistic believer in the ethic of responsibility finds to be naive, Gutman finds to be, not only true, but also realistic. As long as Western leaders, to realize their values, make pacts with diabolical powers, only evil can follow. In Gutman's work, the ethic of ultimate values transcends and dissolves the paradox of consequences. The transcendence, moreover, is grounded in both experience and reason. Until Western leaders take morally principled action in the Balkans, the situation remains utterly unstable and totally undesirable. Gutman is as intolerant of political reasoning grounded in the paradox of consequences as Judah is of political reasoning grounded the discourse of moral prophets. Consider the following strong example of this point.

> There are those who say moral sentiments should not drive civilization. It is true that you cannot let your moral feelings control your every policy. But you cannot divorce policy from moral objectives: not in a democracy, where policy must ultimately find support in the general public. I have yet to find anyone who will argue that we should stand by and watch genocide be committed or the principles of international order be flouted. What our response should be is the real question. The way our governments have addressed genocide is by pretending it didn't happen, by devising euphemisms such as "acts of genocide." That is a moral evasion.... Evading the moral implications does not serve anyone well. It simply doesn't work.[40]

[39]Gutman, "Conversation with History."

[40]Roy Gutman, "Immorality Play," *Freedom Review* 25, issue 5 (September/October 1994), 4, 9.

Politicians and Pundits Reviewed

Together, Judah and Gutman dramatize the ethical tension and moral confusion of Western political leaders. They amplify in singular ways the ethical persuasions of several politicians and diplomats influencing events in Bosnia.[41] For instance, David Owen, like Judah, devalues the ethic of ultimate ends in deference to an ethic of responsibility.[42] Moreover, Owen uses the paradox of consequences (upon which an ethic of responsibility stakes its reputation) to discredit positions that he disagrees with.

> The policy of providing "safe areas" was inadvertently given a substantial boost at this time when the President of the International Committee of the Red Cross (ICRC), Mr. Cornelio Sommaruga, talked to the heads of the permanent missions in Geneva and launched the ICRC recommendation for the immediate setting-up of agreed "protected zones" to accommodate vulnerable groups within Bosnia-Herzegovina.... [A]s Vance and I explained to Sommaruga, the danger was that his well-intentioned proposal, which was based on obtaining the consent of the Bosnian Serbs and the Bosnian Muslims' agreement to effective demilitarization would be changed by the Security Council so that there was neither consent nor demilitarization, which is exactly what happened. The ICFY was doing everything possible to build up its moral authority to halt ethnic cleansing and we thought that to make it apparent that Muslims pushed out of their homes could go into safe areas would be to flash a green light to the Serbs that ethnic cleansing could go ahead. UNHCR agreed with us, but felt inhibited in publicly criticizing governments who were advocating the policy.[43]

[41]The ethic of responsibility dies hard in diplomatic circles. Consider the following remark after the chief prosecutor of the Yugoslav War Crimes Tribunal, Louise Arbour, announced an indictment against Slobodan Milošević and issued an arrest warrent: "'I do not approve of this initiative. It does not serve peace,' France's interior minister, Jean-Pierre Chevenement, said today, criticizing the court for having a 'pseudo-moral' vision instead of a political one" ("U.N. Tribunal Charges Milošević and Four Others with War Crimes," *New York Times* [May 27, 1999]: <http://www.nytimes.com>).

[42]"U.S. opinion would not face up to the reality that wider air strikes threatened the UN humanitarian mission since they were strung out all over the country in small groups, vulnerable to being sized as hostages and capable of being blocked in position for weeks on end or just turned around with the convoys. The Pentagon knew these realities but for some reason could not get the message through to Vice-President Gore or Ambassador Madeleine Albright, both of whom appeared to think these issues could be resolved by bombing the Serbs irrespective of where we were in negotiations or where the UN was on the ground. The State Department seemed to be paralyzed by its own divisions while the White House wanted to practice realpolik and simultaneously preach moralism" (Owen, *Odyssey,* 198–99).

[43]Owen, *Odyssey,* 66. Consider again how the too frequently used term, "ethnic cleansing," co-opts the social complacency and moral inertia of its speakers and their

Drawing upon an ethic of responsibility, Owen coopts the moral concern support-ing the establishment of safe-areas. He argues that the policy gives a "green light" to the Serbs that ethnic cleansing could go ahead. The desire to provide "safe-areas" is based on an ethic of ultimate ends, but it leads to consequences that undermine and subvert the high-minded intent of the policy. Owen capital-izes on the paradox of consequences to belie political initiatives grounded in the ethic of ultimate ends. He cleverly coopts the moral argument in the position he opposes, in this case, to demonstrate to the Serbs that they cannot go on with eth-nic cleansing, and uses it to defend his own position, which opposes the creation of safe-areas.

In contrast to Owen, Bob Dole's commentaries on events in Bosnia and, even more dramatically, Kosovo represent a commitment to an ethic of ultimate ends. Dole, the former majority leader of the U.S. Senate, sharply critiques the actions of the Clinton administration as pathetically limited to and blindly con-strained by an ethic of responsibility. Criticizing Vice President Al Gore's desire to bring in Russia and include Russian foreign minister Primakov to rescue NATO with a diplomatic solution, Dole writes, "[T]hese ideas reflect a combina-tion of political expediency, historical amnesia, suspension of disbelief, and a lack of morality." To conclude his pointed commentary, Dole says,

> After 10 years of conflict in the Balkans, why would we want to guarantee more bloodshed, repression and instability into the millennium? The only thing Milošević deserves is a swift trial at the Hague and a life sentence for geno-cide—not a deal that preserves his power and position. The U.S. cannot claim to assert moral leadership in this world and allow Milošević to remain in power or even at large.[44]

Henry Kissinger, like Dole, sharply critiques Clinton's foreign policy in Bos-nia and Kosovo, but Kissinger, unlike Dole, draws upon an ethic of responsibility rather than an ethic of ultimate ends to do so. While Dole attacks the perception that Clinton is unconscionably constrained by an ethic of responsibility in the face of moral imperatives, Kissinger attacks the perception that Clinton is

---

audience. The phonetic similarity between "ethnic" and "ethic," a minimal pairing, invites a befuddling and grotesque malapropism, namely, that ethnic cleansing is somehow ethi-cal cleansing. The phonetic pairing implies a semantic linkage that is not only ludicrous but obscene.

[44]Bob Dole, April 30, 1999, "Two Bad Ideas for Settling Kosovo Crises," *Chicago Tribune, Bosnet Digest* 6, no. 1,235. See also Bob Dole, April 15, 1999, "Too Little, Too Late In Kosovo," *Wall Street Journal, Bosnet Digest* 6, no. 1,208.

obsessed and disfigured, as a political leader, by an ethic of ultimate ends. Kissinger says the following about Clinton:

> And from the beginning, he never adapted the level of force necessary to achieve these large aims. From the beginning, he proposed objectives that were totally incompatible with the means proposed for achieving those objectives. These commitments to higher moral principles unmatched by higher use of force led to a gradual emasculation of the people we were supposed to be protecting.... We drifted into a pattern of behavior in which we were not willing to stop the war by force. But we were also not willing to accept a peace plan that could stop it by diplomacy. Thus we inflamed the situation without providing the means for dealing with that inflammation.[45]

The ethic of responsibility focuses on the rational interconnectedness of ends and means independently of what these ends and means are.

As a protégé of Henry Kissinger, Richard Holbrooke exemplifies a mixture of the ethic of ultimate ends and the ethic of responsibility. On the one hand, Holbrooke's compassion for Bosnian government reflects an ethic of ultimate ends. On the other hand, his strong-arm methods to achieve the Dayton Peace Accord at any cost reflects the ethic of responsibility. "'This may not be a just peace,' [Holbrooke] told his people, 'but it is more just than a continuation of war.... In the world as it is, a better peace could not have been achieved."[46]

With the publication of his book on Bosnia and the Dayton Peace Accord, entitled *To End a War*, Holbrooke holds himself up as an American hero. When the Europeans fall short, Holbrooke succeeds. Only the American, Holbrooke suggests, could have achieved what he did with the Dayton Peace Accord. Here is the message of Holbrooke's book, and it is a message with which Americans like to identify. What, then does it mean to be an American hero? On the one hand, Holbrooke holds himself up as a defender of moral principle, integrity, and the idea of justice. On the other hand, he is also personally comfortable with Milošević and seems to admire the political savy of the man who started the Balkan wars. What do Holbrooke and Milošević have in common such that they could act like partners, if not friends? They seem to share a clear understanding of an ethic of responsibility and a disciplined ability to follow this commitment as the conditions demand.

Like Holbrooke, Madeleine Albright, Clinton's secretary of state, exemplifies the same ethical ambivalence toward events in Kosovo. On the one hand, her leadership influenced Western nations to confront Milošević militarily in Kosovo, and her leadership, in collusion with the British political leaders Tony Cook

[45]Henry Kissinger cited in Mark Danner, "Slouching Toward Dayton," *New York Review of Books* (April 23, 1998), 62, 64.

[46]Rieff, "Almost Justice," 37.

and Robin Blair, is based on her commitment to an ethic of ultimate ends. On the other hand, her decision to rebuff the request of the KLA (Kosovo Liberation Army) for arms to defend themselves and their families during the ethnic cleansing of Albanians from Kosovo reflects her commitment to the ethic of responsibility. Clinton's defense secretary, William Cohen, articulates the paternalistic rationalization behind this position in the following way: "If we start to support arming the KLA...you will then invite others to start rearming the Serbs and you will intesify the combat and the conflict there rather than demilitarizing it."[47]

Like most modern scholars, Schluchter categorically speaks against an ethic of ultimate values in favor of an ethic of responsibility. He says that "Whatever may be the justification and content of principled action in politics, it detracts from the conditions of the present; it requires the sacrifice of the intellect or of empirical lessons or of both."[48] Given events in Bosnia and Kosovo and the world's response to these events, what Schluchter says against an ethic of ultimate ends may now be said against an ethic of responsibility. As world events, Bosnia and Kosovo challenge and completely invert the hierarchy of values that Schluchter promotes. Bosnia and Kosovo expose the amoral teleology behind the cloak of objectivity under which an ethic of responsibility drapes itself. I, for one, am grateful to Bosnia for this achievement, although I know that the costs were unconscionably high. To sustain a commitment to an ethic of responsibility after Bosnia and Kosovo "requires the sacrifice of the intellect or of empirical lessons or of both." It not only detracts but also distorts the conditions of the present, namely, the sadistic violence, murder, and rape of not thousands of people, but thousands of thousands of people. No means justifies this end, and no end justifies this means. An ethic of responsibility cannot live without an ethic of ultimate ends any more than the adherents to an ethic of responsibility claim that an ethic of ultimate ends cannot live without an ethic of responsibility. Alone, each is equally sophistic, and Dr. Martin Luther King, Jr., explains why.

> But we will never have peace in the world until men everywhere recognize that ends are not cut off from means, because the means represent the ideal in the making, and the end in process, and ultimately you can't reach good ends through evil means, because the means represent the seed and the end represents the tree.[49]

---

[47]William Cohen cited in "Army Says NATO Mission May Help KLA," *Christian Science Monitor* (April 16, 1999).

[48]Schluchter, "Value-Neutrality," 92.

[49]Martin Luther King, Jr., "A Christmas Sermon on Peace," in *A Testament of Hope: The Essential Writings of Martin Luther King Jr.,* ed. James Melvin Washington (San Francisco: Harper and Row, 1986), 255.

Chapter 11

Chomsky's Problem: Fairness First

Act in accordance with all political rules, national and international laws whose infringement you would disapprove of even in the case of just one citizen (or one nation). This is the moral maxim and the political principle of (political) *justice*.... Recognize all human needs, as long as their satisfaction is conceivable without collisions with the maxims of liberty, justice and (rational) equality. This is the moral maxim and the political principle of *fairness*.... In this understanding, "fairness" is not identical with justice, it is something *beyond justice*. Justice can only serve as a limiting factor of fairness in the event of a collision of the two, in which case justice *should* serve as a limiting factor for justice is superior to fairness.

—Anges Heller and Ferenc Fehér
The Postmodern Political Condition

AS SEEN IN THE PRECEDING chapter, it is difficult to account for the dialectical relation between an ethic of responsibility and an ethic of ultimate ends. One reason this is so is that Weber formulates the distinction in empirical rather than metaphysical terms. At the same time, Weber yearns for a meaningful synthesis of the two ethics. At one point, Weber advises, "This is not to say that an ethic of ultimate ends is identical with irresponsibility, or that an ethic of responsibility is identical with unprincipled opportunism."[1] Weber also suggests that truth lies in the synthesis of the two positions: "An ethic of ultimate ends and an ethic of

---

[1] Max Weber, *Politics as a Vocation,* trans. H. H. Gerth and C. Wright Mills (Philadelphia: Fortress Press, 1965), 46.

responsibility are not absolute contrasts but rather supplements, which only in unison constitute a genuine man—a man who *can* have the 'calling for politics.'"[2] As long as the distinction is cast in strict empirical terms, it is difficult to provide for their dialectic. The ethic of responsibility is privileged and an ethic of ultimate ends degraded.[3] Neither benefits from being stratified from the other.

Thus, it is too radical to say with Tzvetan Todorov that the ethic of responsibility is no ethic at all.[4] If this were true, the ethic of responsibility would be tantamount to the crudity of realpolitik and shallowness of Machiavellianism. This reading disrespects Weber's own conviction on the matter. Weber believes that an ethic of responsibility is superior to an ethic of ultimate ends because it is more ethical than an ethic of ultimate ends. Schluchter understands this point better than anyone:

> Whereas an adherent of an ethic of conviction takes on, as it were, a single responsibility, namely, for the convictional value of his action, the adherent of an ethic of responsibility has to carry a double responsibility, namely, for the convictional value and for its relationship to other values, especially success values, in an ethically irrational world.[5]

To resolve this issue and to step outside of the polemic, it is necessary to formulate this dichotomy in metaphysical rather than empirical terms. Weber and Schluchter each entertain this possibility, but neither pursues it.[6]

What is the metaphysical content of the two ethics, respectively? We understand their difference empiricially, but what is their difference metaphysically? An ethic of responsibility is ethical insofar as it reflects a commitment to the principle of fairness. Fairness, as formulated in the liberal philosophy of John Rawls, focuses on the good of cooperation. Fairness works to achieve an overlap-

---

[2]Weber, *Politics*, 54.

[3]Consider the following passage, which privileges an ethic of responsibility: "One could say that the maxims of an ethic of responsibility demand a careful weighing of alternative goods in ethical terms before any action is taken, something not required by the maxims of an ethic of conviction" (Wolfgang Schluchter, *Paradoxes of Modernity: Culture and Conduct in the Theory of Max Weber*, trans. Neil Solomon [Stanford, Calif.: Stanford University Press, 1996], 88).

[4]Tzvetan Todorov, *On Human Diversity: Nationalism, Racism, and Exoticism in French Thought*, trans. Catherine Porter (Cambridge: Harvard University Press, 1993), 207.

[5]Schluchter, *Paradoxes*, 88.

[6]Schluchter restricts the range of his theoretical narrative when he writes, "I will, however, confine my analysis to the diagnostic aspect, touching on the therapeutic only occasionally" (Schluchter, *Paradoxes,* 50). Notice that to pursue questions of a therapeutic rather than diagnostic nature would be to examine questions on how we should and should not live our lives, a forbidden subject in Weber's sociology.

ping consensus by institutionalizing practices of cooperation in a liberal and democratic fashion. For Rawls, this achievement represents a social utopia where individuals are recognized and respected as both free and equal. Rawls calls this position justice as fairness.

Like an ethic of responsibility, fairness recognizes the ethical irrationality of the world and confronts it practically. From the viewpoint of fairness, there is not "one rational conception of the good." Instead, "there are many conflicting and incommensurable conceptions of the good, each compatible with the full rationality of human persons."[7] This understanding within the principle of fairness guides the moral philosophy of political liberalism.

In contrast, an ethic of ultimate ends is ethical insofar as it reflects a commitment to the principle of justice. From Rawls's critique, we learn the following about the principle of justice vis-à-vis justice as fairness: "Indeed, since classical times the dominant tradition seems to have been that there is but one rational conception of the good, and that the aim of moral philosophy, together with theology and metaphysics, is to determine its nature." This is how Weber brings Marxism and Christianity together as representing the same social ethic. Each is passionately committed in different ways to the principle of justice. The problem with adherents to an ethic of ultimate ends is that they take the principle of justice too seriously. They believe that there is one rational conception of the good. They reject the argument that "there are many conflicting and incommensurable conceptions of the good, each compatible with the full rationality of human persons."[8] For this reason, adherents of an ethic of ultimate ends are viewed as intolerant and fundamentalist.

Justice is based on an a priori knowledge of what is true from a universal and rational point of view, and therefore necessary to the human community. The problem for Rawls and the moral philosophy of liberalism is that justice, as a universal rather than general notion, rests upon "metaphysical" propositions that are not subject to empirical verification or public agreement. By reformulating and diminishing the metaphysical significance of the principle of justice with the idea of justice as fairness, Rawls sees himself resolving this problem.

Fairness is based on a posteriori knowledge, a recognition of empirical conditions and their essential relation to ethical understanding. Fairness is aware of the practical consequences and everyday history of what is done and acts with an eye to what Schluchter calls "success" values.[9] Success values focus upon empirical consequences for their measure.

To synthesize an ethic of responsibility and an ethic of ultimate ends, it is necessary to recover the metaphysical substance of each ethic. Schluchter sug-

---

[7]John Rawls, "Justice as Fairness: Political not Metaphysical," *Philosophy and Public Affairs* 14 (1984): 248.

[8]Rawls, "Justice as Fairness," 248.

[9]Schluchter, *Paradoxes*, 88.

gests such a project when he writes, "In order to avoid terminological confusion, I suggest distinguishing between the 'bridging principle of hierarchy' and the 'bridging principle of balance.' Either can be adopted by a moral actor who has to solve the problem of relating convictional values to success values."[10] The way an ethic of ultimate ends links itself to an ethic of responsibility is with a bridging principle of hierarchy. For example, Kant's categorical imperative of goodwill recognizes justice as a universal feature of the human condition. As a universalizing principle, the principle of justice provides rules for "examining" rather than "producing" ethical maxims.

In contrast, fairness links itself to an ethic of ultimate ends with a bridging principle of balance. Through the good of cooperation and dialogue, fairness provides rules for producing rather than examining ethical maxims.[11] Rawls describes this work in the following way: "Since justice as fairness is intended as a political conception of justice for a democratic society, it tries to draw *solely* upon basic intuitive ideas that are embedded in the political institutions of a constitutional democratic regime and the public traditions of their interpretation" [my italics].[12] Unlike justice, fairness does not draw upon an a priori knowledge. Metaphysical ghosts do not haunt or intimidate the work of fairness; in fact, to heed such ghosts in the labor of fairness belies the principle of fairness.

The above distinction between justice and fairness informs the intellectual debates on the morality of the NATO bombing of Serbia and Kosovo. Many intellectuals passionately argued against NATO's bombing of Serbia. They demanded that NATO stop the war. Noam Chomsky was a notable and articulate pundit opposing NATO's war.

The persuasive power of Chomsky's critique is his unconditional commitment to the principle of fairness and his ability to expose innumerable examples of unfairness throughout the world. His critiques highlight the ethical irrationality of the world and the jingoistic character of nation-states that presume to act in the interests of justice.

It is useful to understand Chomsky's arguments in light of the moral philosophy of Rawls. For example, in promoting justice as fairness, Rawl argues, "The essential point is this: as a practical political matter no general moral conception can provide a publicly recognized basis for a conception of justice in a modern democratic state." Then, Rawls says that "Philosophy as the search for truth about an independent metaphysical and moral order cannot, I believe, provide a workable and shared basis for a political conception of justice in a democratic society."[13] In a comparable manner, Chomsky asserts that "Recognizing principles of international law and world order, solemn treaty obligations, decisions by

---

[10]Schluchter, *Paradoxes,* 88–89.
[11]Schluchter, *Paradoxes*, 90.
[12]Rawls, "Justice as Fairness," 225.
[13]Rawls, "Justice as Fairness," 225, 230.

the World Court, considered pronouncements by the most respected commentators—these do not automatically solve particular problems. Each issue has to be considered on its merits."[14]

Chomsky argues that, when considered on its merits, the NATO bombing in Serbia and Kosovo is unequivocally unfair. It is unfair not only to the Serbian nation and its people, given the loss of civilian lives and enormous material damage, but also to the Albanians in Kosovo on whose behalf the bombing, it is claimed, is carried out. Chomsky makes the following point:

> The threat of NATO bombing, predictably, led to a sharp escalation of atrocities by the Serbian Army and paramilitaries, and to the departure of international observers, which of course had the same effect. Commanding General Wesley Clark declared that it was "entirely predictable" that Serbian terror and violence would intensify after the NATO bombing exactly as happened. The terror for the first time reached the capital city of Pristina, and there are credible reports of large-scale destruction of villages, assassinations, generation of an enormous refugee flow, perhaps an effort to expel a good part of the Albanian population—all an "entirely predictable" consequence of the threat and then the use of force, as General Clark rightly observes.[15]

In terms of an ethic of responsibility, Clark is culpable. Clark knew that the bombings would be directly responsible for what happened to the Albanians in Kosovo, the violent murders and unconscionable destruction, and he proceeded anyway.

Another distinguishing feature of Chomsky's critique is the way he juxtaposes the situation in Kosovo with other places in the world. Remember the definition of fairness provided by Heller and Fehér: "Recognize all human needs, as long as their satisfaction is conceivable without collisions with the maxims of liberty, justice and (rational) equality. This is the moral maxim and the political principle of *fairness*."[16] From the viewpont of fairness, why are the human needs of the Albanians in Kosovo greater than other oppressed groups in the world? The need for fairness is as great if not greater in other parts of the world, Chomsky argues.

> Now the term genocide, as applied to Kosovo, is an insult to the victims of Hitler. [It is "unfair" to the victims of Hitler.] In fact, it's revisionist to an extreme. If this is genocide, then there is genocide going on all over the world. And Bill Clinton is decisively implementing a lot of it. If this is genocide, then what do

---

[14]Noam Chomsky, "The Current Bombings: Behind the Rhetoric," 1999 <http://www.zmag.org/current_bombings.htm>, [accessed May 25, 1999].

[15]Chomsky, "The Current Bombings."

[16]Agnes Heller and Ferenc Fehér, *The Postmodern Political Condition* (Oxford: Polity Press, 1988), 69.

you call what is happening in the southeast of Turkey? The number of refugees there is huge, it's already reached about half the level of Palestinians expelled from Palestine. If it increases further, it may reach the number of refugees in Colombia, where the number of people killed every year by the army and para-military groups armed and trained by the United States is approximately the same as the number of people killed in Kosovo last year. Ethnic cleansing, on the other hand, is real. Unfortunately, it's something that goes on and has been going on for a long time. It's no big innovation. How come I'm living where I am instead of the original people who lived here. Did they happily walk away?[17]

There seems to be no refuting Chomsky on these points. Given the ethical irratio-nality of the world, unfairness is everywhere. The best thing to do is to expose the "just" actions of political actors who presume to act morally so as to disclose their hypocrisy. Chomsky focuses on the irrationality of the world as a way to reduce the irrationality of the world and restore the human world to the rules and procedures of international law.

Chomsky's work as both a linguist and a critic is grounded in a strong empir-ical commitment. Justice for Chomsky is represented by international law based on the UN Charter and subsequent resolutions and World Court decisions. Justice or rather justice as fairness is not the moral principle to which these institutions make reference and seek to respect; instead, justice, as a knowable entity, is these institutions themselves and their historical documents. When international law is not respected, the practice is both unfair and unjust. The empirical phenomena is the reality.

Consider how Chomsky formulates the problem of knowledge. Chomsky says, "The whole issue of whether there's a 'physical' basis for mental structures is a rather empty issue." Why is it an empty issue? Chomsky explains, "The con-cept of 'physical' has been extended step by step to cover anything we under-stand." Chomsky is saying that the concept of physical or the idea of empirical demonstration is extended step by step to cover everything science touches. Sci-ence is basically imperialistic; its commitment to empirical demonstration subju-gates every subject to its interest in control. Nothing, not a spiritual being, the principle of goodwill, knowledge of a person's mental structures, not even the parameters of universal grammar, will escape this domain. Chomsky states, "[W]hen we ultimately begin to understand the properties of the mind, we shall...simply extend the notion 'physical' to cover these properties as well."[18] Chomsky does not have ground on which to resist the imminent development of

---

[17]Noam Chomsky, "Print Interview," April 8, 1999 <http: //www.zmag.org/chomint-yug.htm>, [accessed May 23, 1999].

[18]Noam Chomsky quoted in John Lyons, *Noam Chomsky* (New York: Viking Press, 1970), 120.

modern science. He suggests no compelling foundation from which to emancipate social knowledge from the conquest of empirical demonstration.

It is important, however, to ask whether fairness is the same thing as justice. If we lived where there was fairness for everyone, would such a world be a just world? This issue is the controversy surrounding Chomsky's infamous support of Professor Robert Faurisson, who published a book in France claiming that the Nazi gas chambers never existed. Since Chomsky believes in justice as fairness, he not only spoke but also wrote in favor of freedom of speech on behalf of Faurisson's book. Chomsky's writing was used as a preface to Faurisson's book. To defend Faurisson, Chomsky distinguishes between one's right to express one's views (a matter of fairness) and one's right to defend the views expressed (a matter of justice). For Chomsky fairness always comes first. While justice demands that the state censor Faurisson's inflamatory comments, fairness demands that society respect Faurisson's right to express his views, no matter what they are. Chomsky doggedly defends fairness over and above justice because to his mind "the state ought not to have the right to determine historical right and then punish people who deviate from it." To protect people from autocratic rule, Chomsky defends freedom of speech in its absolute sense and so Faurisson's right to argue that the Nazi gas chambers never existed. Chomsky resists any self-righteous commitment that would coerce another individual. At the same time, Chomsky's opposition to this danger becomes another self-righteous commitment.

By exclusively pursuing the rigor of fairness, does society achieve justice? Fairness recognizes all human needs, including the need for private happiness.

> If the pursuit of private happiness is not unjust, if it does not presuppose the use of other persons as mere means (which is an offense against the liberty of others), if it does not infringe the norm of rational equality (which is an offense against positive freedom), it has to be acknowledged and guaranteed in full. Put simply, neither the principle of justice, nor the principle of rational equality (positive freedom) applies to negative freedom, for an obvious reason. Human beings are unique, in this sense they are not equal, they cannot and must be equalized as far as the pursuit of happiness (the satisfaction of their multifarious needs) is concerned. The inequality, or, more precisely the uniqueness, of human beings is intrinsic in the very idea of negative freedom.[19]

The good of fairness is that it protects the private happiness of the individual. The sin of fairness is that it hopes both fatalistically and irresponsibly that this singular commitment does not violate the requirements of justice.

Liberalism argues that, in the modern world, justice and fairness are essentially the same. Liberalism does not recognize the weight of justice vis-à-vis the

---

[19]Heller and Fehér, *The Postmodern Condition*, 70–71.

pragmatic demands of fairness. For liberalism the demands of fairness supersede the principle of justice.[20] Against the principle of justice, Rawls writes, "[T]he aim of justice as fairness as a political conception is practical, and not metaphysical or epistemological." Rawls continues, "That is, it presents itself not as a conception of justice that is true, but one that can serve as a basis of informed and willing political agreement between citizens viewed as free and equal persons." Then, after making this point, Rawls warns, "The only alternative to a principle of toleration is the autocratic use of state power. Thus, justice as fairness deliberately stays on the surface, philosophically speaking."[21] What is it that makes fairness right? What is it that makes fairness more right than justice? According to Rawls, it is wrong to choose justice before fairness because the decision leads to "the autocratic use of state power." Choosing fairness lessens this possibility. As a liberal philosopher, Rawls does not recognize the authority in traditions grounded in one rational conception of the good. Fairness, in contrast, recognizes that "there are many conflicting and incommensurable conceptions of the good, each compatible with the full rationality of human persons."[22]

G. W. F. Hegel helps us comprehend the notion of self in the philosophy of liberalism:

> There is, therefore, in general, no ground for feeling elevated or for lamenting or repenting: all that sort of thing arises from a reflection which imagines another content and another inner nature than is to be found in the original nature of the individual and the actual carrying of it out in reality.[23]

On what grounds do we repent, lament, or feel elevated? Hegel asserts that it is not the original nature of the individual. Rawls reinforces this notion in a positive rather than negative way.

> We introduce an idea like that of the original position because there is no better way to elaborate a political conception of justice for the basic structure from the fundamental intuitive idea of society as a fair system of cooperation between citizens as free and equal persons.... The veil of ignorance, to mention one prominent feature of that position, has no metaphysical implications concerning

---

[20]Consider Prosecutor Louis Arbour's reported fear behind the indictment of Slobodan Milošević: "Arbour obviously took seriously rumours of recent weeks that Milošević was seeking a guarantee of immunity from international criminal prosecution—or even a 'golden exile' in South Africa or some other country—in exchange for his assent to a political solution for the current crises" (Mirko Klarin, "Arbour's Preemptive Strike," *Balkan Crises Report* 39 [May 29, 1999]).

[21]Rawls, "Justice as Fairness," 230.

[22]Rawls, "Justice as Fairness," 248.

[23]G. W. F. Hegel, *The Phenomenology of Mind*, trans. with an introduction and notes by J. B. Baillie (New York: Humanities Press, 1977), 435.

the nature of the self; it does not imply that the self is ontologically prior to the facts about persons that the parties are excluded knowing.[24]

Liberalism, as Hegel suggests, does not go beyond the original nature of an individual. It limits itself to the original position of an individual as the basis on which to surmise justice as fairness. As a matter of politically correct theorizing, liberalism does not imagine another content or another inner nature to be found in the individual, for example, a soul within the individual with an original nature. Another content or another inner nature, according to liberalism, cannot be found. By not imagining another content or another inner nature, the possibilities of repenting, lamenting, or feeling elated do not exist. The possibilities exist only as speculative states on the part of the individual whose ultimate foundation is nothing more or less than the individual's original nature.

For a comparable commentary on the concept of self in Rawls's liberalism, consider the following passage from Michael J. Sandel's *Liberalism and the Limits of Justice:*

> But in Rawls's moral epistemology, the scope for reflection would appear seriously limited. Self-knowledge seems not to be a possibility in the relevant sense, for the bounds it would define are taken as given in advance, unreflectively, once and for all, by a principle of antecedent individuation. But once these bounds are seen to fall away, there is nothing to take their place. For a subject such as Rawls the paradigmatic moral question is not 'Who am I?', for the answer to this question is regarded as self-evident, but rather 'What ends shall I choose?', and this is a question addressed to the will. Rawls's subject would thus appear epistemologically impoverished where the self is concerned, conceptually ill-equipped to engage in the sort of self-reflection capable of going beyond an attention to its preferences and desires to contemplate, and so to redescribe, the subject that contains them.[25]

To return to Hegel, the question "Who am I?" suggests that there is another content or another inner nature to be found in the individual than the individual's original nature. The question "What ends shall I choose?" suggests that the original nature of the individual is all there is to the individual.

Sociology on the whole takes for granted and promotes the notion of self in

[24]Rawls, "Justice as Fairness," 238.

[25]Michael J. Sandel, *Liberalism and the Limits of Justice* (Cambridge: Cambridge University Press, 1982), 153. To cite another example of Sandel's argument against Rawls on the nature of self, consider this passage: "Since for Rawls the faculty of self-reflection is limited to weighing the relative intensity of existing wants and desires, the deliberation it entails cannot inquire into the identity of the agent ('Who *am* I, really?') only into the feelings and sentiments of the agent ('What do I really *feel* like or most *prefer*?')," (Sandel, *Liberalism*, 159).

liberalism. Whether negatively or positively, sociology understands the self within the context of liberal ideology. To give just one example, consider the following passages from Erving Goffman's *The Presentation of Self in Everyday Life*.

> In their capacity as performers, individuals will be concerned with maintaining the impression that they are living up to the many standards by which they and their products are judged. Because these standards are so numerous and so pervasive, the individuals who are performers dwell more than we might think in a moral world. But, *qua* performers, individuals are concerned not with the moral issue of realizing these standards, but with the amoral issue of engineering a convincing impression that these standards are being realized.[26]

Then, to explain his notion of the deontological self, Goffman makes the following analogy.

> In analyzing the self then we are drawn from its possessor, from the person who will profit or lose most by it, for he and his body merely provide the peg on which something of collaborative manufacture will be hung for a time. And the means for producing and maintaining selves do not reside inside the peg; in fact these means are often bolted down in social establishments.[27]

The tension between fairness and justice and their competing ideas of self inform the discussion of people trying to make sense of the NATO bombing in Serbia as well as the unconscionable events by Serb militia in Kosovo. Consider the commonsense resistance that Max Boehnel gives Chomsky during their exchange: "Do you think that people are also affected by the interviews with refugees, including the people who were supposedly bombed by NATO by mistake, who say, well it was a tragedy of course but we don't care, tell NATO to keep on, we are with NATO, NATO's doing the right thing." At first, Chomsky deflects this question by replying, "There are many people around the world who think you ought to bomb Washington, that doesn't make it a wise course of action."[28]

Where, though, are the refugees coming from when they say that, while they are being killed not only by barbaric Serb forces but also by arbitary NATO bombing, the NATO bombing is the right thing to do? These comments are striking. How does Chomsky explain them? The NATO bombing, as Chomsky says, is unfair to the Albanians in Kosovo. The Albanians in Kosovo, however, know themselves that the NATO bombing is unfair to them. Still, they insist that the NATO bombing is the right thing to do. Why?

---

[26]Erving Goffman, *The Presentation of Self in Everyday Life* (Garden City, N.Y.: Doubleday Anchor Books, 1959), 251.

[27]Goffman, *Presentation of Self*, 253.

[28]Chomsky, "Print Interview, April 8."

Chomsky eventually gets around to addressing this challenging question and here is his answer:

> When you are a refugee, what you hate is the person who most immediately drove you out with a gun, of course. If people sitting in Toronto can't think through the fact that the US, Canadian, and British actions escalated the atrocities, predictably, how do you expect a refugee on the ground to think about it?[29]

The refugees, Chomsky reasons, hate the Serbs rather than NATO because of the promixity of the Serbs. Chomsky imagines that, if NATO were as near as the Serbs, the refugees would hate NATO as much as they hate the Serbs. Is hatred toward the people who drove you out of your homes with guns and sadistically murdered your family members the reason why Albanians believe that the NATO bombing is the right thing to do? Is revenge and malice all that guides the Albanians' opinion? Chomsky suggests that it is. For this reason he suggests that we dismiss the credibility of the refugees' opinion. He indicates that the people are not thinking and reasoning the way that he does and, since they are not, they are not really thinking.

The refugees, however, are thinking. They do not simply hate the people who drove them from their homes and murdered their family members and destroyed their communities. The refugees have been living under people who have controlled them with guns for some time. Natural right as an eye for an eye is not the notion that guides the refugees' belief that it is right for NATO to bomb. The refugees understand their situation and they understand that the NATO bombing is unfair to them.

The refugees, however, understand, in contrast to Chomsky, that justice is more important than fairness. This understanding reflects their thinking, and it is a thinking that is conspicuously absent in Chomsky's thinking. The refugees know that they cannot expect fairness until justice is achieved. The NATO bombing is not itself inherently just. It may become nothing more than a screen for the ethnic cleansing in Kosovo. The NATO bombing, however, could lead to justice. To expect fairness without respecting the demands of justice is not to think. Chomsky pities the refugees; he refuses to hear the refugees' account of their needs, that is, their need for justice rather than fairness. He does not consider the principle of justice and its implications for the limits of fairness. The refugees yearn for justice. Their yearning makes them both enlightened and realistic.

The refugees think clearly about their situation because they grasp the importance of justice. It is the complete lack of fairness in their situation that makes them recognize the requirement of justice. Their long-term deprivation puts them in what Rawls might call the original position. What Rawls says is true: there is no better way to surmise a conception of justice than from the orig-

[29]Chomsky, "Print Interview, April 8."

inal position. What the Albanians surmise from this position, however, is different from what Rawls anticipates. The experience of being denied fairness leads to a clearer recognition of the principle of justice, not the principle of justice as fairness. From the original position, the Albanians in Kosovo learn that justice as fairness is not viable.

It is not claimed here that NATO or Western leaders recognize the difference between fairness and justice. Nor is it claimed that Chomsky's critique of jingoistic nation-states acting indifferently to international law are ill-founded. It, however, is claimed that, by simply comparing specific instances of unfairness and measuring their degrees of unfairness, Chomsky negates the particularity of the situation in Kosovo as well as the particularity of other places in the world. Chomsky denies the particularity of the situation in Kosovo by ignoring its relation to what is universally true. If Kosovo is distinctive vis-à-vis other situations in the world, it is because Kosovo's exemplification of the distance between the principle of justice and social life is most striking. The reality of the problem is clearer in Kosovo than other places, which is not to deny the reality of the problem in other places.

A group of Albanian intellectuals posted a collective statement against the kind of antiwar discussion that Chomsky ferments.

> A propaganda war is going on in the international media about the reasonability of the NATO bombing against Serbia's military machine. The Serbian propaganda and a part of the western media are trying to present Serbia as the victim of aggression and NATO as the aggressor. They put forth the idea that the bombing has nothing to do with the protection of the expelled Albanians from Kosovo, but is part of the geostrategic aims of the imperialist western Alliance.[30]

This collective statement by a group of Albanian intellectuals summarizes the nature of Chomsky's argument. The group, however, replies in this way.

> It is also forgotten that before the start of NATO bombardments the Serbian military forces have realized a "scorched earth" policy including the systematic destruction of towns, plundering, expulsion of hundred thousands of Albanians. Also forgotten are the killings, pogroms, massacres, wrappings, masse deportations, destruction of documents and all signs of cultural and religious identity of Albanians. We, the deported Albanian intellectuals would, once again, want to protest against these propagandistic manipulations, which in essence provide an alibi to Serbia's genocidal policies. We want to tell world democratic opinion that we are, without any doubt, in favor of punishing Serbia. The Serbian military machine, which has caused all the wars in former Yugoslavia, should be

---

[30]Rexhep Ismajli, Ali Podrimja, Ali Aliu, Hivzi Islami, Ramiz Kelmendi, Shkeblzen Maliqi, Astrit Salihu, Kim Mehmeti, Mufail Limani, "An Appeal to World Opinion," May 14, 1999 *Bosnet Digest* 6, no. 1,252, <http: //www.bosnet.org>.

broken and annihilated by all means. We hope that the imminent defeat of the Serbian military forces will make possible the return of the deported people to Kosovo, the normalization of the life, and the creation of a milieu for development of a democratic system.[31]

The demand here is clear: justice first, then fairness. What is not an option is fairness first and then justice. If the latter option is pursued, it means justice never. And without justice there is never fairness.

What is it about liberalism and its passion for fairness that creates this tacit alliance with the Belgrade regime and provides alibis for the Serbian genocide in Bosnia and now Kosovo? Consider the assumptions behind Chomsky's proposed, ideal solution to the NATO bombing:

Well, there were three choices. One was to act in such a way as to escalate the atrocities, that's what was chosen. A second choice was do nothing. A third choice is to act as to mitigate the atrocities. Now if you can't think of any way to mitigate atrocities the best choice was to do nothing. Okay, was there any way to mitigate the atrocities? Well, I suppose there were diplomatic options that were open; the Serbian parliament passed a resolution on March 23rd, the day before the bombing, in which it said that they would not accept a NATO force (hardly surprising, Canada wouldn't accept a Warsaw pact force) but they proposed that there could be a move toward autonomy in Kosovo, and that after that, there should be an international force. Well, is that an acceptable offer? We don't know, because the US wouldn't even pay any attention to it. But pursuing that offer, through the mechanisms of world order such as the UN Security Council or neutral countries like India or others would certainly have been better than doing nothing and vastly better than acting to escalate the atrocities.[32]

Here the United States is unfair. The United States would not pay any attention to the constructive initiative of the Serbian parliament the day before the NATO bombing started. For Chomsky, the Serbian parliament represents the closest thing that Serbia has to a democratic institution. The United States was obliged to cooperate and heed the demands of fair play; the Serbian parliament, according to Chomsky, deserved to be listened to.

Why, according to Chomsky, is the United States not free to ignore the Serbian parliament? From a liberal point of view, cooperation is primary. Fairness recognizes that "there are many conflicting and incommensurable conceptions of the good, each compatible with the full rationality of human persons."[33] Given this understanding, it is wrong for the United States to assume that it has a monopoly on the conception of what is good and that the Serbian parliament necessarily

[31]Ismajli et al., "An Appeal."
[32]Chomsky, "Print Interview, April 8."
[33]Rawls, "Justice as Fairness," 248.

lacks such a conception. Fairness rejects the assumption that there is one rational conception of the good. For Chomsky, a commitment to the concept that there is one rational good is not only irrelevant in politics, but hypocritical, not only misleading, but obscene. In the moral philosophy of liberalism, fairness displaces the principle of justice.

In *Liberalism and the Limits of Justice* Sandel provides an incisive critique of Rawls's liberalism. His book, nevertheless, concludes in a disturbing manner. The conclusion demonstrates what Sandel means by the limit of justice and what it is that limits justice, that is, what it is that is better than justice. Sandel puts forth his alternative to Rawls's deontological ethic in which "we view ourselves as independent selves, independent in the sense that our identity is never tied to our aims and attachments."[34] Here, then, is Sandel's alternative:

> We cannot regard ourselves as independent in this way without great cost to those loyalties and convictions whose moral force consists partly in the fact that living by them is inseparable from understanding ourselves as the particular persons we are—as members of this family or community or nations or people, as bearers of this history, as sons and daughters of that revolution, as citizens of this republic. Allegiances such as these are more than values I happen to have or aims I "espouse at any given time." They go beyond obligations I voluntarily incur and the "natural duties" I owe to human beings as such. They allow that to some I owe more than justice requires or even permits, not by reason of agreements I have made but instead in virtue of those more or less enduring attachments and commitments which taken together partly define the person I am.[35]

What are these allegiances that demand that I owe more than justice "requires or even permits"? What are these allegiances that are more than values and go beyond obligations? What allegiances does the United States have to the Serbian parliament such that, in all fairness, it owes the Serbian parliament more than its duty to the Albanians in Kosovo? What are these allegiances that encourage ignoring the requirements of justice? Do these allegiances promote injustice?

To reinforce the unquestionable character of his argument on the limit of justice and to remove it from the realm of refutable exchange, Sandel then writes, "To imagine a person incapable of constitutive attachments such as these is not to conceive an ideally free and rational agent, but to imagine a person wholly without character, without moral depth."[36] Who wants to consider or take a position from which one could be accused of being wholly without character, without moral depth? Sandel intimidates the reader to accept his position or suffer condemnation. According to Sandel, the strength of a person's constitutive attachments, whether they be familial, social, nationalistic, or ideological, stand against

---

[34]Sandel, *Liberalism*, 179.
[35]Sandel, *Liberalism*, 179.
[36]Sandel, *Liberalism*, 179.

the requirements of justice, and to question this notion is tantamount to moral idiocy. According to Sandel, historical traditions surpass the categorical imperative of justice and become themselves the categorical imperative that displaces the imperative of morality. In the end, Sandel's theorizing shirks the weight of justice as much as Rawls's. In the end, Sandel's moral rhetoric is disturbingly analogous to Serbian nationalism, something the Kosovar Albanians understand all too well.

Chapter 12

On the Injustice of Postmodernism: Peter Handke in Serbia

But justice as a value is neither outmoded nor suspect. We must thus arrive at an idea and practice of justice that is not linked to that of consensus...any consensus on the rule defining a game and the "moves" playable within it *must* be local, in other words, agreed on by its present players and subject to eventual cancellation.

—Jean-Francois Lyotard
The Postmodern Condition: A Report on Knowledge

WHEN ADDRESSING THE significance of postmodernism, for purposes of clarity and understanding, it is helpful to keep in mind that the founders of postmodernism—Michel Foucault, Jean-Francois Lyotard, and Jacques Derrida—are all admirers of the ancient Sophists. Foucault, for instance, identifies positively with Callicles in the *Gorgias* and Thrasymachus in the *Republic*. He resents the "reassuring dialectic" that Socrates employs to refute his ancient friends, and it is as if Foucault believed that, if he were himself to encounter Socrates or someone like him, he, unlike his ancient friends, would remain firm in his defense of sophistry and antipathy toward Platonic philosophy. Postmodernism is the serious revival and unabashed celebration of the Sophist's overturning of philosophy.

With the publication of *A Journey to the Rivers: Justice for Serbia*, Peter Handke exemplifies the postmodern perspective within the context of Bosnia.[1] Shortly before the

---

[1] For positive and critical discussions of this approach in this context, see Zsuzsa Baross, "On the Ethics of Writing, after 'Bosnia': The Revenant," *International Studies in Philosophy* 30 (1997): 1–17 and David Campbell *National Deconstruction: Violence, Identity, and Justice in Bosnia* (Minneapolis: University of Minnesota Press, 1998).

signing of the Dayton Peace Accord, Handke traveled to Belgrade and drove to the Drina River, thirty kilometers from the Srebrenica enclave, where five months earlier the Bosnian Serb army and the Yugoslav People's Army methodically massacred approximately eight thousand men and sadistically abused women and children in a United Nations declared safe haven.

Why does Handke travel to Serbia and record his reflections on its people?

> It was principally because of the war that I wanted to go to Serbia, into the country of the so-called aggressors.... Nearly all the photographs and reports of the last four years came from one side of the fronts or borders. When they occasionally came from the other side they seemed to me increasingly to be simply mirroring of the usual coordinated perspectives—distorted reflections in the very cells of our eyes and not eyewitness accounts. I felt the need to go behind the mirror; I felt the need to travel into the Serbia that became, with every article, every commentary, every analysis, less recognizable and more worthy of study, more worthy, simply of being seen.[2]

Handke opposes what he perceives to be the one-sided news coverage of the violence in Bosnia. The more analysis and commentary there is about Serbia, the less understood Serbia is. Most news coverage, Handke believes, simply bears witness against the people of Serbia. To counter this tendency, Handke wants to bear witness on behalf of the people of Serbia. According to Handke, Serbia deserves to be seen or, more correctly, "simply, to be seen."

What, though, do we get behind this mirror where journalistic representations no longer disfigure our vision? Handke makes this observation:

> And on Serbian state television that farewell scene of President Milošović, immediately prior to his departure for the peace talks in Dayton, Ohio: walking down a long line of military and civilian people on the runway and hugging each one long and hard, the whole time visible only from the back—the departing man for long minutes only as a picture from the back.[3]

When Handke watches Milošović depart for Dayton, Ohio, what does he see? More importantly, what do the people of Serbia see? Does Handke believe that the people of Serbia "simply" see?

At its best, Handke's narrative takes pictures. As few words as possible are connected with these pictures. As little discourse as necessary frames the photographs and their significance. Whatever meanings are connected to the images appear random. The notion of arbitrariness holds together the photograph and what it signifies. Walking on the Serbian bank of the Drina, Handke asks, "Was I being observed from the opposite bank? Nothing moved there in the ruins, or was

---

[2]Peter Handke, *A Journey to the Rivers: Justice for Serbia* (New York: Viking, 1997), 2.
[3]Handke, *Journey*, 37.

it an unfinished building?"[4] What do we see? Perhaps a destroyed building; perhaps an unfinished house. Who knows? Concretely speaking, who can say? With the empirical logic of probability, Handke protects the people of Serbia from the metaphysical certitude of Western journalists. Meaning is conditional. There are no absolutes, no necessary significance behind a picture. With the knife of deconstruction, Handke cuts free the people of Serbia from the ropes of moral indignation. Such is the mantle of anti-righteousness that Handke, the postmodern prophet, dons.[5]

Simulation

According to Handke, the problem with most accounts of the violence in Bosnia is that they are constructions disfigured by moral perspectives, and, according to Handke, these accounts of the violence in Bosnia are unconnected to the actuality of events.

> Who can tell me I am mistaken or even malicious when, looking at the picture of the unrestrainedly crying face of a woman in close-up behind the bars of a prison camp, I see also the obedient following of directions given by the photographer of the international press agency outside the camp fence; and even in the way the woman clings to the wire I see something suggested by the picture merchant?[6]

In a way, Handke is right. The relationship between a photograph and its meaning, an image and its significance, a signifier and its signified, is never absolute or impregnable; like any discursive relationship, the photograph of the unrestrained crying face of a woman and its meaning is subject to doubt. When one claims to be an eyewitness, however, one's perceptions seem to be more natural than social; one's perceptions seem to eschew moral construction and social judgment.

Handke wants to teach his readers that there is never an authentic relationship between an image and its significance except the randomness of its construction. There is never an essential, compelling, or integral relationship between a sign and its significance. The relationship is always contrived, never

[4]Handke, *Journey,* 37–38.

[5]Here is how Campbell describes this work: "Deconstruction is a form of 'projectional interpretation' that 'proceeds by projecting ontological presumptions explicitly into detailed interpretations of actuality, acknowledging that its implicit projections surely exceed its explicit formulation of them and that its explicit formulation—constructed relative to other identifiable positions—always exceeds its current capacity to demonstrate its truth" (Campbell, *National Deconstruction,* 23).

[6]Handke, *Journey,* 20–21.

authentic. Here is the postmodern truth that Handke heralds.[7] Here is the notion of intelligibility, which, according to Handke, is true not only for others' but also for his own representations. Handke's advantage is simply that he embraces the postmodern epistemology that insists upon the randomness of what we assume we understand and disavows any principled character of discourse.

Consider Handke's conduct as reported in the news media at the public lectures following the publication of his book: "He adjusts his glasses, peers at the audience, and with nary a word of introduction, embarks on a 90-minute reading from his new book"; "In Frankfurt, a survivor of the concentration camp at Omarska asked to speak, and Handke angrily stormed out of the hall"; "In Vienna.... when an individual in the hall rose to observe that Handke had never been in the war zone, whereas he, the speaker, had visited Sarajevo twenty times, Handke interrupted him: 'Then drive there for the twenty-first time, asshole!'"; and, finally, "When the man who translated six of Handke's books into Slovenian protested in an open letter that Handke was twisting the facts, Handke denied that the man was his translator."[8] Where is Handke coming from? An aphorism on the Nazi era and the pathos of modern warfare from Walter Benjamin helps us locate the foundation of Handke's narrative and public behavior: "All efforts to render politics aesthetic culminate in one thing: war."[9]

One journalist who covered the war for *Der Spiegel* and who is a target of Handke's derision is Peter Schneider. Handke writes, "But what was my generation's response to Yugoslavia,...I know...mechanical scribbling, infatuated with images of enemies and war, collaborating instead of wall jumping, by the author Peter Schneider."[10] Handke sees Schneider's writing collaborating with the Bosnian side; Handke sees Schneider insist upon a Manichean frame of reference, which creates misleading and moralistic dichotomies; in contrast, Handke sees himself wall jumping. Such are the calisthenics of a postmodern prophet.

Schneider, in his own review of Handke's book for the *New Republic*, says, "I am not complaining that Handke is seeking to understand the Serbs, that he is demanding a more accurate view of them. When he forsakes the vanity of the heroic dissenter, when he is animated by a genuine curiosity about the landscape

---

[7]Jean Baudrillard describes this truth in the following way: "So it is with simulation, insofar as it is opposed to representation. Representation starts from the principle that the sign and the real are equivalent (even if this equivalence is Utopian, it is a fundamental axiom). Conversely, simulation starts from the Utopia of this principle of equivalence, *from the radical negation of the sign as value*, from the sign as reversion and death sentence of every reference" (Jean Baudrillard, *Jean Baudrillard: Selected Writings*, ed. with an introduction by Mark Poster [Stanford, Calif.: Stanford University Press, 1988], 170).

[8]Peter Schneider, "A Writer Takes a Hike," *New Republic* (March 3, 1997): 34–38.

[9]Walter Benjamin, "The Work of Art in the Age of Mechanical Reproduction," *Illuminations* (New York: Harcourt Brace and Co., 1968), 243–44.

[10]Handke, *Journey,* 80–81.

and the 'people of Cain,' Handke's book is an attempt to build a bridge between enemies. But he dynamites his own bridge with his tirades, with his groundless, sweeping suspicions of all the critics of the Serbs."[11] Handke wants to understand the Serbian people in an unfiltered way; he takes exception to authors who are unwilling to understand Serbs on their own terms, who fail "simply, to see" the people in Serbia. We understand Handke's motive. We comprehend the conditions that provoke his action and the situation that centers it. What we, however, need to consider carefully is the normative orientation that makes sense of the author, his motive, his conditions, and his situation, that is, the value commitment that holds these elements of his action together as a meaningful course of action.[12]

According to Handke, to understand the people of Serbia, one needs to become like the people of Serbia:

> And how would I, as a Serb in Croatia, have related to such a state, established as an enemy to me and my people? Would I have emigrated "home" over the Danube to Serbia, although perhaps deeply bound to the place, in part by generations of ancestors? Perhaps. Would I, even if suddenly a second-class citizen, even if a coerced citizen of Croatia, have remained in the country, reluctantly to be sure, sad, full of gallows humor, but in the service of precious peace? Perhaps. Or, had it been in my power, would I have taken up arms—naturally, only with many others of my peers and, in an emergency, even with the help of a disintegrating, aimless Yugoslavian army? Probably, or, if I were, as such a Serb, halfway young and without a family of my own, almost certainly.[13]

Handke imagines himself as a Serb. He simulates what, according to him, it means to be a Serb. Notice the escalating and final content of each progression: "Would I have taken up arms...if I were, as such a Serb, halfway young and without a family of my own, almost certainly. And wasn't that how the war began, as is well known, with the marching of the first Croatian state militia into the Serbian villages around Vukovar?"[14] What would Handke have done during the war in Bosnia, and why would he have done it?

If Handke bears witness on behalf of the people of Serbia, how does he do so? What is the self-consciousness Handke ascribes to the Serbian people?

---

[11]Schneider, "A Writer," 36.

[12]For a discussion of the action frame of reference and its importance to social understanding, see either Kenneth Burke, "The Nature of Human Action," in *On Symbols and Society,* ed. with an introduction by Joseph Gusfield (Chicago: University of Chicago Press, 1989), 53–55 or Talcott Parsons, *The Structure of Social Action: A Study in Social Theory with Special Reference to a Group of Recent European Writers* (New York: Free Press, 1968), 43–51.

[13]Handke, *Journey,* 16.

[14]Handke, *Journey,* 16.

Handke's particular mirroring of the Serbian self-consciousness resonates with the barbarian's rejection of the stranger. There is, Georg Simmel argues, a positive meaning in the expression, "the stranger." The stranger is a member of the group itself. The stranger is simultaneously familiar and remote, near and far, close and estranged. The expression "the stranger" indicates how differences are preserved and not encompassed, cherished and not collapsed in the culture of modern societies.

The barbarian, though, is intolerant of the stranger. Simmel writes on this matter.

> The relation of the Greeks to the barbarians is a typical example; so are all the cases in which the general characteristics one takes as peculiarly and merely human are disallowed to the other. But here the expression "the stranger" no longer has any positive meaning. The relation with him is a non-relation.[15]

To the stranger, the barbarian says, "We cannot live together." For the barbarian, there is no relation to the stranger. When, moreover, the stranger, culturally and historically, is a member of the group, the barbarian's rejection of the stranger is violent. The more the stranger is a familiar member of the group, the more violent the barbarian's rejection. The barbarian disallows the stranger "the general characteristics one takes as peculiarly and merely human."[16]

Let us take an example directly from Handke's writing, "How, my immediate thought had been, is that ever supposed to end well, the high-handed establishment of a state by a single people—if the Serbo-Croatian-speaking Muslim descendants of Serbs in Bosnia are in fact a people—in a region to which two other peoples have a right, and the same right!" Handke's conditional phrase, "If the Serbo-Croatian-speaking Muslim descendants of Serbs in Bosnia are in fact a people," rejects the particular cultural identity of Bosniaks and denies the history of Bosnians in general. Handke negates the historical notion that Bosniaks as well as Bosnians are distinctive. It is true that the history of Bosnians is intertwined with the history of Serbs, but it is also true that the history of Bosnians is independent of the Serbs. For example, Adrian Hastings points out that only after the modern establishment of the Patriarchate of Belgrade did Orthodox Bosnians begin to see themselves as Bosnian Serbs.[17] Under Turkish rule, the Orthodox Church was more favored in Bosnia than the Catholic Church; the Orthodox Church grew while the Catholic Church declined. Before the establishment of the Patriarchate of Belgrade, Bosnian Serbs did not think of themselves as Serbs; they thought of themselves as Orthodox Bosnians. Not only Bosniaks or Bosnian

---

[15]Georg Simmel, "The Stranger," in *The Sociology of Georg Simmel* (Glencoe, Ill.: Free Press, 1950), 407.

[16]Simmel, "The Stranger," 407.

[17]Adrian Hastings, *SOS Bosnia,* 3d ed. (Leeds: Margaret Fenton Ltd., 1994).

Muslims but also Bosnian Serbs have a distinct history from the Serbs in Serbia.

Notice the loose, loose logic that undergirds Handke's statement, "If the Serbo-Croatian-speaking Muslim descendants of Serbs in Bosnia are in fact a people."[18] On the one hand, if Bosniaks are distinct from Serbs, they have no relation to Serbs. On the other hand, if Bosniaks are not distinct from Serbs, they are the same as Serbs. They are derivative and do not exist as Bosniaks. Here is the disingenuous rationalization that animated Serb propaganda and guided their genocidal activities in Bosnia. Not only does Handke simply hear; he also simply echoes.

How does Handke's travelogue help us understand what happened in the former Yugoslavia? Taking another enigmatic picture, Handke writes the following:

> In the main hall of the bus station, the destination board, as large as a monumental painting. Here the Cyrillic letters I had grown accustomed to felt like calligraphy: [Srebrenica] and under it, at the end [Žepa]. This tremendous and seemingly ancient board, however, was no longer valid. The current timetable had been pasted over a corner, a tiny, formlessly lettered piece of paper, and there were, for the two last-named places as well as others, no more departures.[19]

From the barbarian point of view, this lonely destination board in the main hall of the bus station is no longer valid. Strangers who were members of the society formerly called Yugoslavia (the Serbo-Croatian-speaking Muslims who lived in Srebrenica and Tuzla) have been assaulted and unjustly rejected. They have been either driven out of their homes with unconscionable terror or sadistically murdered. How ancient, however, is this destination board? What culture, what values, and what normative orientation within a community does this tremendous and seemingly ancient monumental-like painting represent? Handke takes pictures; he takes pictures randomly and indifferently, feeding parasitically off the interior meaning of the images that his prosaic camera captures indifferently.

The Drina

There is, however, one image in Handke's travelogue whose significance is not arbitrary, and this image is the Drina. The Drina becomes the guiding trope in Handke's narrative.

> And I squatted down there, which made the river stretch a little wider, nothing now from the tips of my Serbian winter shoes to the Bosnian bank except the

---

[18]Handke, *Journey*, 18.
[19]Handke, *Journey*, 71–72.

water of the Drina, smoky cold.... Downriver, perhaps fewer than thirty kilometers, began, apparently, the region of the Srebrenica enclave. A child's sandal broke the surface at my feet.[20]

What now links Handke's Serbian winter boots with the Bosnian shore? Nothing. Nothing except the cold water of the Drina. Handke is not, as Schneider naively suggests, trying to build a bridge between enemies. If Handke were, standing there on the Serbian side of the Drina is where he would begin to build such a bridge. "A child's sandal broke the surface at my feet." Why didn't Handke pick up the sandal? Why didn't he ask where the sandal came from? Where is the child now? Handke allows the image to float by him and sink into the smoky, dark waters of indefinite possibilities.

For one brief moment, Handke crossed a bridge over the Drina from Serbia to Bosnia. Before quietly turning back, here is what he reports: "The border guard with the eyes of a sniper—or wasn't it rather a kind of incurable, inaccessible sadness? Only a god could have relieved him of it, and in my eyes the empty, dark Drina flowed past as such a god, if a completely powerless one."[21] In Handke's narrative, the Drina is an image whose significance is not arbitrary. The Drina is Hanke's ineffable muse from whom he discovers no foundation upon which to build a bridge between Bosnia and Serbia. This is the political point of his book. For Handke, the Drina represents a postmodern god, a living, metaphysical, bottomless, impotent chasm, over whose waters it is impossible to build a bridge between Bosnia and Serbia. Even postmodern prophets lapse into grand metanarratives, grand narratives whose import is totalizing and oppressive. Handke is human; he, too, needs order, a limit.

Handke admires the self-consciousness of the Serbian people, and he believes that the Serbian people live closer to reality than any other people. Today, the Serbian nation lives in a Hobbesian jungle where the randomness of force and fraud and the inconsistency of untempered self-interest are the normative orientations guiding society. Yes, an order exists in Serbia, but it is simply a factual order. It is not a normative order, and this fact is the normative order. Talcott Parsons explains this paradox and the problem it presents in the following way: "Thus a social order is always a factual order in so far as it is susceptible of scientific analysis but, as will be later maintained, it is one which cannot have stability without the effective functioning of certain normative elements."[22] How long can the people of Serbia sustain themselves and their community without the effective functioning of certain normative elements? Are sociologists taking up this question that challenges the root of their discipline? Serbia has become an experiment of postmodern social theory.

[20]Handke, *Journey,* 73.
[21]Handke, *Journey,* 60.
[22]Parsons, *Structure of Action,* 92.

What normative element, what principle of justice, does Handke see himself bring to the people of Serbia? Is it the justice they need? Handke recounts a truly striking event in Belgrade, and his narration of it shows the degree to which he is riveted to his simulation.

> A kind of panel discussion was now supposed to take place about general conditions, about the Bosnian war, about the Bosnian Serbia, Serbian Serbia role in the war. For a long time we sat in near silence, edgy, at a loss, with a huge bottle of Frascati, and an ancient one at that.... And then gradually, as a matter of course, the subject changed to contemporary Yugoslavia. One man in the room finally literally screamed at how guilty the Serbia leaders were for the present suffering of their people, from the oppression of the Albanians in Kosovo to the thoughtless recognition of the Krajina Republic. It was an outcry, not an expression of opinion, not simply an oppositional voice from a cultural gathering in a dark room.[23]

Handke has trouble tolerating this stranger, who, in fact, is a Serb. When the man speaks, Handke hears a scream expressing no opinion. Handke hears an animal rather than a human.

For Handke, if conditions are such that to speak one can only speak like a voiceless animal, the decision that preserves one's humanity is silence. This man failed Handke's criteria of what would preserve his humanity. Why? "And this Serb spoke only about his own leaders; the war dogs elsewhere were spared, as if their deeds themselves screamed to heaven, or to somewhere else."[24] For Handke, the man's words (no matter how valid and compelling) carry no weight because they are only about Serbian leaders and not about other war dogs. Here is the logic behind Handke's critique: one must first speak negatively of "them" before one can speak positively about "us." Loyalty must first be demonstrated, and loyalty is demonstrated by speaking negatively about "them" and never about "us." Handke's account itself displays this rule of loyalty.

In Handke's report, we hear of a voice that resists. From a moral point of view, this event is heartening. We are not interested in the self-consciousness of the Serbian people, however cosmopolitan it may or may not be; we are interested in their conscience. The reason Handke finds the Serbian people "overly self-conscious" is because the gap between their self-consciousness and conscience is great. For Handke, the Drina now symbolizes the void seperating the self-consciousness and conscience of the Serbian people. "Only a god could have relieved him of it, and in my eyes the empty, dark Drina flowed past as such a god, if a completely powerless one."[25]

---

[23]Handke, *Journey*, 48–49.
[24]Handke, *Journey*, 50.
[25]Handke, *Journey*, 60.

Handke rejects the man who speaks up; Handke rejects as well the part of himself which identifies with this man:

> Strange, however: although in this man's presence I finally lost my sense that anything was official or calculated about the situation—rather than making statements, he suffered, angrily and transparently—I did not want to hear his damnation of his leaders; not here, in this space, nor in the city or the country; and not now, when a peace was perhaps in the works, after a war that had been started and finally probably decided with the help of foreign, utterly different powers. (That he then hugged me as we parted was, I thought there, because he felt understood, and I ask myself now whether his motivation wasn't rather that he hadn't.)[26]

This man abandons the role of voiceless barbarian, but Handke suffocates him with the nationalistic rhetoric from which the man himself wishes to escape. Handke disallows the man "the general characteristics one takes as peculiarly and merely human." Instead, Handke returns the man to the void from within which the man objects to having been placed. In this interaction, Handke refuses to see an authentic human being living in an inauthentic society. Instead, Handke stipulates the barbarian line of reasoning: the Serbian leaders are not the ones who started the war; the war was started by foreign powers, foreign powers which are "utterly different," in other words, non-Serbian.

Recovering Justice

It is important now not to treat Handke in the same way that he treats the man who speaks up. It is important to hear Handke as best as we can. What version of justice does Handke promote? What version of justice does he shun? Handke asks the critical question:

> Didn't my generation fail to grow up during the wars in Yugoslavia?... In what way?... What was my generation's response to Yugoslavia, in the case that was for us ... of earth-shattering importance ... from those of my approximate age, I know ... Peter Schneider, arguing for the intervention of NATO against the criminal Bosno-Serbs.... To grow up, to do justice to, to not only embody a reaction to the century's night and thus add to the darkening, but to break out of this night.[27]

For Handke justice, not only embodies a reaction to the century's night, but also breaks out of the century's night. According to Handke, a NATO intervention against the criminal Bosno-Serbs would just be a reaction to the century's night; it would only add to the darkening. To do justice to the criminal Bosno-Serbs

[26]Handke, *Journey,* 50.
[27]Handke, *Journey,* 80–81.

begets an action that is another use of force and equal in kind to the force against which it reacts, equally criminal. For Handke, to do justice to the criminal Bosno-Serbs is not grown-up. Handke equates justice on behalf of the thousands and thousands of victims in Bosnia and now Kosovo with unjust consequences for the criminal Bosno-Serb. For Handke, bringing justice to bear on the criminal Bosno-Serbs only adds to the darkening of the century's night; it does not bring light to the thousands and thousands of victims. Nor does it, for Handke, bring light to the criminal Bosno-Serbs.

Handke denies the Platonic notion that justice for the victims of wrong-doers is also justice for the wrong-doers. In the *Gorgias*, Socrates clearly identifies the logic that Handke rebuffs.

> SOCRATES: Will a man who does wrong be happy if he is brought to justice and punished?
>
> POLUS: On the contrary, he will then be most miserable.
>
> SOCRATES: But, by your account, if he isn't brought to justice he will be happy?
>
> POLUS: Yes.
>
> SOCRATES: On the other hand, Polus, my opinion is that the wicked man and the doer of wicked acts is miserable in any case, but more miserable if he does not pay the penalty and suffer punishment for his crimes, and less miserable if he does pay the penalty and suffer punishment in this world.
>
> POLUS: What an extraordinary proposition to maintain, Socrates.[28]

Is doing justice to the criminal Bosno-Serbs advantageous only to their victims? Does it only bring light to the victims of injustice? According to Socrates, bringing justice to bear on doers of wicked acts is advantageous to doers of wicked acts. It brings the light of fairness and human dignity not only to the thousands and thousands of victims in Bosnia and Kosovo but also to their victimizers. This and only this creates the possiblity of social reintegration. Tragically, Bosnians wait for this necessary development.

Handke suggests that bringing justice to bear on the criminal Bosno-Serbs would bring unjust consequences for the criminal Bosno-Serbs. To accept such reasoning, one must believe, with Polus, that bringing justice to bear on wicked men makes wicked men miserable and unhappy. To promote such reasoning, one must believe, with Polus, that the doers of wicked acts who escape penalty remain happy. One must believe, moreover, that the greater the injustice of the

---

[28]Plato, *Gorgias,* trans. Walter Hamilton (Middlesex, England: Penguin, 1960), 59.

wrongdoer, the greater the misery the wrongdoer will experience if brought to justice. Therefore, those responsible for acts of genocide would experience the greatest misery imaginable if brought to justice. This logic grounds the apparent sympathy in the actions of European and American political leaders toward the criminal Bosno-Serbs who remain free. European and American political leaders anticipate the pain that the criminal Bosno-Serbs will feel upon being brought to justice. The message in the behavior of European and American political leaders is that the pain that the criminal Bosno-Serbs would feel upon being brought to justice would equal if not exceed the suffering their horrid crimes brought to thousands and thousands of human beings. Why, European and American political leaders reason, perpetuate the cycle of pain? Someone has to stop the cycle; the victims need to forget what happened.

Here is how European and American political leaders display their sense of goodwill toward the situation in Bosnia. European and American political leaders think that they do not have the right to make a human being feel as miserable and unhappy as the criminal Bosno-Serbs will feel upon being brought to justice. European and American political leaders imply that it would be inappropriate on their part to bring the criminal Bosno-Serbs to justice.

The apparent sympathy that European and American political leaders show the criminal Bosno-Serbs is ill-founded. Their sympathy displays moral ignorance. For one thing, it collapses the distinction between pleasure and good. European and American political leaders assume that whatever is painful is bad and that whatever is not painful is good. Since the criminal Bosno-Serbs would experience tremendous pain upon being brought to justice for their crimes against humanity, bringing them to justice would be bad. It is difficult for American and European political leaders to imagine a pain greater than being brought to justice for crimes against humanity and acts of genocide.

Socrates makes the exact opposite argument. Socrates argues that it is hard to imagine a pain greater than not being brought to justice for one's crimes against humanity and acts of genocide. The Serbian soldiers leaving Kosovo and returning to Serbia after their war crimes are more unhappy than their victims, which is not to deny the profound unhappiness of their victims. For Socrates it is hard to imagine a pain greater than not being brought to justice for ordering the rape and murder of thousands and thousands of human beings, who were neighbors, friends, and relatives. It is unconscionable, Socrates argues, to leave human beings in such a state of despair. Socrates cannot imagine that any rational human being would do such a thing to another human being, and yet this is exactly what European and American leaders are doing to the Bosno-Serb criminals. Why, then, do American and European political leaders do what Socrates finds most unconscionable?[29]

[29]Consider President Clinton's moral ambivalence on arresting Milošević: "Even though I strongly support the decision of the War Crimes Tribunal—or the prosecutor, Mrs. Arbour, too, to make the charges she did, I think it's important that we not in any way

The actions of American and European political leaders are based on their deference to Slobodan Milošević and his successful but ultimately self-defeating representation of natural right. In Plato's *Gorgias*, Callicles says to Socrates, "I tell you frankly that natural good and right consist in this, that the man who is going to live as a man ought should encourage his appetites to be as strong as possible instead of repressing them, and be able by means of his courage and intelligence to satisfy them in all their intensity by providing them with whatever they happen to desire."[30] From the perspective of natural right, it is baser to suffer wrong than to do wrong. It is baser to be murdered than to murder; it is baser to be raped than to be a rapist. From the perspective of natural right, before suffering wrong, it is smarter to do wrong to the person from whom one anticipates wrongdoing.

Again, Socrates argues the opposite point of view. Moral understanding is simple. It is not esoteric. Moral understanding is the recognition that it is baser to do wrong than to suffer wrong. It is baser to be a murderer than to be murdered; it is baser to be a rapist than to be raped. The recognition that it is baser to do wrong than to suffer wrong establishes a normative order rather than a factual order. Sarajevo, as a community, exemplified this recognition throughout the war.

Tragically, the attitudes of European and American political leaders toward the genocide in Bosnia seem to mirror the logic of the criminals. European and

---

mislead people about what happens next. Our heaviest responsibility, the NATO allies, is to get the Kosovars back home in safety, and then to give them self-government, autonomy, and rebuilding assistance, and then work on the region. Under the rules that we have followed, any of us, if we had jurisdiction over Mr. Milošević, would turn him over, or anyone else who had been charged, just as we do in Bosnia. If he remains inside the confines of Serbia, presumably he's beyond the reach of the extradition powers of the other governments. But sometimes these things take a good while to bear fruit. I think we'll just have to wait and see how that develops.... But I do not believe that the NATO allies can invade Belgrade to try to deliver the indictment, if you will. And I don't think we should be—that does not mean that this is not an important thing, or that there won't someday be a trial, but we need to focus on our obligations, our fundamental humanitarian obligations to get the Kosovars home and to continue to uncover whatever evidence of war crimes there is in Kosovo as well" (Bill Clinton cited on Saturday 19, 1999, *Bosnet Digest* 99, no. 32). This dichotomy between "our fundamental obligations" to the Kosovars and the moral duty to apprehend Milošević is specious and self-contradictory. Practically speaking, Clinton's position is self-defeating. Our fundamental duty is to apprehend Milošević. Morally speaking, Clinton's self-interest moves him to engage in sophistry and act in bad faith. While he says that it is important not to mislead people in any way, he profoundly misleads people.

[30]Callicles to Socrates in Plato, *Gorgias*, 90.

American political leaders act as if it is baser to suffer wrong than to do wrong. When American and European political leaders model this reasoning, they identify themselves with the unjust acts of the criminal Bosno-Serbs and they also ask the world to identify with these acts. They ask the world to abandon the normative orientation and moral understanding of their communities and adapt the factual order of natural right.

What would have been a mature response "on the part of our generation to Yugoslavia"? Handke asks the critical question, but he does not answer it. A mature response recognizes the need of the Serbian people to reduce the gap between their self-consciousness and their conscience. What triggered the grotesque and immense violence in 1999 against Albanians in Kosovo? The gap between their self-cosciousness and their conscience of the Serbian people triggered the war. Events in Kosovo are a cry of pain on the part of the Serbian people as well as the Albanian people, although the reason for the Serbian cry of pain is quite different. The Serbian people cannot do what they must do to become a community; they cannot bring justice to bear upon themselves. The violence in Kosovo is the only way that the Serbian people know how to force American and European political leaders to do for the Serbian people what the Serbian people can no longer do for themselves. Tragically, American and European leaders do not get the message.

A mature response intervenes in Kosovo not only on behalf of the thousands and thousand of victims in Bosnia and Kosovo, but also on behalf of the Bosnian Serbs and Serbian Serbs guilty of genocide and crimes against humanity. "Neither the man who establishes a dictatorship by crime nor the man who is punished for attempting to do so can ever be described as the happier; you can't compare the happiness of two people who are both miserable. But the man who gets away with it and becomes a dictator is the more miserable. What's this, Polus? Laughing?"[31]   ·

---

[31]Plato, *Gorgias*, 61.

Chapter 13

Against the Positivistic-Utilitarian Understanding of Bosnia

For unless one has transcended the positivistic framework, even a consciousness of the abstractness of the theory does not open up any new *theoretical* possibilities.

—Talcott Parsons
The Structure of Social Action

THIS CHAPTER EXAMINES the positivistic-utilitarian understanding of events in Bosnia as a preliminary discussion to the concluding chapter. The work of Robert M. Hayden is a clear and articulate example of this perspective. In particular, I discuss the position that Hayden puts forth on April 3–6, 1996, in his keynote address at the Peace-Making and Peace Enforcement: Beyond the Iron Curtain mini-conference at University of Missouri-Columbia. While the discussion focuses primarily on Hayden's keynote address, the position that he articulates is repeated in his published writing on Bosnia. Hayden's work presents the positivistic-utilitarian perspective clearly and strongly.[1]

Hayden starts his lecture in a rhetorically effective fashion. First, he notes

[1]The lecture, "War and Peace in Bosnia: Peace Agreements and Peace Enforcement," was given in the Gannett Auditorium at the University of Missouri School of Journalism on April 4, 1996, the day after Secretary of Commerce Brown was killed in a plane crash in Croatia. The conference was organized by Robin Remington in the Political Science Department at the University of Missouri-Columbia, and sponsored by several departments and colleges at the University of Missouri-Columbia as well as several departments and organizations at other universities.

that many pundits say that "the wars in former Yugoslavia have been in some way irrational and that it has been difficult to understand how something like this could happen in contemporary Europe." He then says, "I don't think that it is hard to understand the wars in Yugoslavia at all actually." Hayden does not make this assertion for simply rhetorical reasons. He continues, "I think that the logics involved and the politics involved have been fairly simple to understand."[2]

What are the assumptions upon which Hayden makes this assertion? First, Hayden articulates what he sees as a tempting but false assumption. "The premise of the former Yugoslavia," he said, "was that all these peoples were so closely related that they could co-exist and that they lived so intermingled that they had to co-exist." Hayden notes, "Empirically, both of these parts of the equation were quite true." Why do the parts of the equation no longer add up? What renders this empirically true equation false?[3]

I will summarize the answer that Hayden provides. Hayden introduces the concept of the nation-state, which, he says, is often misunderstood by North Americans because the concept has a particular meaning within the context of European history. North Americans interchange the terms nation and state. In Europe, the terms have distinct meanings. In order for a state to have a stable configuration (one in which "democracy is safe"), it is first necessary to establish a nation. Nation, Hayden said, refers to ethnic group. Historically, the nation, Hayden says, "gets the state, the territory, the government." This concept, Hayden says, is the standard European model, and "it works."[4]

The major problem in Bosnia, Hayden continues, is that there is no ethnic majority that could be said to constitute a nation upon which to build a state. According to Hayden, it is ignorance on the part of the European Community and the United States to recognize Bosnia-Herzegovina as an independent state. Bosnia, he says, is "a legal fiction." "It does not exist on the ground."[5] It is impossible to declare Bosnia a state because there is not one nation upon which to establish the state.

When discussing a map showing the ethnic composition of Bosnia before the war, Hayden notes, as others have, that "It is like a leopard's skin, wherever you tear it, it is going to bleed. The logic of the situation was that it was going to be torn. The map needed to be rationalized, homogenized. That was what the war was all about." Here, in a nutshell, according to Hayden, are the logics and politics that guided the war in Bosnia.[6]

What frame of reference supports this understanding of the war in Bosnia?

---

[2]Robert Hayden, "War and Peace in Bosnia: Peace Agreements and Peace Enforcement," Peace Studies, University of Missouri-Columbia (1996), Videocassette.

[3]Hayden, "War and Peace in Bosnia."

[4]Hayden, "War and Peace in Bosnia."

[5]Hayden, "War and Peace in Bosnia."

[6]Hayden, "War and Peace in Bosnia."

As a sociologist, I would characterize Hayden's account as representative of the positivistic-utilitarian system of social thought. The end of the war in Bosnia was to establish a nation upon which to build a stable state. The means to achieve this end was called ethnic cleansing. The choice of this means was rational, from a political point of view, given the conditions, in that it was the most efficient means available, "it worked." Speaking of Thomas Hobbes and his conception of human nature, Talcott Parsons writes, "Man is not devoid of reason. But reason is essentially a servant of the passions—it is the faculty of devising ways and means to secure what one desires. Desires are random, there is 'no common rule of good and evil to be taken from the nature of the objects themselves.'"[7] Given the positivistic-utilitarian understanding of social action, the wars, according to Hayden, reflect a rational process.

At this point, I have different choices on how to proceed. One choice is to draw attention, as I already have, to several exceptional books—*Bosnia and Herzegovina: A Tradition Betrayed*, *Bosnia: A Short History*, and *Twisted Politics: Readings of History and Community Relationships in Bosnia*—and point out that these books argue quite persuasively that to understand Bosnia authentically, it is necessary to understand that there is a culture, tradition, and history (that is, a nation based on more than ethnic affiliation) that serves as a basis for a sustainable state.

Hayden, however, would counter this position with competing examples and note that, when given the choice, Bosnian Croats and Bosnian Serbs chose to live in a state in which their ethnic group constituted not simply a plurality but an immense majority. When given the choice, Bosnian Croats and Bosnian Serbs chose to live in a place where they would be the immense majority. This choice is rational. Given the notion that might is right, it makes sense to live where one can be on the side of might. People do what is necessary to survive.

There are, though, notable exceptions to this generalization. In the TV documentary based on Laura Silber and Allan Little's book, *Yugoslavia: Death of a Nation*, we observe Bogić Bogićević, a Bosnian Serb, who was Bosnia-Herzegovina's representative on the Yugoslav federal presidency in 1991, resist the pressure on him at an emergency session of the federal presidency, to vote with the Serbs. Bogićević does not put himself on the side of the majority. Bogićević instead voted on behalf of Yugoslavia, which was a state at that time, as well as on behalf of Bosnia, which was a multi-national Republic. It was a heroic moment. What logic influences Bogićević's action to resist the pressure to align himself with the Serbian power elite? Was Bogićević irrational?

Consider also the leadership of Jovan Divjak, the general deputy commander of the Bosnian government army. Divjak defended Sarajevo against the national-

---

[7]Talcott Parsons, *The Structure of Social Action: A Study in Social Theory with Special Reference to a Group of Recent Eurpean Writers* (New York: Free Press, 1968), 89.

ist Serbs during the long siege. Popular and well-respected, Divjak is a Serb, or Bosnian Serb, whose orders Bosniaks followed and respected. What social logic governs Divjak's actions?

Comparing and contrasting different facts and discussing their significance, however, may not be the best way to examine Hayden's position. Such a discussion would seesaw back and forth with different examples of each position. A second choice is to bring to bear the compelling critiques of the positivistic-utilitarian perspective upon which Hayden's account relies. There are two notable examples of this critique in the social science literature. In *The Structure of Social Action*, Parsons's theorizing surpasses the assumptions of the positivistic-utilitarian theory of social action. Utilitarianism has been an important tradition in sociology, but Parsons shows how the perspective is inadequate for explaining social action for both theoretical and empirical reaons.[8]

It is possible as well to draw upon the critique that the legal theorist Ronald Dworkin makes of utilitarianism and its hegemonic influence in jurisprudence. In *Taking Rights Seriously,* Dworkin exposes the conceptual problems of the utilitarian perspective within the tradition of legal theory; he makes a strong case for the principle of human rights, an idea the utilitarian philosopher Jeremy Bentham called "nonsense on stilts." Rather than question the facts upon which Hayden's position draws, it is possible to question the theory that he uses to explain these facts.

I think, though, that the best way to proceed is to explicate the issues that arise in Hayden's writing. From a positivistic-utilitarian perspective, Hayden successfully explains the reason for the war in Bosnia, but overall his presentation is quite enigmatic. After his lecture, Hayden takes questions and the first questioner asks about people from mixed marriages. Hayden repeats the question, "What is that person who is the product of intermarriage?" He then says, "Probably, if lucky, an emigre" [Laughter is heard from members of the audience]. Hayden continues, "Because there is no place where you belong. If you are not a Croat, you do not belong in Croatia, if you are not a Slovene, you do not belong in Slovenia, if you are not a Serb, you do not belong in Serbia. It is not wise to call yourself a Yugoslav.... And there are people who knew this when the 1991 census was taken.... Now, if you are now engaged in a mixed marriage, you will choose an identity for your child and try very hard to hide the other identity. That is what you do."[9]

No matter how descriptively accurate, these comments are disheartening. They contrast sharply with the thoughtful reflections of Aleš Debeljak in *Twilight*

---

[8]"It will be maintained, and the attempt made in considerable detail to prove, that *in this sense all of the versions of positivistic social thought constitute untenable positions*, for both empirical and methodological reasons [Parsons's italics]" (Parsons, *Structure*, 125).

[9]Hayden, "War and Peace in Bosnia."

of the Idols: Recollections of a Lost Yugoslavia on what it means to be a Yugoslav. Indeed, Hayden himself contradicts the sentiment in his answer when responding to a subsequent question. He said that "In 1989–90 the majority of Yugoslavs everywhere in Yugoslavia were in favor of maintaining Yugoslavia together." "That option," Professor Hayden continued, "should have been preserved."[10] If Yugoslavs were comfortable with their identity as Yugoslavs in 1989–90 and if Yugoslavs constituted a political majority, why are they now pariahs? What happened? Even in his own writing, Hayden says, "As late as May 1990, much of the population of Bosnia and Herzegovina did not share the sentiments of the nationalist parities and viewed the formation of such parities as dangerous."[11]

Hayden articulates one answer grounded in the positivistic-utilitarian tradition. He observes that "The more well-integrated people are the more violence is required to separate them."[12] Given how closely integrated Bosnians were, much violence was required to seperate them. Hayden notes as well that it was politics from outside these areas that initiated the violence that separated the people. For instance, Serbs from outside Bosnia killed, not only non-Serbs, but also Bosnian Serbs who did not cooperate with or support the policy of ethnic cleansing. These dynamics were common, Hayden adds.

The question now is no longer whether the relation between the means and the ends is rational. Given the rational norm of efficiency, one can say that, following the positivistic-utilitarian perspective, there is a rational relation between the means and the end. Violence was an efficient means to a desired end. Nobody has trouble understanding this point. Note, however, that the ends stand independently of a common rule of good and evil. Thus, the question is whether the end, the end of creating a nation-state, say, a Greater Serbia or a Greater Croatia, is justifiable. If it is not justifiable, it cannot serve as a basis for stability, and Parsons explains why: "What may be called value ideas are, on the contrary, of the greatest importance to the understanding of social equilibrium."[13]

Hayden himself insists that "All this stuff about these people always hating each other is nonsense. It really is nonsense. When permitted to live together, they did so fairly successfully."[14] Is it possible to reconcile Hayden's own positive report on Bosnia's history with the utilitarian frame of reference embedded in his explanation?

At times, Hayden stipulates facts as if their utilitarian logic were unbreakable. For example, Hayden says, "You cannot reconstruct Bosnia without recon-

[10]Hayden, "War and Peace in Bosnia."

[11]Robert Hayden, "The Partition of Bosnia and Herzegovina, 1990–1993," *Radio Free Europe/Radio Liberty Research Paper* 2, no. 22 (May 28, 1993): 3.

[12]Hayden, "War and Peace in Bosnia."

[13]Parsons, *Structure of Action*, 277.

[14]Hayden, "War and Peace in Bosnia."

structing the former Yugoslavia, and you cannot reconstruct the former Yugoslavia." For Hayden, the statement is a truism. What does it mean, though, to stipulate that, "You cannot reconstruct Bosnia without reconstructing the former Yugoslavia, and you cannot reconstruct the former Yugoslavia"?[15]

It is helpful to compare Hayden's comment with one made by Ivo Banac. Banac says, "I view Bosnia as primarily a functioning society which Yugoslavia never was. My question is how does one keep a complicated, complex entity like Bosnia-Herzegovina together? Undoubtedly the answer presupposes an interest in the maintenance of Bosnia-Herzegovina by its neighbors."[16] Notice the contrast. For Hayden, Yugoslavia is a model for the Republics of Yugoslavia. If Yugoslavia dies, it is necessary for the rest of Yugoslavia to die. For Banac, Bosnia is a model for the rest of Yugoslavia. If Yugoslavia dies, why must Bosnia also die? Why must Bosnia sacrifice itself if Bosnia itself represents the reality from which Yugoslavia drew its inspiration?

Notice the egocentric logic of the child here—if I cannot have it, neither can you. Or, in this context, if the newly formed Yugoslavia cannot have Bosnia, Bosnia cannot have itself. Banac explains the problem in this perspective:

> If Bosnia were a collectivity of separate entities, then it would have been a mini-Yugoslavia. But it is not that. Bosnia is a historical entity which has its own identity and its own history. In other words it is not a Yugoslavia: it cannot be construed to be a mini-Yugoslavia. There is a temptation to do this precisely by people who seek to divide it. The argument goes more or less the way you put it: Yugoslavia disintegrated as a multinational state and so must multinational Bosnia. This is basically a Serbian argument.[17]

The sociologically compelling question at this point is what made Bosnia, according to both Hayden and Banac, "primarily a functioning society"? The answer lies in Parsons's critique of the positivistic-utilitarian understanding of social order: "There has been, on the whole, a common standard of rationality and, equally important, the absence of any other 'positive' conception of a normative element governing the means-end relationship."[18] In Hayden's account, the standard of rationality dominates. Equally important, there is an absence of any other positive conception of a normative element governing the means-end relationship. What would a positive conception of a normative element governing the means-end relationship look like? Was it present in Bosnia? Is this "posi-

---

[15]Hayden, "War and Peace in Bosnia."

[16]Ivo Banac, "Separating History from Myth: An Interview with Ivo Banac," in *Why Bosnia? Writings on the Balkan War*, Rabia Ali and Lawrence Lifshultz, eds. (Stony Creek, Conn.: Pamphleteer's Press, 1993), 139.

[17]Banac, "Separating History from Myth," 138–39.

[18]Parsons, *Structure of Action*, 59.

tive conception of a normative element governing the means-end relationship" what made Bosnia primarily a functioning society in a way that Yugoslavia never was?

Recall Hayden's observation: "As late as May 1990, much of the population of Bosnia and Herzegovina did not share the sentiments of the nationalist parities and viewed the formation of such parities as dangerous."[19] What were the sentiments, the collective sentiments of "much of the population of Bosnia and Herzegovina," such that this sentiment found the leaders of the nationalist parties to be dangerous? How was the normative orientation of "much of the population of Bosnia and Herzegovina" qualitatively different from the normative orientation of the leaders of the nationalist parties? What was the moral substance of this normative orientation that distinguished itself from the nationalist political parties?

What has happened in Bosnia is that, in the interest of creating a nation, a functional society was killed. It was not just genocide—it was sociocide. The question now is whether a nation can expect to become a functional society when the manner in which the nation established itself destroyed the state as well as the nation that preceded it and upon which it, too, depended. Can a nation expect to establish itself if the principle upon which the nation stakes its legitimacy is a principle of apartheid based upon the murder of a community? Sociologically, we know the answer to this question; historically, we are waiting to witness the answer.

A central argument in the positivistic-utilitarian perspective is that social scientists cannot provide accounts of events and, at the same time, reference moral or metaphysical arguments. This restriction is a feature of the positivistic-utilitarian tradition upon which Hayden's reasoning depends. My position, which is not unscientific, is that, unless reference to the values in the normative orientations is made, the values expressed in these normative orientations are left unexamined. Our understanding of society remains deficient. Moreover, it becomes impossible to distinguish the viewpoint of the scientific observer from the viewpoint of the actors being observed, in this case, the actors engaged in ethnic cleansing.

Hayden argues that it is now impossible for people from different ethnic groups, that is, Bosnian Serbs, Bosnian Croats, and Bosnian Muslims, to live together given the nationalist practices of the political parties. Not only has partition happened, but it had to happen. For this reason, Hayden says that it is a tempting but false assumption to believe that much of the population in Bosnia and Herzegovina could still live together.

The sociological question, however, still stands: What was the normative orientation of "much of the population" such that much of the population did coexist? What were the shared values and common understandings that provided

[19]Hayden, "The Partition," 3.

a foundation for coexistence among people from different ethnic groups? What has happened to this collective sentiment that Hayden himself observed? Is it correct to say that it no longer exists? Is it wishful thinking on the part of nationalist leaders and their intelligentsia to assert that these common understandings no longer exist? Are the normative orientations of much of the population that found the nationalist parties to be dangerous no longer present? Unless the moral beliefs that undergird the collective sentiment of much of the population are explicated and examined, it becomes impossible to distinguish the viewpoint of the scientific observer from the viewpoint of the actors being observed. If the scientific observer and the social actors simply share the positivistic-utilitarian perspective, the scientific observer can only be a mouthpiece for the social actors.

As critical social scientists, our task is to explain the normative orientation of the collective sentiment and to examine whether it is true that this normative orientation has been destroyed. The work of social scientists is different from the work of natural scientists. To explicate the difference, it helps to mention Kenneth Burke's three guiding principles for the study of symbolic action.

> (1) There can be no action without motion—that is, even the "symbolic action" of pure thought requires corresponding motions of the brain. (2) There can be motion without action. (For instance, the motions of the tides, of sunlight, of growth and decay.) (3) Action is not reducible to terms of motion. For instance, the "essence" or "meaning" of a sentence is not reducible to its sheer physical existence as sounds in the air or marks on the page, although material motions of some sort are necessary for the production, transmission, and reception of the sentence.[20]

To apply these points to the subject at hand, there has been a lot of motion in Bosnia and a lot of motion in response to the motions in Bosnia. Here is what natural scientists account for. There has also been a lot of action in Bosnia and a lot of action in response to the actions in Bosnia. Here is what social scientists account for. What is called for today is an account of the actions in Bosnia. Actions are not reducible to terms of motion. Can a nation that created itself through acts of genocide become a stable state? Social scientists address the sentiments that make action not only meaningful but also stable.

At times, Hayden himself steps outside the positivistic-utilitarian account of social action to explain events pertaining to Bosnia. He, too, explains events as if they were not reducible to terms of motion. For example, Hayden's argument against the Dayton Accord is grounded in the perception that the manner in which the Dayton Accord was constructed reflects a crude understanding of

---

[20]Kenneth Burke, *On Symbols and Society*, ed. with an introduction by Joseph R. Gusfield (Chicago: University of Chicago Press, 1989), 53–54.

social structure. In "Focus: Constitutionalism and Nationalism in the Balkans," Hayden makes the following point:

> The Dayton Constitution...gives priority to human rights. Yet these are meaningless. As James Madison notes in 1787, "In framing a government...the great difficulty lies in this: you must first enable the government to control the governed; and in the next place oblige it to control itself."[21]

This citation from Madison is problematic but helpful. First, how does a government control the governed? One way in which the government controls the governed is through the use of force and fraud. Hobbes even says that it is rational for the government to use force. The government qua government uses force for one reason and one reason alone—to protect the governed from using force and fraud against themselves. For this reason, the governed accept the government's use of force.

Madison, however, indicates that a government is not truly a government if the only thing that it does is control the governed. If all the government does is control the governed, no matter how efficiently and effectively, it is not a government. If a government maintains a factual order by homogenizing a population through the use of murder, rape, and coercion and does so with impunity, it is not a government. Madison says that the government is also obliged to control itself. When the only thing that a government does is control the governed, say, through fear and terror, the government is out of control. Such a government can only use increasingly sophisticated forms of force and fraud, and this road, as events in Kosovo make clear, is the road to hell.

What, then, obliges a government to control itself? The U.S. State Department officials and European leaders seem to think that the threat of sanctions can oblige a government to control itself. A government will control itself when a force greater than itself insists that it control itself. A government will control itself when it is no longer rational from a utilitarian perspective to fail to control itself. Airstrikes and sanctions are geared to force a government to act rationally by creating conditions that force a government to see what is against its self-interest. This approach is based on an uncritical acceptance of the positivistic-utilitarian understanding of social order. It assumes that a government is obliged to control itself for extrinsic rather than intrinsic reasons.

What, though, truly obliges a government to control itself? Is it really the threat of an external force greater than the government itself? What happens when this threat no longer exists? There is only one way to oblige a government to control itself. When a government gives priority to human rights, the government is obliged to control itself. Giving priority to human rights is tantamount to

---

[21]Robert Hayden, "Focus: Constitutionalism and Nationalism in the Balkans" *East European Constitutional Review* (fall 1995): 68.

the government controlling itself.[22] What else besides a commitment to human rights obliges a government to control itself as it controls the governed? What else besides a commitment to human rights wins the consent of the governed to be governed, to be controlled, by the government? Human rights are a positive conception of a normative element governing the means-end relationship that stands independently of the common standard of rationality.

Hayden points out how Madison identifies what is essential to the framing of a government. The Dayton Accord is flawed insofar as it sees the task of framing a government as a utilitarian rather than principled exercise. If the Dayton Accord gives lip service to the idea of human rights, then there are self-defeating contradictions within the Dayton Accord. Human rights are meaningful because they are the foundation upon which to establish a state. The self-defeating contradictions of the framers of the Dayton Accord undermined their intention.

Human rights are meaningful in and of themselves and human rights are required for social stability. They are a required ingredient to the establishment of a viable state. The best, the most efficient, and so ultimately the most rational way for a government to control the governed is to demonstrate respect for human rights. Human rights oblige a government to control itself. Respecting human rights wins the consent of the governed to be controlled by what controls the government. Hayden's dissatisfaction with the Dayton Accord and his reference to Madison are based on his own perception of the inadequacies of the positivistic-utilitarian understanding of social action. In the concluding chapter, we will complete the argument on this matter.

[22]See Ronald Dworkin, *Taking Rights Seriously* (Cambridge: Harvard University Press, 1977).

Chapter 14

Justice and Peace before Utilitarianism

But, the evil observed, what is its cause and what can be its remedy?

—Emile Durkheim
The Division of Labor in Society

ON JULY 11, 1995, on PBS Evening News, the U.S. secretary of state Warren Christopher was interviewed as Srebrenica was falling to the invasion of the Serbian army. At one point the secretary of state said, "So for the time being in a situation where the parties apparently still are not ready to solve the matter themselves, I think that the UN presence is the best of the available alternatives."[1] What is Christopher saying, and why is he saying it at this time? He is saying that for him to change his behavior toward the injustices occurring in Bosnia, the parties first must be ready to solve the matter themselves. Until this point is reached, the United States is unwilling to do any more than it already is. What, though, will make the parties ready to solve the matter themselves? How will this come about?[2]

Christopher believes that, after experiencing enough pain, the parties will

[1] Warren Christopher interviewed by Jim Lehrer, Public Broadcasting Evening News (July 11, 1995).

[2] "To define the war as a tribal feud or a civil war is simply an easy way of dismissing the whole thing. The argument then is that if something has been going on forever, presumably, it will continue forever and hence nothing need be done to alleviate the situation. The best thing to do, therefore, is simply to sit back and watch as this hellish situation plays itself out.... It all adds up to...intellectual laziness" (Ivo Banac, "Separating History from Myth: An Interview with Ivo Banac," in *Why Bosnia: Writings on the Balkan War,* Rabia Ali and Lawrence Lifschultz, eds. [Stony Creek, Conn.: Pamphleteer's Press, 1993], 136).

begin to do what he expects, namely, solve the matter themselves. Christopher's opinions are governed by his understanding of the Hobbesian theory of social order. In the eyes of Christopher, Bosnia is a Hobbesian jungle. In Bosnia, it is every man and woman for himself and herself. Force and fraud are the two cardinal virtues. Life is short, nasty, and brutish.

Christopher reasons that, after experiencing this kind of life for a sufficient length of time, the parties will be ready to solve the matter themselves. The parties will be willing to sit down and talk, that is, to form a social contract. They will make agreements that they can count on.

Christopher's belief is that only the establishment of a social contract can stop the violence in Bosnia. After creating a social contract, the parties, in the interest of a longer and more peaceful life, will suspend their use of force and fraud against each other. "I would have to say, Jim [Lehrer], after having worked on this problem for two and a half years, until the parties get ready to resolve it, it probably won't be resolved."[3]

There is no more or less willingness among people in Bosnia to solve the matter themselves than there is in any other place in the world where there is conflict. Think of the talks over the federal budget between President Clinton and the Republican-led Congress. References to the conflict in Bosnia as a unique place where tribal hatreds reign are specious, to say the least.[4]

Christopher's comments on the PBS Evening News are meant to save face. Erving Goffman openly acknowledges that Hobbes' understanding of social order is the basis for his analysis of face-work. The light of reason that Hobbes assumes will arise out of the Hobbesian jungle, and that Christopher believes will arise out of Bosnia, is represented, Goffman says, in the individual's willingness and ability to take on the chores and duties of face-work. Goffman writes of this matter:

> A person's performance of face-work...represents his willingness to abide by the ground rules of social interaction. Here is the hallmark of his socialization as an interactant. If he and the others were not socialized in this way, interaction in most societies and most situations would be a much more hazardous thing for feelings and faces.[5]

There is something amiss, however, in the Hobbesian understanding of social order, whether it appears in the reasoning of world leaders or the inquiry of

---

[3]Christopher, PBS, 1995.

[4]"There is no sane reason," Ivo Banac observes, "to believe that in this particular corner of the world there is some sort of special concentration of hate. Human beings are human beings everywhere" (Banac, "Separating History from Myth," 164).

[5]Erving Goffman, *Interaction Ritual: Essays on Face-to-Face Behavior* (New York: Pantheon Books, 1967), 31.

sociology. While it is possible to turn to the work of Talcott Parsons at this point, it is better to stay with this context and work out Parsons's points in terms of this context.[6]

What would it take for the Bosnian government to get ready to resolve this matter themselves in diplomatic talks with the nationalist Serbs? (Notice Christopher's reductionism when he equates the Republic of Bosnia and Herzegovia, which fights for an open, pluralistic society and a rights-based government, with the nationalist Serb party, now recognized by the Dayton Accord as the Republika Srpska, which stands for an ethnically cleansed community and legally sanctioned apartheid state.) Must the Bosnian government accept the right of nationalist Serbs to maim, rape, degrade, and murder its citizens with impunity? Must the Bosnian government accept the power of the Bosnian Serb army in collusion with the Yugoslav National Army, to deny its people the right to live, either because its people are non-Serbs or because its people are Serbs who chose not to live in a fascist state?

At first glance, Christopher's reasoning is Hobbesian. After experiencing enough pain, the parties will be ready to solve the matter themselves. Thus, Christopher chooses to wait until this point is reached, no matter how bad it gets. Christopher's reasoning, however, is more Darwinian than it is Hobbesian, and the Darwinian part, while latent, is the more powerful. Like his European counterparts at this time, especially in Britain and France, Christopher is upholding the notion that the strongest prevail, the principle that spurs on the nationalist Serbs.

In *The Division of Labor in Society* Émile Durkheim writes on the problem of social order.

> To be sure, the strongest succeed in completely demolishing the weakest, or in subordinating them. But if the conquered, for a time, must suffer subordination under compulsion, they do not consent to it, and consequently this cannot constitute a stable equilibrium. Truces, arrived at after violence, are never anything but provisional, and satisfy no one. Human passions stop only before a moral power they respect. If all authority of this kind is wanting, the law of the strongest prevails, and latent or active, the state of war is necessarily chronic.[7]

Durkheim's writing provides an apt critique of the Dayton peace agreement. At Dayton, the parties were never ready to solve the matter themselves; they were, however, ready to let the United States solve it. Durkheim says that a "truce," basically what Hobbes means by the social contract, lacks the weight required to

---

[6]Talcott Parsons, *The Structure of Social Action: A Study in Social Theory with Special Reference to a Group of Recent European Writers* (New York: Free Press, 1968).

[7]Émile Durkheim, *The Division of Labor in Society,* trans. George Simpson (New York: Free Press, 1964), 2–3.

counter the law that the strongest prevail. A truce qua social contract lacks the power to command respect and win agreement. Human passions do not willingly defer to a truce, which is not to say that there is nothing to which human passions defer.

Impartiality is not itself a moral position, despite the pretense of UN officials that it is. Impartiality is simply what Goffman would call a front, a dramaturgical performance of bogus and hypocritical fairness. While impartiality sometimes carries weight and status with respect to the achievement of objectivity in scientific inquiry, the UN's impartiality has never commanded respect nor established significant limits.

Western leaders did not want to lift the arms embargo against former Yugoslavia, and Western leaders rely upon the Hobbesian understanding of social order to justify their decision. What is needed in Bosnia, Western leaders argue, is not more force (there is enough force already), but more reason. Reason will be exemplified in the willingness of the parties to establish a social contract, a social contract that limits the use of force and fraud for the safety of all. Lifting the arms embargo, Western leaders reasoned, would hinder this development. It would prevent the light of reason from arising out of the Hobbesian jungle. Lifting the arms embargo would lead to more fighting and even worse atrocities. It would empower the Bosnian army and enable it to match, if not defeat, the Serb army. The same reasoning was used in discussions of whether to arm the Kosovo Liberation Army fighting the Serbian forces in Kosovo. But more fighting and worse atrocities continued in Bosnia and in Kosovo.

There is a flaw with this argument of Western leaders, even in terms of its own frame of reference. The Hobbesian solution, which comes so highly and exclusively recommended, works only if there is an equality among the participants, when, as Hobbes says, no one, given the fragility of human nature, is capable of overpowering another for any sustained length of time. In the state of nature, given the equality of human beings in terms of power and cunning, people surmise that their situation is senseless. People reason that nobody is going to win and everybody is going to lose. Human reason prevails, and a peaceful society is established. The social contract is created.

The situation in Bosnia, however, is different. As long as there is a significant power imbalance and one party believes itself to be invincible, it is thoughtless (to say the least) to argue that the strongest will establish an agreement with the weaker or that the weaker will trust whatever agreement it is forced to make with the stronger. The situation in Bosnia is unnatural, and the arms embargo ensures that the situation remains unnatural. As long as the arms embargo holds, the Hobbesian solution cannot take hold.

"No one," Saul D. Alinksy says, "can negotiate without the power to compel negotiation."[8] (In the Hobbesian jungle, what compels negotiation is that nobody can compel negotiation, which means all can compel negotiation.) Given the lack of military arms vis-à-vis the Serbian army, the Bosnian government cannot compel serious negotiation with the nationalist Serbs on any issue. The Bosnian government depends upon the UN, NATO, or the United States to compel negotiation.[9] Western leaders, however, exercise this power only sporadically and only when it suits their interests rather than the interests of the Bosnian government. For instance, to justify the deployment of NATO troops in Bosnia, Western leaders argue that the deployment is required to hold NATO together and preserve NATO's integrity. What, though, about holding the Republic of Bosnia and Herzegovina together and preserving its integrity?

The times Western leaders are most willing to employ their power to compel negotiation are when the Bosnian government itself is on the verge of realizing this power for itself, for instance, when, in August 1995 its military forces threatened Banja Luka, the Serbian stronghold in Western Bosnia, or when, given the advice of the U.S. international lawyer Francis Boyle, its government considered filing lawsuits at the World Court against UN Security Council members for abetting genocide.[10]

Frequently, the Bosnian government is subject to double-standards. Paradoxically, the fairer the Bosnian government is toward its citizens as well as its enemies, the more abused the Bosnian government is. Likewise, the more unfair the nationalist Serbs are toward non-Serbs as well as Serbs, the more admired the nationalist Serbs are for their audacity. This treatment by Western leaders pressures the Bosnian government in that, to be treated fairly, it is as if the Bosnian government must be morally pure. It is remarkable that the Bosnian government has acted with as much probity as it has. For instance, the corruption and nepotism in the current government are criticized as if they were tantamount to the genocidal practices of the nationalist Serbs.[11]

The assertion by Western leaders that the Hobbesian solution (and only the

---

[8]Saul D. Alinsky, *Rules for Radicals*, excerpted in William A. Gamson's *SIMSOC: Simulated Society, Participants Manual with Selected Reading*, 4th ed. (New York: Free Press, 1991), 69.

[9]David Owen took advantage of this situation on behalf the Bosnian Serbs. His opportunism, however, did not succeed. The question now is whether the Dayton accord is any more or less opportunistic than Owen's work was, which could explain why Owen is envious of the Dayton accord.

[10]The same dynamic holds true in Kosovo. After a former Croatian general with considerable military experience was appointed commander of the KLA in the spring of 1999, it may have been only a matter of time before the KLA turned back the Serbian forces in Kosovo.

[11]"The United States has another reason to keep the Bosnians at arm's length: their

Hobbesian solution) must be given a chance justified the arms embargo. The lop-sided advantage of the nationalist Serbs, however, ensured that the nationalist Serb leaders never had to think in terms other than might is right. Experience taught the nationalist Serbs that, with respect to achieving their interests, force and fraud were very "efficient."[12] It is difficult to see why the nationalist Serbs would even begin to consider abandoning these methods given the gains they reaped.

"Universal human nature," Goffman writes, "is not a very human thing. By acquiring it, the person becomes a kind of construct, built up not from inner psychic propensities but from moral rules that are impressed upon him from without."[13] With this statement, Goffman shows his acceptance of the Hobbesian understanding of human nature. Why should nationalist Serbs take on these "moral rules which are impressed upon them from without" if they do not have to? The nationalist Serbs are rational. It would be irrational for them to adapt a Hobbesian logic when the Darwinian logic remains to their advantage. For instance, while negotiations were taking place in Dayton (and a cease-fire was in effect), the Bosnian Serb army in Banja Luka was refurbished and resupplied by the Serbian federal army in Belgrade, which Milošević (who was in Dayton) controls.[14]

The vainglory of the nationalist Serbs is that they are both stronger and more cunning than the UN and NATO together, who, logically, ought to be stronger and smarter given their size and strength. The Western press sensationalizes this perception, which helps nationalist Serbs save face. Nationalist Serbs wonder why U.S. diplomats insist that Bosnian Muslims and Bosnian Croats form a Federation as if the two groups have nothing in common except their need to be powerful vis-à-vis the nationalist Serbs. From the viewpoint of nationalist Serbs, the only authority of this Federation, as proposed by Western leaders, is sheer number. U.S. diplomacy simply reinforces the nationalist Serbs' own point of view. From the viewpoint of nationalist Serbs, their actions and U.S. diplomacy are the same in that both are committed to the same notion—might is right. This per-

---

Government is rife with corruption...a 'Balkan Tammany Hall'" (George Kenney, "If the U.S. Takes Sides," *New York Times* [December 12, 1995]).

[12]"Lying is a form of our patriotism and is evidence of our innate intelligence. We lie in a creative, imaginative, and inventive way" (Dobrica Ćosić, former president of self-styled Yugoslavia and a Member of Serb Academy of Arts and Sciences), <http://www.alb-net.com>.

[13]Goffman, *Interaction Ritual,* 45.

[14]"What Milošević has done," Ivo Banac observes, "and with greater effectiveness than many realize, is to demonstrate that there are no real restrictions on aggressive behavior" (Banac, "Seperating History from Myth," 150).

spective also informs the rationalization that nationalist Serbs give to explain their murders of non-Serbs—Serbs are afraid to live in a community in which they are not a majority.

Do Western leaders have to meet force with force, asocial behavior with asocial behavior, to change the situation? Clinically, the behavior of the nationalist Serbs can be described as "asocial" behavior. It can then be said that asocial behavior is untreatable because asocial behavior is incorrigible. Neither reason nor treatment changes asocial behavior. Only behavior that is itself asocial can "redirect" asocial behavior. The face-saving argument against military intervention in Bosnia is that military or forceful intervention is as "uncivilized" as the behavior it is meant to confront. To meet force with force means to enter the Hobbesian jungle and to be no different from the animals already in it. Whenever NATO bombs Serb military targets, nationalist Serbs play up this argument to their people and the media. While nationalist Serbs find the use of NATO military force abhorrent, they also identify with it and employ it for purposes of self-justification and self-confirmation.

In the *Structure of Social Action*, Parsons laments the innocence of the Hobbesian understanding of social order.

> There is nothing in the theory dealing with the relations of ends to each other, but only with the character of the means-end relationship.... For the failure to state anything positive about the relations of ends to each other can then have only one meaning—that there are no significant relations, that is, that ends are random in the statistical sense.[15]

To understand Bosnia in terms other than the theater analogy, it is necessary to locate what is absent in the Hobbesian understanding of social order. "There has been [in the Hobbesian account of social order]...a common standard of rationality and, equally important," Parsons adds, "the absence of any other *positive* conception of a normative element governing the means-end relationship."[16] Can we state something positive about the relations of ends to each other? What positive conception of a normative element governing the means-end relationship is there? In Goffman's dramaturgical account, ends are random. They are statistically related. Ends reflect the random self-interests of individuals. Parsons calls it atomism. Without a positive notion of the relations of ends to each other, it is impossible to oppose the exceptional dramaturgical behavior of the nationalist Serbs. The best Western leaders can do is match that behavior.

What is the Hobbesian social contract? For Hobbes, the social contract is the birth of the distinction between being obliged, for example, obeying at the point

[15]Parsons, *Structure of Action*, 56.
[16]Parsons, *Structure of Action*, 59.

of a gun, and being obligated, for example, complying out of deference to authority. According to Hobbes, authority is based on the notion that a group of people (a society) collectively accepts a rule as binding upon the group. Without this contract, life is short and brutish. Force and fraud are the only two virtues, that is, the only viable methods of achieving self-interest in social interaction. Since experience shows that, with respect to acheiving self-interest, force and fraud are very efficient, it is difficult to explain why, from a utilitarian point of view, these methods should no longer be employed.

Society is created when a collection of people recognizes that life becomes longer and more peaceful when they agree to suspend their use of force and fraud against each other and when this agreement is viewed as binding. This recognition lifts people out of the Hobbesian jungle, where interactions remain simply a matter of every man and woman for himself or herself. Hobbes theorizes that, when the limitless use of force and fraud becomes exceedingly painful, people recognize the superior rationality of the social contract. People recognize that the social contract is better with respect to attaining a longer life because it is more efficient than the unchecked use of force and fraud. What convinces people to accept the social contract? The answer that Hobbes gives is that the hellish experience of a war of all against all and our primal memory of this experience compel us to accept the superior rationality of the social contract. Social history is a record of forgetting and remembering this lesson, the ebb and flow of irrational and rational behavior.

An upshot of the social contract is that now society, the omnipotent Leviathan, uses force to secure its purpose, and the justification for this use of force is that it is an effective way of protecting people from each other's use of force. Society ensures order by employing the very device which, when employed by individuals, leads to disorder.

Notice the destabilizing feature of the utilitarian account: If an alternative were found that proved itself to be more efficient, it would only be rational to displace the social contract and adapt this more efficient alternative. For instance, what prevents an individual or group from employing the same means that the state employs? Is society's claim to an advantage vis-à-vis the individual that it is bigger in that it serves the self-interest of all rather than the self-interest of one? Is such a claim grounded in any other notion than that the strongest prevail? What is the difference between the self-interest of all, as an aggregate of isolated individuals, and the self-interest of one? In the utilitarian account, there is none. In the utilitarian account, the self-interest of all is not distinct from the self-interest of one except in terms of sheer number, that is, power.

In the utilitarian acount, society is a rational construct. For Parsons, this assumption is positive. The problem with the utilitarian account is that it is not sufficiently rational. Within Hobbes' idea of the social contract, society is conceived of as a means, a means to an end that is external to society itself. Society is a way to attain the adequate satisfaction of everyone's individual self-interest in peace and safety. This narrow perspective leads to sociocide.

Self-interest as the motivation of action is the cornerstone of utilitarianism, and Parsons does not reject this assumption. Parsons, however, rejects the narrow way in which utilitarianism formulates self-interest. "Departures from the rational norm have been described in such negatiave terms as 'irrational' and 'nonrational.'"[17] What would make the self-interest of all qualitatively different from the self-interest of one? What would make the self-interest of one and the self-interest of all indistinguishable? Parsons insists that there is a force greater than the social contract that governs the structure of society. What is this force? "What may be called value ideas are, on the contrary, of the greatest importance to the understanding of the social equilibrium."[18] "That men have this attitude of respect toward normative rules, rather than the calculating attitude, is, if true, an explanation of the existence of order."[19] Parsons argues that action, in the best sense of the term, is neither the pursuit of self-interest in the most efficient fashion within a given social context, nor the clever response of a group of human beings to their dominating and material conditions. Action exemplifies one's values as a social member of a community whose character is itself an essential part of one's own character. "Just as society cannot be said to exist in any concrete sense apart from the concrete individuals who make it up, so the concrete human individual whom we know cannot be accounted for in terms of 'individual' elements alone, but there is a social component of his personality."[20]

Plato helps. In the *Gorgias*, Socrates appears to lose face, as Goffman would say, when he takes a seemingly irrational or nonrational position, a position that belies his self-interest. The young sophist Polus laughs when he hears Socrates' "bottom line." Socrates says that the person who does wrong with impunity is more unhappy and more miserable than the person who does wrong and is justly punished. Polus (like nationalist Serbs) believes that the person who does wrong without being punished is the happier one, even happier than the righteous person. To Polus, Socrates' comments are "out of line," "unreal," "irrational."

Let us say Socrates' comment represents a parameter of morality that is relevant in every community albeit in specific ways. If so, Socrates' comment generates telltale points for Bosnia. Notice that Socrates' comment imagines a positive conception of a normative element governing the means-end relationship.[21] Socrates' comment surpasses the Hobbesian understanding of what governs the

---

[17]Parsons, *Structure*, 56.

[18]Parsons, *Structure*, 227.

[19]Parsons, *Structure*, 386.

[20]Parsons, *Structure*, 337.

[21]Richard McKim makes an interesting argument on this matter of how to read Plato. He says that Socrates' ability to refute the sophists has nothing at all to do with reason. "If we demand a logical proof that shameful acts are harmful to their agents, instead of

means-end relationships because it points to a foundation upon which the social contract commands respect, which is what limits as well as transforms human passions.

Intervention is necessary in Croatia, Bosnia, Kosovo, and Serbia not only for the sake of the victims of aggression but also for the sake of aggressors, murders, rapists, and thieves. Without intervention, the aggressors remain the most unhappy and most miserable people in the world.[22] Why else is the observing world so interested in these hidden lives? Why else is the media prevented from viewing these concealed regions? What are the consequences of sadistic actions for sadistic actors? When an individual, no longer cloaked in the "crowd" mentality of a paramilitary group, reflects and feels guilt, one possible consequence is suicide. Intervention is necessary to relieve the nationalist Serbs of their misery (a misery which they seem too proud to share but cannot avoid sharing). Relief for wrong actions comes only from being punished justly for wrong actions. The souls of the nationalist Serbs are ill, wretched with the disease of injustice, and justice, absolute justice, is the only medicine that can cure these souls.

This argument is not esoteric, nor is it archaic. In an interview cited by Anthony Lewis on November 20, 1995, in the *New York Times*, Judge Goldstone points out that "If individuals are not brought to book then there is collective guilt. The victims and their survivors cry out for justice against a group." To support his point, Goldstone adds that "I'm not sure the re-integration of Germany into Europe would have been achieved as it was if those trials [the Nuremberg trials of Nazi leaders after World War II] had not been held."[23] Unless justice is achieved, peace is impossible. Here is the anterior but abused idea in the Western official's comment on the Dayton Accord, discussed in chapter 1: "But there comes a time, when you have to choose between some absolute justice and moving forward in peace." No one can move forward in peace and simultaneously accept injustice as not requiring punishment. The comment reflects moral ignorance; it speaks of a time that has never and will never exist. This is a fact as

---

acknowledging, as Polus must in the end, that we feel them to be shameful because we already believe this, we lower ourselves in Plato's view to the level of sophistic debaters, refusing to admit what we really believe in order to 'win' the argument regardless of the truth," ("Shame and Truth in Plato's *Gorgias*" in *Platonic Writings, Platonic Readings,* ed. Charles L. Grisworld, Jr. [New York: Routledge, 1988], 48).

[22]"The military defeat of Serbia would be good not only for everybody who was subjected to Serbian aggression, but it would be good for Serbia too" (Banac, "Separating History from Myth," 162).

[23]Richard Goldstone cited in Anthony Lewis, "Abroad at Home: No Peace without Justice," *New York Times* (November 20, 1995): 15.

powerful as any fact of nature. Peace and justice are as interdependent in society as are life and light in nature.

The Western official's comment conceals not only how necessary but also how pragmatic it is to achieve justice. Justice is attained when it is achieved absolutely, that is, categorically. Goldstone observes, "I can't believe that many Serbs would condone the kinds of atrocities with which these men have been charged. The evidence, if it is upheld, shows that they are people who should not be leaders of any society." Few Serbs want to be forced at gun point to murder their non-Serb neighbors, whom they have lived with their entire lives and befriended.[24] It is both essential and pragmatic to achieve justice because it is necessary that justice governs Serbs as a collective. Serbs themselves realize that no justice is exemplified in the notion that might is right.

Catering to Milošević the way that U.S. diplomats do prevents the Serbs throughout former Yugoslavia from becoming who they are. Western leaders condemn this group of people to a life far worse than the life of the citizens of Bosnia, who have enjoyed the freedom and richness of an open and pluralistic society. Serbs are forced to live in a community governed by barbarians who have committed unspeakable crimes (and can no longer live with themselves). These barbarians dominate the communities in which they live, and the tacit political support of Western leaders helps them do so. Consider how disheartening the following comments from President Clinton must be, not only to the victims of Milošević's crimes, but also to the Serbs living under Milošević and even the Serbs who carried out Milošević's orders.

President Clinton on Thursday advocated a "wait-and-see" approach on seizing Yugoslav President Slobodan Milošević to stand trial for atrocities in Kosovo, saying NATO's first obligation is to get the refugees home. "I do not believe that the NATO allies can invade Belgrade to try to deliver the indictment," Clinton said, when asked about prosecuting Milošević, who has been indicted as a war criminal by an international tribunal in the Netherlands. "We need to focus on our obligations—fundamental humanitarian obligations to get the Kosovars home and to continue to uncover whatever evidence of war crimes there is in Kosovo," Clinton said.[25]

In the *Gorgias* Socrates says that it is better to suffer wrong than it is to do wrong, and Polus thinks that Socrates is crazy. While no person, Socrates says, willingly suffers wrong, if the choice is between suffering wrong and doing wrong, the better choice is to suffer wrong. Polus cannot believe that any one

---

[24]See Norman Cigar, *Genocide in Bosnia: The Policy of "Ethnic Cleansing"* (College Station: Texas A&M University Press).

[25]"Clinton Says NATO Will Not Go after Milosevic in Serbia," *New York Times* (June 17, 1999).

would seriously make this argument. Still, the position explains much of what is true in Bosnia. The people to be most pitied in Bosnia are those who are responsible for war crimes, whether Serbs, Croats, or Muslims. Many citizens in Bosnia know this, which accounts for their contemptuous attitude toward Europe and which accounts for their capacity to survive with integrity. As Jean Baudrillard says, the people in Sarajevo are to be envied, not pitied, and, while Baudrillard, as a postmodern intellectual, would not formulate it this way, the reason is that the people in Sarajevo understand Plato's insight—it is better to suffer wrong than to do wrong. What surprises people in Sarajevo is that nobody else in the world seems to understand this truth.[26] People in Sarajevo wonder themselves how long they can preserve it.

The reason that the nationalist Serbs persist in breaking agreement after agreement and violating truce after truce is because they, too, know what they need. They do not need Western leaders to tolerate their unconscionable actions. Western tolerance only spurs on the nationalist Serbs. The nationalist Serbs need justice, not for the sake of their victims, but for the sake of themselves. The nationalist Serbs lack the will to stop themselves. Their wills are ill. By not only continuing, but also increasing the degree of their injustices, they seek, not unconditional acceptance, but a just response. The nationalist Serbs are being provocative. Their souls are stunned, deeply stunned, by the unexpected tolerance of Western nations for ethnic cleansing. Nationalist Serbs cross moral line after moral line because their souls cannot rest with their actions and because their souls cannot allow others to rest with their actions. Here is the small but unbreakable thread of shared values in the souls of the nationalist Serbs, which will ensure that they are brought to book.

An essential feature of evil is its need to be witnessed. The greater the evil is, the greater its need to be witnessed. The reason Serb troops and paramilitary forces are vacating Kosovo so readily is because Serb troops need their crimes against Kosovars to be witnessed. There is still a thread of superego within their egos. Serb troops could cover up their enormous crimes better than they do, but they do not want to. The Serb troops want the world to see what the world allowed them to do. This is the only form of revenge that the Serb troops have against not only the world but also their leader, Milošević.

If NATO does not do everything it can to apprehend the war criminals, the guilty will continue gleefully to coopt NATO's collusion. The cost will be high for NATO, and the rewards great for the guilty. The desire of the guilty to show that those who have power over them are, morally speaking, no different from them is a far greater motivation than the fear of apprehension.

What ought to be the motivation of Western leaders? Again, Plato helps.

[26]See Jean Baudrillard, "No Pity for Sarajevo," trans. James Petterson, *Libération* (January 7, 1993).

Socrates would say that, in Dayton, U.S. Assistant Secretary of State Holbrooke was anything but Milošević's friend. Indeed, in Holbrooke, Milošević could not have found a worse enemy. It is a crime for Holbrooke to help Milošević avoid punishment for his crimes against humanity.[27] If Holbrooke were truly concerned for the well-being of Milošević, the Serbian community, and the world at large, Holbrooke, as a friend, would empathetically insist that Milošević "force himself and others not to play the coward, but to submit to the law with closed eyes like a man, as one would to surgery or cautery, ignoring the pain for the sake of the good result which it will bring."[28] By not doing so, Holbrooke and all Western leaders, who follow this example, ensure that Milošević lives the most wretched of lives and that all those subject to him live equally wretched lives. The one way that Western leaders and diplomats can atone for their complicity is to do everything within their powers to place Milošević in the hands of the prosecutor at the International War Crimes Tribunal. The reward for all would be immeasurable.

Western leaders need to intervene in the Balkans for their own sake. If they do not, they allow the nationalist Serbs to determine their own self-concept. Western leaders allow nationalist Serbs to encourage their citizens to assume that the law of the strongest prevails rather than the principle of justice.[29] They allow nationalist Serbs to determine their citizens' values, which will then guide their citizens' behavior. Intervening in Bosnia is not only in the national interest of Western nations, but also in the highest interest of Western nations.

If, say, the racist leaders of the Ku Klux Klan were able to gain control of every TV and radio broadcast in the United States, what would prevent what happened in Bosnia from happening in the United States? Every society, like every person, has a faultline. Milošević put incredible pressure on the faultline of former Yugoslavia. Such a faultline exists in all communities, and there are people in all communities who could apply the pressure that Milošević did and in the

[27]Playing the devil's advocate, Socrates says, "If the enemy injures a third party, one must clearly make every effort, both in speech and action, to prevent his being brought to book and coming before the judge at all; if that is impossible one must contrive that he gets off unpunished.... The most desirable thing would be that he should never die, but live for ever in an immortality of crime; the next best that he should live as long as possible in that condition" (Plato, *Gorgias* [Middlesex, England: Penguin, 1960], 74). Socrates ironically describes how one brings the greatest harm to an individual, and it is exactly what Holbrooke is doing to Milošević.

[28]Plato, *Gorgias*, 73.

[29]The concluding sentence of *Yugoslavia: Death of a Nation* reads, "Victory, in former Yugoslavia, will fall not to the just, but to the strong" (Laura Silber and Allan Little, *Yugoslavia: Death of a Nation* [New York: Penguin, 1996], 372). No matter how informed Silber and Little are, their last sentence, which serves as an epitaph not so much for former Yugoslavia, but for the Republic of Bosnia-Herzegovina, is misguided. Silber and Little's resignation prevents them from going beyond a Hobbesian understanding of their subject, which moves them, however unwittingly, to echo the reasoning of the strong.

same manner. "You must imagine a United States with every little TV station everywhere taking exactly the same editorial line—a line dictated by David Duke. You too would have war in five years."[30] If Western leaders cannot bring justice to bear on the nationalist Serbs, how do they expect to bring justice to bear on the people in their own countries who model their thinking and their actions after the nationalist Serbs? Intervening in Bosnia is in the vital interest of the world. It is in the interest of Western leaders to fight evil abroad, because the longer they collude with evil abroad, the sooner they will need to deal at home with the evil they have fermented.

[30]Miloš Vasić in Noel Malcolm, *Bosnia: A Short History* (Washington Square: New York University Press, 1994), 252.

Afterword

> Fuck, the minute I even think that in some book of world history some asshole is going to write about this war as a conflict of national and religious interests between ethnic groups located in a perpetually unstable region of the Balkans, which lasted from 1991 to whenever, I could just blow this whole planet to bits so that not a particle of it remains.
>
> —Elma Softić
> *Sarajevo Days, Sarajevo Nights*

THE LESSON OF THE children's tale, "The Adventures of Pinocchio," is to encourage respect for the idea of honesty. Whenever Pinocchio lies, his nose grows longer and he gets into deeper trouble. The integrity of the tale is based on the notion that the truth is good for you and that it is good for you to tell the truth, even when the truth is not something that others want to hear and even when the truth says something bad about yourself. Call it moral education. The well-known story conveys this lesson by dramatizing the consequences of not telling the truth.

In 1996, I took my daughters to the movie theater to see the new version of "The Adventures of Pinocchio." What was amazing about this new version is that it "deconstructs" the integrity of the original story. As a postmodern reviewer might say, this new version "erases" the metanarrative, the moral mythology within the story that is inherently controlling and oppressive. The result is that the style of telling the story and the unique manner in which the story is told, the aestethics of the production, become the exclusive point. The moral idea embedded in the tradition story, which could be said to carry universal import, becomes a nonpoint. In this new version, Pinocchio is no longer a "goody two-shoes."

For instance, the new version provides an interesting twist on how Pinocchio and his father get out of the whale's belly. To escape, Pinocchio begins to say, "I hate you, Papa;" "I never, ever missed you;" "I wish I never found you;" "I never wanted to be your son; I want to stay a puppet." With each lie, Pinocchio's wooden nose grows and grows. "Lies! All lies!" Papa says, amazed and pleased. Finally, Pinocchio's wooden nose becomes so long that it pushes on the whale's throat and the whale chokes Pinocchio and Papa into the sea. Pinocchio is a smart boy.

As Pinocchio started lying to his Papa, my six-year-old daughter whispered, "Dad, look, he is lying in order to save himself and his father." I was amazed. What was the socialization that my daughter was getting from viewing this new version of Pinocchio and to what degree did this new version stand as a sign of our times? At the end of the movie, Pinocchio, who was now a real boy rather than a wooden puppet, tells a lie with no compunction. We watch Pinocchio tell the "bad" guys, who are greedy for gold, about a valley where, if they drink the water while holding rocks, the rocks will turn into gold. Earlier, we had learned that drinking the water means you turn into a jackass. At this point, Pinocchio playfully asks, "Would I lie?" He then walks away, touches the tip of his nose, and grins. He is safe. He can lie with impunity; in real life nothing happens. It is difficult to imagine a more thorough inversion of the original moral mythololology.

The cynicism that undergirds this new version of Pinocchio is no different from the cynicism that undergirds the sophistry of many power elites dealing with the conflict in Bosnia. The reason that the observing world has focused on the conflict in Bosnia more than in other areas is not because the conflict in Bosnia is more evil or more violent or more unjust than in other areas. The reason is because Bosnia became a global media screen, a theater, upon which we witnessed a gripping and horrifying moral tale. Like my daughter, we are influenced by this tale in which dishonesty reigns. Like my daughter, we are amazed as we watch the various power elite defend themselves with lie after lie. Like my daughter, we are stunned as we watch diplomats gainsay the truth, walk away, touch their noses, and grin. Perhaps unlike my daughter, we know that we ought to be offended. Crime, Émile Durkheim says, is an act that offends the collective sentiment. If constant mendacity gives no offense, if thousands of rapes give no offense, if thousands of murders give no offense, is there no crime? Where is society when mendacity, rape, murder, and genocide no longer offend the collective sentiment? Where is human nature without society?

Film and Video Resources for Understanding Events in Bosnia

with Heather Burgess and Daniel Capotosto

Cabaret Balkan: A Film by Goran Paskaljević. (Under the former title, *The Powder Keg*). Belgrade: Eurimages, 1998. Serbo-Croatian with English subtitles (121 min.). Best Film Awards at Venice International Film Festival, Antalya Film Festival in Turkey, and the Haifa Film Festival in Israel.

Produced in contemporary, nocturnal Belgrade, *Cabaret Balkan* dramatizes the self-pity of everyday Serbs. The film is profound because the anterior idea behind each vignette is the possibility as well as the impossibility of love: A man in a drunken stupor murders his close, lifelong friend with a splintered beer bottle; a rapist and his frightened victim commit suicide together with a grenade; a thug, who permanently crippled a policeman, confronts his victim but then gives him a lift from the bar; a bus driver, who had been an esteemed professor in Sarajevo, kills a youth and grieves his deed; a cosmopolitan man, who returns to Belgrade to win back the love of his abandoned wife, is pathetically killed.

The pathos of these eerie stories stems from the Serbs' victimizing not non-Serbs, but themselves. Victimization becomes a form of courtship; self-victimization a mode of seduction. The self-consciousness of the film is the recognition that self-pity subverts the realization of love. The film concludes by demonstrating how today guilt for Serbs is a random circumstance and solipsistic experience, which renders the idea of responsibility futile and the reality of love abstract.

Bosna! New York: Zeitgeist Films, 1994. French with English subtitles (117 min.).

"After Auschwitz, people said, 'We didn't know.' Fifty years later, for Sarajevo, they say, 'We don't understand.'" This documentary reconstructs the events leading up to the assault on Sarajevo and beyond. The narrative flows like a Greek tragedy with French narration and English subtitles. "It was all set, almost a perfect crime. But the tradition of peace in the city was so strong, national or religious conflict so unthinkable, that people knew without knowing, not believing in a war." The confusion that baffled Bosnians now perplexes Americans. If tension existed between the different groups in Bosnia, why did the April 4 attack in 1992 meet with such disbelief? We learn that the former psychiatrist, Radovan Karadžić, the nationalist Bosnian Serb leader, had his own clinic and home in Sarajevo shelled. Why? One person explains, "It's Sarajevo they hate and the part of their lives they left there."

Bosnia: Peace without Honor. Princeton, N.J.: Films for the Humanities and Sciences, 1998. English (40 min.).

This film details the fight for and the eventual failure of the Vance-Owen Plan, primarily through interviews with Lord David Owen. In Owen's opinion, the primary reason for the failure of the plan was the election of U.S. President Bill Clinton, whose unwillingness to put American troops on the ground in Bosnia killed the plan. The Dayton Peace Plan, which was ultimately implemented with the U.S. government at the helm, is really a failure, according to Owen, because it resulted in the partitioning of Bosnia, which was exactly the thing to be avoided. While the film competently addresses this subject matter, it veers into dangerous territory, for instance when it explores the possible Muslim origins for two mortar attacks in Sarajevo. The only conceivable justification for this inclusion is the view that Lord Owen expresses: "There is no use pretending there are any innocents in this business"; the filmmakers themselves promote this view. To suggest that there are no innocent helps conceal that there are perpetrators.

Calling the Ghosts. New York: Bowery, dist. by Women Make Movies, 1996. *Awards:* Emmy, Outstanding Journalism Program; Emmy, News and Documentary; Robert F. Kennedy Award for Journalism; Berlin International Film Festival; Amnesty International European Film Festival Special Jury Prize; others. Serbo-Croatian w/ English subtitles (60 min.).

"Before, when I read in the newspaper that women were suffering somewhere in the world, I took it simply as news and glanced over it." This documentary is the most powerful documentary reviewed here. Language is inept at communicating the cutting and corrosive experience of Omarska survivors (Omarska was a death camp near Prjedor run by nationalist Serbs). This film is essential to any understanding of the systematic degradation that ethnic cleansing is and to making sense of an unintelligible war. The individual testimonies give meaning to the euphemism "ethnic cleansing" and alerts "a heap of uninterested people, millions of uninterested people. Those who aren't hungry, who aren't getting shots fired on them, who would only wake up if a grenade exploded on top of their heads or if a knife appeared." Besides recounting events, the narrative bears witness. Despite the horror of the subject, the tone is sublime. The courageous action of two Bosnian women is inspiring.

The Ethnic Cleansers and the Cleansed: The Unforgiving. Princeton, N.J.: Films for the Humanities and Sciences, 1994. Serbo-Croatian with English subtitles (78 min.).

"Atrocities are not the preserve of one side or another." This apparently impartial attitude guides this confusing documentary. Its story both begins and ends with two Serbian parents' frustrating quest to find their young son's body and the degradation of a Muslim prisoner during their search. The parents' quest, like the documentary, reaches no conclusion. The narration strains to tell both sides, but, in fact, the narrative sensationalizes the chauvinistic and militaristic perspective of Serb nationalism. An attitude of pity rather than sympathy is displayed toward the victims of ethnic cleansing. The rationalizations of Serb militia engaged in ethnic cleansing is highlighted. This documentary "fogs" the moral issues and makes it difficult for viewers to gain objective information on the violence of ethnic cleansing. The documentary is a good example of the pseudo-objective, two-sided reporting that characterized news coverage of events in Bosnia.

Exile in Sarajevo. Atlanta, Ga.: CNN Productions, 1996. English and Serbo-Croatian with English subtitles (96 min.).

This documentary was made by an Australian man whose mother left Bosnia after World War II. He goes to Bosnia during 1995 and vows to stay until the city is liberated, saying, "This [film] is not about Serbia or Bosnia, but about the kind of world we want." The documentary presents a unique perspective, against the voyeuristic perspective that is condemned by the filmmakers. A Bosnian woman who joins the production team comments that "people with cameras are called cockroaches here. They often film us like animals in a zoo." This film does not endeavor to capture the sights of the war and the attack on the city and people of Sarajevo; instead, the filmmakers say, "We are making a film

about Sarajevo's people that will attempt to portray…the positive side
of their struggle to maintain the cultural and practical aspects of their
existence." That singular perspective on the people of Sarajevo as they
struggle to live despite a horrific war makes this film moving.

Killing Memory: Bosnia's Cultural Heritage and Its Destruction. Haverford, Pa.:
Community of Bosnia Foundation, 1994. English (42 min.).

The documentary presents a sensitive and thoughtful narration over still
images. "Before there is a new past, the old must be erased." The narra-
tor, Andras Riedlmayer, explicates the incongruity between the purported Balkan history of antagonism and the social harmony that truly
existed. The documentary points out that the greatest damage is not
physical loss, but the loss of Bosnian culture and history. "When a person dies, it is that person's life, that person's family that's affected.
When a culture is killed, it forecloses the future, and it destroys the
memory of the past. Even if the people to whom those monuments and
documents belong survive, they've lost their anchor, their connection to
who they are, of how they belong to a particular place.… I think that
you cannot separate the sufferings of people from the destruction of
monuments of culture. The killing of memory is as great a tragedy as the
killing of people."

The Land of the Demons. Oak Forest, Ill.: Public Media / Films Inc. Video, 1993.
English (45 min.).

This is an ABC News documentary that explains the historical background of the former Yugoslavia, reasons for the war, and the consequences of Western involvement or lack thereof. The film's treatment of
the historical and social background may seem basic to anyone with any
knowledge of the conflict. The film often falls back upon the "ancient
ethnic hatreds" explanation, even as it asserts that many of the ethnic
groups have lived together in relative harmony since World War II. The
film criticizes Europe's lack of decisive action in the situation and
details political reasons why France, Germany, and Great Britain have
acted as they have. A discussion follows of the benefits and detriments
of possible United States intervention. As this film was made in 1993,
much of the information is outdated.

The Peacekeepers: How the UN Failed in Bosnia. Alexandria, Va.: ABC News,
1995. English (60 min.).

The documentary presents harsh but warranted criticism of the United
Nations' impotence in keeping their promise to the Bosnian people.
Insights into the institutional and political red tape that allowed and

encouraged the massacre of thousands of Bosnians is provided. Bosnian Prime Minister Haris Silajdzić observes, "Behind all this, there is one genuine wish, and that's to take Bosnia off the table—if possible—by all means. And forget about it." The documentary shows how nationalist Serbs, in total disregard of UN threats, were encouraged by conciliatory weakness. Peter Jennings interviews Sir Michael Rose and confronts Rose about his repeated refusal to do anything about Serbian offenses. The film misses the irony that the media failed as well; local scandal updates were more lucrative than the death of a nation and the destruction of a society.

Rape: A Crime of War. Canada: National Film Board, 1996. English (59 min.).

This film profiles the efforts of some women who are working to ensure that for the first time ever, rape will be tried as a crime against humanity at the International War Crimes Tribunal in The Hague. The film centers around the trial of Dusan Tadić, accused of crimes at the concentration camp, Omarska. Captured for the first time on film are the tragic images of cast-off clothing at the Sonja Hotel in Sarajevo. A former site of mass rape and murder, and land-mined since the crimes were committed, time seems to have stood still at the hotel—underwear, shoes, and hairbands lie frozen amid the debris of war. Weaving together testimony from women who survived imprisonment at Omarska and interviews with prosecutors at the war crimes tribunal, the film conveys the stark realities of the crimes committed against women in the former Yugoslavia, and shows the terrible ramifications of the use of mass rape as a weapon of war.

The Road to Nowhere: Yugoslavia. Princeton, N.J.: Films for the Humanities and Sciences, 1994. English (50 min.).

This documentary takes its form from the central metaphor of the Highway of Brotherhood and Unity, which was constructed under authority from Tito to connect the Serbs and Croats. Now, the highway has become the road to nowhere. Instead of symbolizing the unity of the Serbs and Croats, as it was meant to when it was built, the highway now signifies their separation. The filmmakers journey along this highway, alternating through Croat- and Serb-held territory. The film critically examines and condemns the effects of nationalism in both groups. It is revealed through interviews with people whom the filmmakers meet along the way that, although they claim they have nothing in common with the other group, both ethnic groups share a destructive nationalism, both claim to want peace while also desiring an ethnically homogeneous bit of land, and both share a common tendency to destroy the evidence of their interdependent past.

Shot Through the Heart. New York: HBO Home Video, 1998. English (115 min.).

This film is a dramatization of a true story of two men in Sarajevo, a Muslim and a Serb, who were close friends and would have been on the Yugoslavian Olympic rifle team together had Yugoslavia still existed in 1992. Instead, the men found themselves on opposite sides of the battle for Sarajevo. Early in the film, Slavko, the Serb, quickly aligns himself with the nationalists, while Vlado, the Muslim, still holds on to his former identity as a Yugoslav. Slavko immediately obeys his orders to join the Bosnian Serb army and begins using his skill as a rifleman to train snipers to shoot from the hills surrounding Sarajevo; Vlado is hesitant both to engage in the fighting and to leave Sarajevo. Eventually, Vlado chooses to fight and becomes involved in the battle against the snipers. Vlado finds himself crouching in shelled-out buildings near where Sarajevans must go to get water, and as they are shot, he tries to determine from where the shots are coming. At first, he has difficulty returning fire, knowing that he might be shooting at his old friend, Slavko. Eventually, however, Vlado sneaks up the treacherous hills to visit Slavko, and after their nostalgic visit, the next morning Vlado shoots Slavko, sniper-style, as Slavko is leaving home to go "to work." The film is a harrowing and emotionally moving dramatization of a very real phenomenon that took place in Sarajevo, of friend killing friend, neighbor killing neighbor.

We Are All Neighbors. Chicago: Public Media, Inc. and Films, Inc. Video, 1993. English and Serbo-Croatian with English subtitles (52 min.).

This film was made to demonstrate "how war affects family and friendships in a village in Bosnia." The relationships among neighbors are traced over the course of a few months in a village about fifteen miles outside Sarajevo. The village consisted of about two-thirds Muslim and one-third Croatian population. The film documents the transformation of the village from one of inter-ethnic harmony, trust, and friendship, in which the danger is perceived as coming from the Serb soldiers who are attacking Sarajevo, to a village of suspicion, distrust, and violence, in which the danger is perceived as coming from neighbors of the other ethnicity. As the Croatian army takes control of the town, Muslims are murdered, and the Muslim population is forced to relocate. Every Muslim house in the village is burned, shelled, and vandalized. At the end of the film, trust between the two groups has been broken. The people go from saying, "We all get along because we all have to live together. Bosnia could never be any other way," to saying, "We can't live with them any more after what they've done. There can be no more living together." The film recounts the killing of a *Gemeinshaft*. The lament of Tone Bringa for the situation is telling. This Bosnian village was the site of her fieldwork for the important book, *Being Muslim the Bosnian Way*. The film starkly presents the violence of the Croat-Muslim conflict in Bosnia at an everyday level.

Welcome to Sarajevo. Burbank, Calif.: Miramax Home Entertainment and Buena Vista Home Entertainment, 1997. English (102 min.).

In his review of *Welcome to Sarajevo*, Roy Gutman, author of *Witness to Genocide*, evokes the rule that professional journalists never become a part of the story that they cover. Gutman laments that the journalists in *Welcome to Sarajevo* do exactly that: they become involved in the story that they cover to such a degree that they invent rather than report the story. In Gutman's view, *Welcome to Sarajevo* misrepresents the character and discipline of journalistic work. The main storyline is the rivalry between an American and a British journalist. The primary drama is their sportslike competition. Bosnia and what was happening to Bosnians is simply a stage upon which to watch this soap opera in which the egos of two journalists bounce off each other. We do not learn anything about the tragedies and personal struggles of Bosnians, and as Gutman notes, there are many stories about the tragedies and personal struggles of Bosnians from which we could learn much. The British journalist tries to help an orphan leave Bosnia, and adopts her. The film implicitly questions the ambiguity of this altruistic action, but the question takes a backseat to the journalists' rivalry.

Yugoslavia: Death of a Nation. New York: Discovery Channel, 1995. English (250 min.).

The five-part documentary is an extensive and critical study of the breakup of former Yugoslavia. The key players are interviewed and the telltale events in the fragmentation of Yugoslavia are chronicled. The candor of the political players being interviewed is startling because their answers are often self-incriminating. The documentary reveals how Slobodan Milošević ousted the former Serb president Ivan Stambolić, gained control of the Yugoslav army, and seized the presidency of the country. It was a classic example of a coup d'ètat. Pointed testimony from the Serbian warlord, Vojislav Šešelj, implicates Milošević for organizing the ethnic cleansing in Bosnia. This video is indispensable for understanding the contemporary history of former Yugoslavia. Truth springs forth from the dispassionate narration of Christian Amanpour.

Glossary of Sociological Terms

alienation. Loss or estrangement, either from one's self or from society, or from control over social and economic processes.

anomie. A situation in which the norms that guide behavior are no longer appropriate or effective.

behaviorism. The study of observable activity as opposed to reported or inferred mental and emotional processes.

bureaucracy. Formal administrative structure that is responsible for planning, supervising, and coordinating the work of the various segments of an organization.

charisma. Extraordinary personal qualities that can turn an audience into followers.

charismatic authority. Power legitimated through extraordinary personal abilities that inspire devotion and obedience.

crowd. A temporary gathering of people who share some common focus of attention and often influence one another.

deconstruction. A frequently used term to name the methodology of postmodernism in which irony is used to expose and erase the significance of oppressive value paradigms.

degradation ceremony. Any communicative work between persons, whereby the public identity of an actor is transformed into something looked on as lower in the local scheme of social types.

double-voiced discourse. M. M. Bakhtin's term for studying the dialogical rather than monological character of discourse. Jokes, irony, satire, puns, sarcasm are all examples of double-voiced discourse.

dramatism. Kenneth Burke's system of analyzing literary works in terms of their relative emphasis on act, scene, agent, agency, and purpose.

dramaturgical analysis. The analysis of social interaction in terms of theatrical performance.

ego. Freud's designation of the conscious attempt to balance the pleasure-seeking drives of the human organism and the demands and realities of society.

face. The positive social value that a person effectively claims for himself by the line others assume he has taken during a particular interaction.

face-giving. The tactful practice of arranging for another to take a better line than he might otherwise have been able to take.

face-saving. Discretion, or the process by which the person sustains an impression for others that he has not lost face.

functionalism. Functional analysis examines the relationship between the parts and the whole of the social system; the various parts that make up the whole interact in such a way as to create stability.

hyperreality. A postmodern concept in which simulations of reality are perceived as being more real than that which is simulated.

id. Freud's designation of the human being's basic needs, the natural human state including the pleasure instinct including the appetite for food, sex, and comfort.

ideal type. Purified model of a concept against which a real world example can be compared for the purpose of social understanding.

latent function. The unrecognized or unintended consequences of any social pattern.

line. The social actors' agreed-upon definition of their interaction and their roles within the interaction.

manifest function. The recognized and intended consequences of any social pattern.

normative orientation. The value commitment that holds a person's actions together as a meaningful course of action.

norms. Social rules and guidelines that prescribe appropriate behavior in particular situations.

patrimonialism. A system of governing that can be characterized by the offering of positions of power through favors and nepotism.

phenomenology. The study of the various forms and varieties of consciousness and the ways people can comprehend the world in which they live.

positivism. The assertion that science, rather than any other type of human understanding, is the singular path to knowledge.

postmodernism. Any number of trends, movements, theories, or cultural attitudes developing in the 1970s in reaction to or in rejection of the principles or practices of modernism, namely, the culture and ideas resulting from the Enlightenment.

rationality. Deliberate, matter-of-fact calculation of the most efficient means to accomplish any particular goal.

simulacrum. The postmodern concept of a representation bears no relation to any reality except its own; it is a representation that creates reality.

simulation. The postmodern concept of feigning, which does not simply imitate, but threatens to become, or actually becomes, that which is feigned.

sociocide. The killing of a society, its normative orientation, and collective sentiments upon which its people and their community thrive.

species-being. The Marxist principle whereby an individual treats himself or herself as the actual, living species; he or she treats himself or herself as a universal and therefore free being. The origin of this concept may be found in Aristotle's writing.

superego. Freud's designation of the presence of culture within the individual in the form of internalized values and norms.

utilitarianism. The philosophical doctrine that considers utility as the normative criterion of action and the useful as the measure of what is good or worthwhile.

verstehen. The sociological task of learning how individuals in a particular social setting understand their own actions.

wrong face. A social actor can be said to be in wrong face when information is brought forth about him or her which cannot be integrated into the line that is being sustained for him or her.

Glossary of Names

Yasushi Akashi. Senior UN envoy to the former Yugoslavia, 1993–1995. Akashi was promoted to under secretary general for Humanitarian Affairs in 1995.

Madeleine Albright. The U.S. ambassador to the UN, 1993–1997; U.S. secretary of state since 1997.

Jean Baudrillard. French sociologist and social commentator, Baudrillard is perhaps the most representative of the postmodern cultural leftists, who argue that the line between reality and simulation is false.

Kenneth Burke. American literary critic and communications theorist who is best known for his concept of symbolic action.

Noam Chomsky. American linguist and social critic who invented a grammatical system known as transformational grammar. Chomsky has become widely known for outspoken communication of his political ideas.

Warren Christopher. U.S. secretary of state, 1992–1997.

Charles Horton Cooley. An important American sociologist in the early development of the discipline, Cooley is most famous for the concept of the looking-glass self, an important concept in the study of the social self.

Robert Dole. Former U.S. senator and presidential candidate.

Émile Durkheim. An early and influential French sociologist and theorist on the profound connections between the individual and society.

Harold Garfinkel. A sociologist who coined the term *ethnomethodology* in the 1950s. Rather than seeing society as a broad system with a life of its own, Garfinkel looked at familiar everyday experiences to examine the manner in which people constantly formulate understandings of their environment, situation, and surroundings.

Erving Goffman. American sociologist whose approach to understanding society is described as dramaturgical analysis because he emphasizes the ways human beings deliberately act to foster certain impressions in the minds of others.

Peter Handke. Austrian postmodern playwright, novelist, essayist, poet, and translator. Handke was influential in the 1960s in the "overthrow" of the European modernist literary tradition.

Robert R. Hayden. Anthropologist at University of Pittsburgh who has written articles and spoken frequently on Bosnia.

Thomas Hobbes. The English philosopher who suggested that society was a reaction to the fact that human nature was innately selfish.

Richard Holbrooke. The U.S. assistant secretary of state, Holbrooke played an important role during the peace negotiations in Dayton.

Alija Izetbegović. Leader of Muslim Democratic Action Party (SDA); president of Bosnia-Herzegovina since 1990.

Bernard Janvier. Lieutenant general of France, UN force commander in the former Yugoslavia, 1995–1996. Janvier was unwilling to authorize NATO air power, a significant contributor to the division between the United States and the UN.

Radovan Karadžić. Psychiatrist; leader of the Nationalist Bosnian Serb movement; president of Bosnian Serb Republic from 1992 to 1996; indicted for war crimes in 1995 by the International Tribunal in The Hague; Karadzic resigned in 1996 when the Dayton Peace Accord declared that no indicted war criminal could hold public office.

Robert K. Merton. A contemporary American sociologist whose work has been guided by the structural-functional paradigm. Merton was a principal founder of the field of sociology of science and is known for attempting to define researchable theories of the range between pure abstraction and empiricism.

Slobodan Milošević. President of the Republic of Serbia from 1989 to 1997 and president of the Federal Republic of Yugoslavia from 1997. Generally held responsible for the breaking apart of Yugoslavia.

Ratko Mladić. Yugoslav People's Army general, then commander of the Bosnian Serb army from 1992 to 1996; indicted for war crimes by the International Tribunal in The Hague.

David Owen. Co-chairman with Cyrus Vance of the Peace Conference on former Yugoslavia, 1992–1995.

Talcott Parsons. Parsons is the major proponent of the structural-functional paradigm in American sociology, and he is considered the founder of American sociological theory.

John Rawls. Contemporary analytic philosopher; Rawls's theories can be seen as a way of resolving the major political separation of the libertarian right from the egalitarian left.

George Ritzer. Contemporary American sociologist, perhaps most well known for his study of occupational structures and social status based on occupation.

Michael Rose. British lieutenant general and UN commander in Bosnia, 1994–1995.

Georg Simmel. German sociologist and founder, along with Max Weber and Ferdinand Toennies, of the German Sociological Society. Simmel's work rejects the organicist theories of society, instead promoting the concept that society consists of a web of patterned interactions.

Franjo Tudjman. Founding leader of the Croatian Democratic Union (HDZ); president of Croatia from 1991.

Cyrus Vance. UN envoy and cochairman with Lord David Owen of the Peace Conference on former Yugoslavia.

Max Weber. German sociologist who emphasized the importance of understanding society as it is subjectively perceived by individuals.

Bibliography

Ali, Rabia, and Lawrence Lifschultz, eds. *Why Bosnia?: Writings on the Balkan War.* Stony Creek, Conn.: Pamphleteer's, 1993.

Allen, Beverly. *Rape Warfare: The Hidden Genocide in Bosnia-Herzegovina and Croatia.* Minneapolis: University of Minnesota Press, 1996.

Bakhtin, M. M. *The Dialogic Imagination.* Edited by Michael Holquist. Translated by Caryl Emerson and Michael Holquist. Austin: University of Texas Press, 1996.

Banac, Ivo. *The National Question in Yugoslavia: Origins, History, Politics.* Ithaca, N.Y.: Cornell University Press, 1984.

Barthes, Roland. *Mythologies.* Translated by Annette Lavers. New York: Noonday, 1972.

Baudrillard, Jean. *America.* Translated by Chris Turner. New York: Verso, 1993.

———. *The Gulf War Did Not Take Place.* Translated by Paul Patton. Bloomington: Indiana University Press, 1995.

———. *Jean Baudrillard: Selected Writings.* Edited by Mark Poster. Stanford, Calif.: Stanford University Press, 1988.

Bauman, Zygmunt. *Modernity and the Holocaust.* Ithaca: Cornell University Press, 1996.

Benoit, William L. *Accounts, Excuses, and Apologies: A Theory of Image Restoration Strategies.* Albany: State University of New York Press, 1995.

Blackman, Ellen. *Harvest in the Snow: My Crusade to Rescue the Lost Children of Bosnia.* Washington, D.C.: Brassey's, 1997.

Blagojević, Slobodan, ed. *Erewhon: An International Quarterly.* Vol. 1. Amsterdam: Strichting EX-YU PEN Amsterdam, 1994.

Blum, Alan. *Socrates: The Original and Its Images.* London: Routledge and Kegan Paul, 1978.

———. "Victim, Patient, Client, Pariah: Steps in the Self-Understanding of Suffering and Affliction." *Canadian Journal of Visual Impairment* 1 (1992): 56–65.

Bringa, Tone. *Being Muslim the Bosnian Way: Identity and Community in a Central Bosnian Village.* Princeton, N.J.: Princeton University Press, 1995.

Buber, Martin. *I and Thou.* Translated by Ronald Gregor Smith. New York: Macmillan Publishing Company, 1958.

Burke, Kenneth. *A Grammar of Motives.* Berkeley: University of California Press, 1969.

————. *On Symbols and Society.* Edited by Joseph R. Gusfield. Chicago: University of Chicago Press, 1989.

————. *Permanence and Change: An Anatomy of Purpose.* Berkeley: University of California Press, 1984.

Campbell, David. *National Deconstruction: Violence, Identity, and Justice in Bosnia.* Minneapolis: University of Minnesota Press, 1998.

Cataldi, Anna. *Letters from Sarajevo: Voices of a Besieged City.* Translated by Avril Bardoni. Rockport, Mass.: Element, 1994.

Cigar, Norman. *Genocide in Bosnia: The Policy of "Ethnic Cleansing."* College Station: Texas A&M University Press, 1995.

Cohen, Philip J. *Serbia's Secret War: Propaganda and the Deceit of History.* College Station: Texas A&M University Press, 1996.

Cohen, Roger. *Hearts Grown Brutal: Sagas of Sarajevo.* New York: Random House, 1998.

Collins, Randall. *Max Weber: A Skeleton Key.* Beverly Hills, Calif.: Sage, 1986.

Cushman, Thomas, and Stjepan Meštrović, eds. *This Time We Knew: Western Responses to Genocide in Bosnia.* New York: New York University Press, 1996.

Davis, G. Scott, ed. *Religion and Justice in the War Over Bosnia.* New York: Routledge, 1996.

Debeljak, Aleš. *Twilight of the Idols: Recollections of a Lost Yugoslavia.* Translated by Michael Biggins. Fredonia, N.Y.: White Pine, 1994.

Dizdarević, Žlatko. *Portraits of Sarajevo.* Edited by Ammiel Alcalay. Translated by Midhat Ridjanović. New York: Fromm, 1994.

————. *Sarajevo: A War Journal.* Edited by Ammiel Alcalay. Translated by Anselm Hollo. New York: Fromm, 1993.

Donia, Robert J., and John V. A. Fine, Jr. *Bosnia and Hercegovina: A Tradition Betrayed.* New York: Columbia University Press, 1994.

Doubt, Keith. "The Person and the Limit of Empiricism." *Personalist Forum* 10 (spring 1994): 1–13.

Fiipović, Zlata. *Zlata's Diary: A Child's Life in Sarajevo.* Translated with notes by Christina Pribichevich-Zorić. New York. Scholastic, 1994.

Fletcher, Jonathan. *Violence and Civilization.* Malden, Mass.: Blackwell, 1997.

Freire, Paulo. *The Pedagogy of the Oppressed.* Translated by Myra Bergman Ramos. New York: Continuum, 1989.

Freud, Sigmund. *The Ego and the Id.* Edited by James Strachey. Translated by

Joan Riviere. New York: Norton, 1960.

Garfinkel, Harold. *Studies in Ethnomethodology.* Englewood Cliffs, N.J.: Prentice-Hall, 1967.

Gjelten, Tom. *Sarajevo Daily: A City and Its Newspaper under Siege.* New York: HarperCollins, 1995.

Goffman, Erving. *Interaction Ritual: Essays on Face-to-Face Behavior.* New York: Pantheon, 1967.

————. *The Presentation of Self in Everyday Life.* Garden City, N.Y.: Doubleday Anchor, 1959.

Goldberg, Carl. *Speaking with the Devil: A Dialogue with Evil.* New York: Viking, 1994.

Gutman, Roy. *A Witness to Genocide: The 1993 Pulitzer Prize-Winning Dispatches on the "Ethnic Cleansing" of Bosnia.* New York: Macmillan, 1993.

Handke, Peter. *A Journey to the Rivers: Justice for Serbia.* Translated by Scott Abbott. New York: Viking, 1997.

Hatzfeld, Jean. "The Fall of Vukovar." *Granta* 47 (1994): 197–222.

Hayden, Robert M. "The Partition of Bosnia and Herzegovina, 1990–1993." *RFE/RL Research Paper* 2, no. 22 (May 28, 1993): 1–14.

————. "Schindler's Fate: Genocide, Ethnic Cleansing, and Population Transfers." *Slavic Review* 55, no. 4 (winter 1996).

Hegel, G. W. F. *The Phenomenology of Mind.* Translated by J. B. Baillie. New York: Humanities, 1977.

Heller, Agnes, and Ferenc Fehér. *The Postmodern Political Condition.* Oxford: Polity Press, 1988.

Heller, Agnes. *The Power of Shame: A Rational Perspective.* Boston: Routledge, 1985.

Hobbes, Thomas. *Leviathan.* Edited by C. B. Macpherson. Middlesex, England: Penguin, 1968.

Holbrooke, Richard. *To End a War.* New York: Random House, 1998.

Honig, Jan Willem, and Norbert Both. *Srebrenica: Record of a War Crime.* Middlesex, England: Penguin, 1996.

Hukanović, Rezak. *The Tenth Circle of Hell: A Memoir of Life in the Death Camps of Bosnia.* Edited by Ammiel Alcalay. Translated by Colleen London and Midhat Ridjanović. New York: Basic Books, 1996.

Jaspers, Karl. *The Question of German Guilt.* Translated by E. B. Ashton. New York: Capricorn, 1961.

Judah, Tim. *The Serbs: History, Myth, and the Destruction of Yugoslavia.* New Haven: Yale University Press, 1997.

Kurspahić, Kemal. *As Long as Sarajevo Exists.* Translated by Colleen London. Stony Creek, Conn.: Pamphleteer's Press, 1997.

Le Bon, Gustave. *The Crowd: A Study of the Popular Mind.* Marietta, Ga.: Larlin, 1982.

Levinas, Emmanuel. *The Levinas Reader.* Edited by Seán Hand. Cambridge, Mass.: Blackwell, 1989.

Lukács, Georg. *History and Class Consciousness: Studies in Marxist Dialectics.* London: Merlin Press, 1968.

Maass, Peter. *Love Thy Neighbor: A Story of War.* New York: Vintage, 1996.

Machiavelli, Niccolò. *The Prince.* Translated by Luigi Ricci. New York: Vintage, 1952.

MacIntyre, Alasdair. *After Virtue: A Study in Moral Theory.* Notre Dame, Ind.: University of Notre Dame Press, 1981.

Mahmutćehajić, Rusmir. *Twisted Politics: Readings of History and Community Relationships in Bosnia.* Translated by Francis R. Jones and Marina Bowder. Sarajevo: Did, 1998.

———. *Living Bosnia: Political Essays and Interviews.* Edited by Edin Mulać. Translated by Spomenka Beus and Francis R. Jones. Ljubljana, Slovenia: Oslobodenje International, 1995.

Malcolm, Noel. *Bosnia: A Short History.* Washington Square: New York University Press, 1994.

———. *Kosovo: A Short History.* Washington Square: New York University Press, 1998.

Mayerhoff, Milton. *On Caring.* New York: Harper Perennial, 1990.

McHugh, Peter, Stanley Raffel, Daniel C. Foss, and Alan F. Blum. *On the Beginning of Social Inquiry.* Boston: Routledge and Kegan Paul, 1974.

Mead, George Herbert. *On Social Psychology.* Edited by Anselm Strauss. Chicago: University of Chicago Press, 1977.

Meštrović, Stjepan. *The Balkanization of the West: The Confluence of Postmodernism and Postcommunism.* New York: Routledge, 1994.

———. *Genocide After Emotion: The Postemotional Balkan War.* New York: Routledge, 1996.

———, ed. *The Conceit of Innocence: Losing the Conscience of the West in the War Against Bosnia.* College Station: Texas A&M University Press, 1997.

Meštrović, Stjepa, Slaven Letica, and Miroslav Goreta. *Habits of the Balkan Heart: Social Character and the Fall of Communism.* College Station: Texas A&M University Press, 1993.

Mills, C. Wright. *The Sociological Imagination.* New York: Oxford University Press, 1967.

Mommsen, Wolfgang J. *The Age of Bureaucracy: Perspectives on the Political Sociology of Max Weber.* New York: Harper and Row, 1974.

Mousavizadeh, Nader, ed. *The Black Book of Bosnia: The Consequences of Appeasement.* New York: New Republic, 1996.

Neier, Aryeh. *War Crimes: Brutality, Genocide, Terror, and the Struggle for Justice.* New York: Times, 1998.

Parsons, Talcott. *The Structure of Social Action: A Study in Social Theory with*

Special Reference to a Group of Recent European Writers. New York: Free Press, 1968.

Peck, M. Scott. *People of the Lie: The Hope for Healing Human Evil.* New York: Simon and Schuster, 1983.

Pinson, Mark, ed. *The Muslims of Bosnia-Herzegovina: Their Historic Development from the Middle Ages to the Dissolution of Yugoslavia.* Cambridge: Harvard University Press, 1993.

Plato. *Gorgias.* Translated by Walter Hamilton. Middlesex, England: Penguin, 1960.

————. *Protagoras and Meno.* Translated by W. K. C. Guthrie. Baltimore: Penguin, 1975.

Rieff, David. *Slaughterhouse: Bosnia and the Failure of the West.* New York: Simon and Schuster, 1996.

Ritzer, George. *The McDonaldization of Society: An Investigation into the Changing Character of Contemporary Social Life.* Newbury Park, Calif.: Pine Forge, 1993.

Rohde, David. *Endgame: The Betrayal and Fall of Srebrenica, Europe's Worst Massacre since World War II.* New York: Farrar, Straus, and Giroux, 1997.

Roth, Guenther, and Wolfgang Schluchter. *Max Weber's Vision of History: Ethics and Methods.* Berkeley: University of California Press, 1979.

Rubenstein, Richard L. *The Cunning of History: The Holocaust and the American Future.* New York: Harper and Row, 1975.

Sadkovic, James J. *The U.S. Media and Yugoslavia, 1991–1995.* Westport, Conn.: Praeger, 1998.

Sandel, Michael J. *Liberalism and the Limits of Justice.* New York: Cambridge University Press, 1982.

Sartre, Jean-Paul. *Anti-Semite and Jew.* Translated by George J. Becker. New York: Schocken, 1965.

Scharf, Michael P. *Balkan Justice: The Story Behind the First International War Crimes Trial Since Nuremberg.* Durham, N.C.: Carolina Academic Press, 1997.

Sells, Michael A. *The Bridge Betrayed: Religion and Genocide in Bosnia.* Berkeley: University of California Press, 1996.

Silber, Laura, and Allan Little. *Yugoslavia: Death of a Nation.* New York: TV Books, 1996.

Simmel, Georg. *The Sociology of Georg Simmel.* Edited by Kurt H. Wolff. Glencoe, Ill.: Free Press, 1950.

Smajlović, Ljiljana. "From the Heart of the Former Yugoslavia." *Wilson Quarterly* (summer 1995): 100–113.

Softić, Elma. *Sarajevo Days, Sarajevo Nights.* Translated by Nada Conic. St. Paul: Hungry Mind, 1996.

Sontag, Susan. "Godot Comes to Sarajevo." *New York Review of Books* 40

(1993): 52–59.

———. "A Lament for Bosnia." *Nation* 261 (1995): 818–21.

Strauss, Leo. *What Is Political Philosophy? and Other Studies.* Westport, Conn.: Free Press, 1973.

Todorov, Tzvetan. *On Human Diversity: Nationalism, Racism, and Exoticism in French Thought.* Translated by Catherine Porter. Cambridge: Harvard University Press, 1993.

Topčić, Zlatko, ed. *Forgotten Country 1: A Selection of Bosnian-Herzegovinian Stories.* Sarajevo: Association of Writers of Bosnia-Herzegovina, 1997.

———, ed. *Forgotten Country 2: War Prose in Bosnia-Herzegovina (1992– 1995).* Sarajevo: Association of Writers of Bosnia-Herzegovina, 1997.

Ugrešić, Dubravka. *The Culture of Lies: Antipolitical Essays.* Translated by Celia Hawkesworth. University Park: Pennsylvania State University Press, 1998.

Weber, Max. *On Law in Economy and Society.* Edited by Max Rheinstein. Translated by Edward Shils and Max Rheinstein. New York: Clarion, 1967.

———. *Politics as a Vocation.* Translated by H. H. Gerth and C. Wright Mills. Philadelphia: Fortress, 1965.

———. *The Theory of Social and Economic Organization.* Edited by Talcott Parsons. Translated by A. M. Henderson and Talcott Parsons. New York: Free Press, 1964.

Wiesenthal, Simon. *The Sunflower: On the Possibilities and Limits of Forgiveness.* New York: Schocken, 1997.

Zimmerman, Warren. *Origins of a Catastrophe: Yugoslavia and Its Destroyers— America's Last Ambassador Tells What Happened and Why.* New York: Times, 1996.

Index

About the Author

KEITH DOUBT earned his Ph.D. in 1986 in the Graduate Programme of Sociology at York University, Toronto, Canada. He wrote his doctoral dissertation, "Acquaintance, Good Will, and the Problem of Knowing the Other," with Alan Blum and Peter McHugh. He has published numerous articles in different journals on a variety of social theorists. In 1995 he was elected to the Theory Section Council of the American Sociological Association. He is the author of *Towards a Sociology of Schizophrenia: Humanistic Reflections* and is currently associate professor of sociology at Truman State University.